THE POWER AND AUTHORITY OF THE CHURCH

EQUIPPING THE SAINTS TO ADMINISTER GOD'S KINGDOM ON EARTH

"But this Man, after He had offered one sacrifice for sins forever, sat down at the right hand of God, from that time waiting till His enemies are made His footstool" (Hebrews 10:12-13).

ABRAHAM JOHN

The Power and Authority of the Church: *Equipping the Saints to Administer God's Kingdom on Earth*

Copyright © 2016 by Abraham John

Published by Abraham John
Maximum Impact Ministries
P.O. Box 631460
Littleton, CO 80163-1460
www.maximpact.org
email: mim@maximpact.org
(720) 420 9873

ISBN: 978-0-9972591-1-7

Printed and published in the U.S.A

Even if you have read *Kingdom Mandate*, I would strongly recommend reading this book from the beginning because I have made some changes and added more content for clarity.

Let the *Real* Church Arise!

Contents

Preface

For too long the body of Christ has been waiting for revival or the rapture, but let me tell you the good news: The greatest move of God we have all been waiting for is right here in the midst of us. In fact, it started almost two thousand years ago! It is called the *kingdom movement.* Though this movement has been among us for many years, the church as a whole has yet to catch up with it. The time has come for us to fully cooperate with God in what He wants to do here on earth.

Why the kingdom movement? Many think of the kingdom of God futuristically, as something that is going to take place later in time or as a place or state they enter or reach after they die. The entire Bible is about a King, His kingdom, and His royal family. He decided to extend that kingdom to a planet called Earth. To manage that kingdom He created a unique species in His image and likeness called human beings. That is our purpose: to represent God and manage His kingdom on earth.

The first mandate that was given by the King to man was to have dominion over the earth and everything He created in it (Genesis 1:26). According to the law of first mention, when God speaks about something for the first time He reveals His heart and purpose concerning that thing. A mandate is an authorization to act, a charge to get things done, a commission to carry out an injunction, a precept to adhere to, a guideline to follow without deviation, and an important order which must be obeyed. God gave the mandate to Adam and Eve: they were to have dominion over the earth and to subdue and rule everything God created. But Adam failed in his assignment.

Man was deceived by the enemy and lost dominion over the earth. Still, God did not change His purpose concerning man nor His kingdom. He chose individuals and then a nation, the nation of Israel, to represent Him and His kingdom on earth. Eventually, they also rebelled and failed in their assignment. So Jesus said,

> "Therefore say I unto you, the kingdom of God shall be taken from you (Israel), and given to a nation (the church) bringing forth the fruits thereof" (Matthew 21:43).

The church is a holy nation in itself: a nation within the nation you are living in (Peter 2:9). God sent His Son to die for our sins and to reinstate His kingdom purpose. He instituted the church, comprised of both Jews and Gentiles, to represent Him and His kingdom on earth. This is not a new revelation I just discovered or made up. The revelation of God's kingdom is as old as heaven and earth.

Throughout the centuries the church has been asking God for particular benefits and specializing in a few aspects of the kingdom instead of crying out for His kingdom to come. As a result, He sent the salvation movement, healing movement, holiness movement, word of faith movement, and others. They are all different aspects of His kingdom, but not *the* kingdom. The time has come for us to receive the whole kingdom and administer it so that God's will is done on the earth *as it is in heaven.*

Why, in nations where Christians are the majority, do they have no influence in decision-making? Why are nations where mighty revivals once took place now considered post-Christian societies? Why do some nations where Christians are the majority remain poor? Why do the majority of people on this earth remain unreached when two thousand years ago just twelve men reached almost the whole known world in their own lifetime? This is what happens when the church fails to receive and administer the kingdom of God.

I believe there is still hope for the church in the West, but we need to take some emergency steps if we are to turn the ship before it gets wrecked. Just because the church is God's idea does not mean harm won't come to it. History proves that bad things can happen to churches and nations if they don't heed the voice of God, even if they are chosen by Him. We are all familiar with the history of Israel.

The seven churches named in the book of Revelation don't exist today. All of the great churches that Paul established have disappeared from the face of the earth. Europe—once known as the cradle of Christianity and world missions—is now considered a post-Christian society. Many hide behind a form of religion because they know it is written in the end of the Book that God and the church will win. That is true, but just like many historic nations, churches, and empires, you and your nation may not be around to experience it because you were negligent about the warnings written in the Bible.

We have been busy making converts, but have failed to disciple nations. As a result, though we have many converts, we are losing nations. The Lord sent a warning about this. He said, "If the church in the West does not make some course corrections soon, the same thing will happen to them that happened to the early church."

In Matthew 16:18, Jesus said, "I will build My church, and the gates of hades shall not prevail against it." How then were these churches overthrown by the gates of hell? Why are we losing our Christian heritage? Why are hundreds of churches being closed every year? Kingdoms and empires that thought they would last forever have perished. They never thought that would happen, and neither do we. But this can happen to our society. God gave me this book to prevent that from happening. It is not God's will that these things should take place. If we take the appropriate action, what happened to those historic churches and nations will not happen to us.

Why do you go to church? Are you happy with what is going on in the church at large? Are you going to church to socialize, or because you are afraid God will punish you if you do not, or to please your pastor or leader? Do you go to church to fulfill your religious duty or feel good about yourself? If you are a Christian, you go to church. That's what most of us are used to doing on Sunday morning. Afterward we go out to breakfast or lunch, and then home to watch TV and take a nap. Does that sound familiar to anyone?

But if you are a kingdom citizen, you know that when you come together as a church you assemble to exercise kingdom authority. If nothing changed when you came together, it was a fruitless exercise. There should be an improvement in the mindset of the people present or their spiritual condition. Either that or there should be a shift in the spirit world. Otherwise there is no benefit from the time spent together on a Sunday morning, regardless of how elaborate the production was. If that was the case, it would have been better if we had played a game; at least the people would have benefitted from the physical exercise.

THE POWER AND AUTHORITY OF THE CHURCH

The churches in Europe and North America are still doing the same things they have done all along. They have been doing the same things, again and again, thinking someday the results they are hoping for will appear in their midst. Dear brothers and sisters and pastors, it will not happen. It's getting late and it is time to wake from our sleep.

If we do things differently and if Jesus tarries for the next ten years, I believe we can truly change the nations with the wisdom and the grace of God. That is what this book is all about. Jesus did not come to give us a religion, revival, a building, or a particular form of worship—He came to give us a kingdom.

> "Do not fear, little flock, for it is your Father's good pleasure to *give you the kingdom*" (Luke 12:32).

> "And *I bestow upon you a kingdom*, just as My Father bestowed *one* upon Me" (Luke 22:29).

Any nation or kingdom is only as good as the people who administer it. Wherever I go, people are dissatisfied and complaining about the government in their nation. They are expecting unsaved men and women who are part of the government to be good and execute righteousness in their nations. It will not happen. Though God gave us a kingdom, most people don't know how to administer a kingdom. We are like little children whose father gave them all the wealth of this earth, but we are still crying for a little piece of candy because we do not understand the vast wealth He already gave to us.

The governing influence of the church is supposed to extend to every sphere of our lives: spiritual, natural, political, and economic—every area. The church is not supposed to be excluded or separate from any part of our life. *It should all be connected.*

If there is one agency that God put on this earth to bring any necessary changes to our community and the nations, it is the church. The church is the hope of the nations. This book is not about evangelism or church planting. This book is about how to administer the kingdom of God now, to the nations of the world and the immediate communities around us. Evangelism and church planting are by-products of that administration. God has wanted to see His kingdom established on the earth from the very beginning. When the phrase "God's kingdom on this earth" is used, it is normal for a person to wonder what that looks like in the natural in this age and time.

PREFACE

I am very excited to bring understanding to you from the Holy Scriptures. Establishing His kingdom does not mean overthrowing governments and taking over the geopolitical systems of this world, or building palaces and thrones and armies. It means to bring the influence of the kingdom of heaven into the kingdoms of men. It is to make known to the people of this earth that there is a God in heaven whose kingdom reigns over all.

> "Therefore know this day, and consider *it* in your heart, that the Lord Himself *is* God in heaven above and on the earth beneath; *there is* no other" (Deuteronomy 4:39).

> "And as soon as we heard *these things,* our hearts melted; neither did there remain any more courage in anyone because of you [the Israelites], for the Lord your God, He *is* God in heaven above and on earth beneath" (Joshua 2:11).

> "Then Jehoshaphat stood in the assembly of Judah and Jerusalem, in the house of the Lord, before the new court, and said: "O Lord God of our fathers, *are* You not God in heaven, and do You *not* rule over all the kingdoms of the nations, and in Your hand *is there not* power and might, so that no one is able to withstand You? *Are* You not our God, *who* drove out the inhabitants of this land before Your people Israel, and gave it to the descendants of Abraham Your friend forever?" (2 Chronicles 20:5-7).

> "The Lord has established His throne in heaven, and His kingdom rules over all" (Psalm 103:19).

> "In order that the living may know that the Most High rules in the kingdom of men" (Daniel 4:17).

> "Then fear came upon every soul, and many wonders and signs were done through the apostles" (Acts 2:43).

Joseph and Daniel are great examples of how, in a time and age like ours, we are supposed to administer God's kingdom in the nations we are living in. They did not overthrow the king and sit on his throne to establish God's kingdom. But, as a result of exercising the *wisdom* and *spiritual authority* God gave them, the king and all the people in the land came to recognize that there is a God in heaven and they worshiped Him.

THE POWER AND AUTHORITY OF THE CHURCH

That is what I mean by administering God's kingdom now on this earth. But it is not exclusive. There are certain times we need to remove rulers and change the laws of governments through the prayers of the church. Believe me, the *ekklesia*[1] has the power to do this, and it happened in the New Testament.

If individuals like Joseph and Daniel could bring great kings and kingdoms to their knees and the demonic forces that ruled those kingdoms could not touch them, and twelve men could reach the entire known world in their lifetime, how much more can nearly one billion believers who are filled with the Spirit of God accomplish in our time? What was it like when a whole city or even entire nations turned to Jesus during the New Testament times? Modern countries like Turkey, Syria, and many others were once Christian countries. Is it possible that something like that can happen in our day and time? I totally believe it is possible and it is God's will. This book is intended to teach us how to do it.

In the next decade, things are going to change drastically in the political arenas of the nations. There will be a tremendous shift in the economy and in our ways of thinking and living. Many things we believed theologically to be true will be challenged. Many will fall prey to the enemy's lies, but there will be a remnant who will remain faithful to their Savior, no matter the cost. I dedicate this book to those precious ones who are going through various trials and temptations right now. Actually, these are the birth pangs for the next move of God.

To administer a kingdom, we have to be willing to learn to think differently and adopt new ways of doing things. This book will change your perception and understanding about yourself and the *ekklesia* (church) of which you are a part. If we apply the principles outlined in this book and the one I will mention at the end of this, we will see any nation coming to Christ within ten to fifteen years of time without a single gospel crusade or healing rally.

Abraham John

---

1. This refers to the governing body of the kingdom of God as a whole. Please see page 38 for a complete definition.

Introduction

Introduction

On August 21, 2013, in the suburbs of Damascus, Syria, rockets and artillery shells containing a chemical agent called *sarin* were fired from government positions toward rebel-held villages in the eastern and southern parts of the city. This caused the death of more than 1,400 civilians, including hundreds of children.

The United Nations and the West gave the Syrian regime an ultimatum to either destroy their chemical weapons or hand them over to the U.N. If they didn't comply and allow the sites to be inspected, they would face dire consequences.

There was another element involved in Syria that could propel the situation into a possible world war if a battle broke out: the involvement of Russia. The Syrian regime that was backed by the Russians was not willing to step down and give up their power that easily. A scenario was set for a possible world war to break out at any moment.

On September 1, 2013, the president of the United States approached Congress for approval to take military action against Syria. The whole world was looking at the nation of Syria to see what would happen next. Everyone was afraid another war might break out in the Middle East, which could potentially turn into a global war because of Russia's involvement. No one wanted that.

Five U.S. aircraft carriers were ordered to move to eastern Mediterranean waters; they were waiting for the order to fire cruise missiles into Syria to attack and destroy the chemical weapons and their plants. The U.S. Secretary of State gave the Syrian government one week to hand over its chemical weapons and allow a U.N. inspection to avoid military attack.

Time was running out. There was no positive response from the Syrian government for the first five days, but something was about to change the whole game.

A Choice to Make

On September 3, nearly seven thousand miles away from Syria, in Denver, Colorado, I was scheduled to speak. The message God gave me to share was entitled "How to Reach the World." He told me that if we are going to reach the world, we must know what it is made of.

Only a few hours were left to decide the fate of thousands of innocent people. The destruction could never be justified. Children would have lost their parents and siblings; and in addition to loss of life, hundreds of people might have become handicapped or maimed. The devastation would have been horrific. The devil wants to kill as many people as possible and take them to hell with him before they ever hear the name of Jesus and the salvation He offers. That is the reason for the increase of wars and natural disasters.

There I was, preparing to preach about how to reach the world, when most of the world was in fear and turmoil because another war was about to break forth. I had two options before me: the first was to preach a nice sermon to please the crowd, pray for them at the end, and many would come and tell me how wonderful the sermon was.

> There I was, preparing to preach about how to reach the world, when most of the world was in fear and turmoil because another war was about to break forth.

But I had another option before me: to do something in the spirit about what was imminent in Syria, for the thousands of people who had not yet heard the gospel of Christ and the salvation He offers. They could go to hell and we wouldn't even know they ever existed.

Ekklesia is a Greek term that describes the governing body of a kingdom, which we call the church. The Holy Spirit, the Governor of the *Ekklesia*, stepped in and told me to lead the *ekklesia* in prayer for what was going on in Syria, so there would not be another war. The Bible says God's house shall be called a house of prayer for all nations and His kingdom reigns over the kingdoms of men.

We prayed fervently that night. We prayed and declared that there would not be another war in Syria. We exercised our God-given authority to intervene to save the lives of thousands of innocent people. Something dramatic happened in the world of international politics within the following eight hours. The Syrian regime consented to the demands of the United Nations for the destruction of their chemical weapons and allowed them to inspect the sites. It was a temporary victory, and as I write, the problems are still raging. They need our continued prayers.

I am not saying the above result came just because of *our* prayers. There might have been thousands of other members of the *ekklesia* around the world who were also praying. The reason I mention the above incident is to show what our prayers could do if the *ekklesia* really prayed. What could happen in our country if believers spent at least a fraction of their Sunday morning services praying for their communities and nations?

> **What could happen in our country if believers spent at least a fraction of their Sunday morning services praying for their communities and nations?**

Have We Missed Our Purpose?

I know that many are waiting for the rapture to take place. Every generation since Christ thought that they were the last generation and that Jesus was going to return in their lifetime. I wish it would happen now, but what if He tarries and does not come for another century? Are we prepared for it? We are supposed to live like His return is imminent but prepare and plan as if there are another hundred years ahead of us.

Could it be possible that we miss God and what He has for us now—like many of the first century Jewish people missed their Messiah—because we're looking for the wrong thing? They were considered the most spiritual people of their time. I strongly believe the season the entire world has been waiting centuries for has come upon us. Perhaps we can't see the forest through the trees.

Why would God give Jesus all authority in heaven and on earth, and He in turn give it to the *ekklesia* if He does not want us to use that authority right here and now? Would He want us to use it after the rapture instead? I don't think so. Is it God's will for the majority of the people alive today to go to hell? That is probably what would happen if the rapture were to take place right now.

The time has come for God's children to take their place on this earth before Jesus comes back. There is one Scripture that is quoted more times from the Old Testament in the New Testament than any other verse. It's not about becoming born again, the rapture, or prayer for revival. In this verse the Father is telling His Son to sit at His right hand until He makes His enemies His footstool. It is quoted seven times in the New Testament.[2] I began to wonder why that particular Scripture was quoted more times than any other and I believe there is a definite reason for it. *In fact, this verse is quoted in the first message Peter preached that was the catalyst for the New Testament church.*

> "For David did not ascend into the heavens, but he says himself: 'The Lord said to my Lord, "Sit at My right hand, till I make Your enemies Your footstool" ' " (Acts 2:34-35).

Though Jesus defeated Satan and his kingdom on the cross, we do not yet see that Jesus' enemies have been made His footstool in the practical sense. When will this happen, and who is going to do the job? Through Jesus' death and resurrection He received all authority in heaven and on earth. In turn, He gave that authority to His church (Ephesians 1:19-23). Now the church has to exercise that authority to bring His enemies to His footstool. He is waiting for this to happen so He can return to the earth.

> "But this Man, after He had offered one sacrifice for sins forever, sat down at the right hand of God, *from that time waiting till His enemies are made His footstool*" (Hebrews 10:12-13).

If someone on TV tells you that Jesus is going to come this year, please don't sell your belongings and pack your stuff. He is not coming until the church overcomes this world and His enemies are made His footstool. How is the Father going to accomplish this task for His Son? In this battle, the Son is not going to fight to make the enemy His footstool. He already finished His work on the cross and received the right to sit at His Father's right hand. The most important part of those two verses is the Son being asked to "sit till" the Father

---

2. See Matthew 22:44; Mark 12:36; Luke 20:42-43; Acts 2:34-35; 1 Corinthians 15: 24-25; Hebrews 1:13; 10:12-13.

makes His enemies His footstool. And the Son has been sitting and waiting for that to happen. Believe it or not, He is not going to come back to earth until that takes place.

Neither is the Father going to come to this earth to fight against the enemy. There is only one way this can be accomplished and that is through the *ekklesia*, the body of Christ on the earth today, under the direction of the Holy Spirit. You and I are part of that body, and subsequently part of the battle to make His enemies His footstool. This book is all about equipping the saints to do just that. If this is to happen, the current church needs to make a U-turn. Fast.

How is the *ekklesia* going to accomplish this task? For this to happen we need to know what the *ekklesia* is all about. Why did Jesus leave us on this earth? Is it to sing to Him? If so, why didn't He ask anyone to sing to Him while He was here? Did God ask Adam to sing to Him? We have been misinformed about our mission and purpose. For too long we have been deceived and robbed of our inheritance and our rights as the children of Almighty God.

When the *ekklesia* exercises her rightful authority and brings Jesus' enemies to His footstool, He in turn will deliver the kingdom to God the Father and then the end will come.

> "Then *comes* the end, when He delivers the kingdom to God the Father, when He puts an end to all rule and all authority and power. For He must reign till He has put all enemies under His feet" (1 Corinthians 15:24-25).

The kingdoms of this world must become the kingdoms of our Lord and of His Christ (Revelation 11:15).

How is this practically realized in this day and age? It does not mean we (the church) need to destroy Satan and all his demons from earth before Jesus can come back. That is not what the above verses mean. They do not say that until all demonic forces are destroyed from this earth Jesus will not return. I believe it means that each believer and family faces a particular battle, or enemy, that fights against them. Though we have the same enemy, we don't all face the battle in the same area of life. He uses a specific strategy against us and we need to overcome it. It is the same with local churches. The battle a local church in New Delhi, India, faces will be different than the one a local church in Los Angeles, California, faces.

When Jesus gave the messages to the seven churches in the book of Revelation, each of those churches faced different challenges and they were commanded to overcome something specific or lose their reward. It was very clear what Jesus was expecting of them. When each individual believer and each local church overcomes their particular battle, they are declaring to the forces of darkness that our Lord has overcome and are in turn bringing the enemies of Jesus to His footstool.

In the book of Romans Paul said to the church in Rome, "And the God of peace will crush Satan under your feet shortly" (Romans 16:20). That does not mean they were going to crush Satan under their feet once and for all and he would not be in existence anymore. No. It meant God was going to give them victory over the enemy that was fighting against the church in Rome. The Roman Empire eventually fell and the demonic forces that ruled Rome were defeated and brought to the footstool of Jesus.

When the Israelites reached the Promised Land they needed to overcome their enemies in order to possess the land. They did not overcome the enemies in the entire world. Their enemies were very specific nations God had told them about. Though God promised them and told them the land was theirs, they were required to fight and defeat their enemies. Just because God promised, that does not mean the enemy was going to let them come and take the land. They had to make a choice either to overcome their enemies or be satisfied with what they had. We are at a crossroad and we are forced to make a choice. Are we going to continue the way we have been going or is it time to reevaluate our programs? If we continue doing the same we will keep reaping the same result.

A New Era

With the year 2000, we entered a new era called the Kingdom Age led by apostles. The church has yet to embrace this. Most are still trying to revamp the past season. The church as a whole is not ready to receive apostolic ministry. When apostles come they don't come

> **With the year 2000, we entered a new era called the Kingdom Age led by apostles.**

with a little "God loves you" message or motivational speech. Instead they come with apostolic doctrines, which for most are difficult to receive. We need

INTRODUCTION

to pray for the church to be ready to receive the ministry of an apostle. This may require a great deal of restructuring in the way things are done.

The Kingdom or Apostolic Age has three major characteristics. One is a greater manifestation of God's wisdom and authority through His people; the second is increased persecution against Christians; and the third is the advancement of the kingdom in the midst of that persecution.

If you look at the early church—or anyone who made a difference for God—you will see these characteristics manifested in their lives. But the good news is that God's kingdom and His *ekklesia* always prevailed if they remained faithful to their Commander-in-Chief. People like Joseph, Daniel, Paul, and the brethren of the early church existed and grew in very hostile environments.

There is something amazing about the kingdom of God: When it is hard pressed, it will bring to nothing everything that opposes it. I like what Jesus said about His kingdom, "Therefore I say to you, the kingdom of God will be taken from you and given to a nation bearing the fruits of it. And whoever falls on this stone will be broken; but on whomever it falls, it will grind him to powder" (Matthew 21:43-44).

Throughout the Bible and history, God raised up certain people and nations to make known His greatness, wisdom, and power to the rest of the earth. The Bible tells why God raised up Pharaoh, the king of Egypt, "For the Scripture says to the Pharaoh, 'For this very purpose I have raised you up, that I may show My power in you, and that My name may be declared in all the earth' " (Romans 9:17).

Jesus said, "My house shall be called a house of prayer for all nations" (Mark 11:17). Today in our churches, we have made what is most important the least important, and the least important things have become the most prominent part of our program. If we spent twenty minutes singing, and took just five minutes of that to pray as a congregation, what would God do through that church? Even when we pray, we spend most of the time asking God for things He has already given us. So, we pray amiss.

> Today in our churches, we have made what is most important the least important, and the least important things have become the most prominent part of our program.

Just before the year 2000, most of the world was caught up (the church included) with Y2K. They thought the world was going to end and Jesus was going to come in that year. Y2K came and went and we are still here. People constantly make claims like that, saying Jesus is going to come this year. I asked the Lord why such things happen and He reminded me that He said that many would rise and say they have found the Messiah.

> "Then if anyone says to you, 'Look, here *is* the Christ!' or 'There!' do not believe *it.* For false christs and false prophets will rise and show great signs and wonders to deceive, if possible, even the elect" (Matthew 24:23-24).

In fact, this will increase in the days ahead. God told us not to be deceived by those people. The reason these false prophets arise is to deceive the church in order to keep her ineffective and disengaged. When they hear Jesus is going to come this year, many people become fearful and do not engage in what is going on in their community and nation. They seclude themselves and wait for the rapture to take place. They give the devil plenty of freedom to do whatever he wants to do, while the church just watches and complains.

Where Is the Everlasting Kingdom?

Vast numbers of people have lost trust in the church. The American church is becoming more secular than Christian, and Europe has become one of the least Christian continents on earth. Have you ever wondered why such things happen? It is not because great revivals did not take place in these regions. To most people in the world, Christianity is just another religion with rules, regulations, and rituals. Jesus never intended His kingdom or His church on earth to be known as a religion. The devil knew that if he could bring Christianity down to the level of a religion, it would lose its very essence and people would stay away from it.

Why would someone who belongs to one religion change to another? In some parts of the world people have changed their religion to gain better material or social benefits, but their lives cannot be used to build God's kingdom on earth because they never had a true revelation of who God is and how His kingdom operates. So, when someone else offers them better benefits, they will change their religion again. This is happening in the United States and in India right now as I write this book.

INTRODUCTION

The devil has a counterfeit for everything God has and does. In fact, he has a false church operating now. Unfortunately, many so-called Christians are part of that pseudo-church. The devil also does better social and charitable works through other religions than most Christians. Additionally, he has people in authority in governments and businesses all over the world to execute his will and purpose.

You might be wondering if I am a propagator of "kingdom now" or "dominion theology." I am not. I am a kingdom *forever* guy because God's kingdom is everlasting and His dominion has no end (Luke 1:33). He reigns forever. Dimensions and manifestations of this vary according to how the people on the earth respond.

In the Old and New Testaments, God used His people to administer His kingdom, and He has given us the power and authority to do the same. The whole world is waiting for the manifestation of the sons of God (Romans 8:19).

If you are part of that end-time army of God, what I write in this book will bear witness in your spirit. I would like to ask you a favor. Just like the believers in Berea did, please refer to the Holy Scriptures to see that what I am sharing here lines up with the Word of God. I also request that you not reject a truth just because it is not popular. Are you ready?

Chapter 1: The *Ekklesia*

Chapter 1: The *Ekklesia*

"The mystery which has been hidden from ages and from generations, but now has been revealed to His saints" (Colossians 1:26).

The *ekklesia* is one of the mysteries that was hidden in the heart of God from eternity past and has been revealed to us in this day and age through His apostles and prophets. Believe it or not, we are part of that era that every prophet and saint we admire in the Old Testament looked forward to seeing. They yearned to see and live in this day and age.

> **The *ekklesia* is one of the mysteries that was hidden in the heart of God from eternity past and has been revealed to us in this day and age.**

A Matter of Perspective

The church we see today is like the poem called "The Blind Men and the Elephant" by John Godfrey Saxe. These blind men had never seen anything before, let alone an elephant. They had heard much from other people about this humongous animal but could not really imagine exactly what it would look like. To end their curiosity, they decided to go and explore for themselves. They would "feel" how an elephant *looks* so they could put together the pieces of their imagination and finally "see" the elephant.

One of them touched the leg of the elephant and thought it felt like a tree. He said the elephant looked like a tree. The second touched the trunk of the elephant and came back saying it looked like a snake. The third touched the tail of the elephant and thought the elephant was like a rope. The fourth touched its ear and returned saying it looked like a big fan. The fifth touched the stomach of the elephant and claimed the elephant was like a wall. The sixth man happened to touch the elephant's tusk, so he told the others it was like a spear.

If we take just one of their reports as the ultimate truth, how accurate will the description of an elephant be? To be honest, an elephant is *like* everything explained above. But if you took only one of their descriptions and came to a conclusion, it would be wrong and not an accurate picture of an elephant. An elephant is not a tree, snake, rope, fan, wall, or spear. Only when we put all of these perceptions together will we get an idea of what an elephant really looks like.

The last stanza of the poem reads:

> So oft in theologic wars,
> The disputants, I ween,
> Rail on in utter ignorance
> Of what each other mean,
> *And prate about an Elephant*
> *Not one of them has seen.*[3]

Just like each of those blind men had a different experience and perception of the elephant, throughout the centuries people got stuck on a particular view or perception of the church and began to fight against each other for their view, rather than fighting against the forces that divided them. They missed the big picture.

For many centuries the church has been arguing and fighting about particular doctrines and traditions. That fight birthed various denominations and sects, each one specializing in different truths or aspects of the church. The church is a multi-faceted organism. Many have tried to "singlify" its objective through the centuries and they all went astray in their portrayal of the church.

Some say the church's focus should be on evangelism and saving sinners. Others say it should be on power, healing, and miracles. Still others say the focus should be on loving others, feeding the hungry, taking care of orphans, and helping the poor. Many believe our purpose is to worship and teach the Word of God. There may be other concepts and descriptions of the church that come to your mind, such as the building and the clergy. It could be faith and prosperity, grace, holiness, or revival.

---

3. Saxe, John Godfrey. "The Blind Men and the Elephant." Public domain.

Just like those blind men missed grasping the full understanding of an elephant, we as believers have missed what God's purpose for the church is, and thus we remain ineffective in our nations. The church is the only hope for the nations. Only the church can offer real solutions to the problems we are facing in our world today. It is time to put all the pieces together, break down the walls that separate us, and embrace one another in the unity of the Spirit—not in the unity of our perceptions.

If you take a look at the Catholic Church, they have a revelation about the natural aspects of how a kingdom operates. They have more than one billion followers and have just one leader. There are many Catholic nations in which almost everyone is Catholic from the leader of the nation to the shopkeeper down the street. They establish schools, hospitals, and charitable institutions in almost every country, including the Muslim nations. What they lack is a true revelation of who Jesus is and what He accomplished in His resurrection. We need to pray that God will give them that revelation.

Other denominations that are good in the natural aspects of the kingdom are the Baptist, Presbyterian, and the Methodist churches. They are very good at administration, starting new businesses, and coming up with products. But they lack the revelation of who the Holy Spirit is and His ministry today. We need to pray that they will have that revelation.

The Pentecostals and the Charismatics are very good at operating in the gifts of the Holy Spirit, but not that good in demonstrating the fruit of the spirit, and lack an understanding of the natural aspects of a kingdom. We need to pray for God to give us a revelation of how His kingdom operates. When we put all the above pieces together we will have an idea of what the church is all about. The same religious spirit works behind all these deceptions to blind the body of Christ and to keep us divided and ineffective.

Jesus Didn't Teach Much about the Church

Jesus used the word *church* only three times in the four Gospels. That shocked me! If Jesus came to establish His church on the earth, why didn't He teach about it more? Why didn't He teach His disciples about church administration, homiletics (the science of preaching), building funds, church picnics, revivals, worship, and choir? They would be the ones leading the church once it began, after all.

For almost twenty years of my life I was focused on evangelism, church planting, training pastors, and taking care of orphans. I was not happy with the results. My mindset was that if I could win more people to Christ and if there were more Christians in a nation, it would be transformed to heaven on earth. Then I realized that the kingdom of darkness was thriving in the nations with a Christian majority! I went to God with my problem.

> Jesus used the word *church* only three times in the four Gospels.

That's when God began to give me revelation and insight. Though I received the revelation of the kingdom of God and preached it, the people who listened to those messages were not able to receive the revelation because they were drenched in a *church mentality* instead of a *kingdom mindset*.

For most of the people I trained, planting another church or baptizing another convert was the most important part of their agenda. They were not concerned about God establishing His kingdom on this earth. When Jesus taught us to pray, His first priority was summed up in this statement, "Let Your kingdom come and Your will be done on earth as it is in heaven." He did not ask us to pray, "Let another church be planted on the other side of the street" or "Take us all to heaven as soon as possible."

So what is the purpose of the church? What did God intend in His heart when He thought of the church? If a company sends its representative overseas to train people about a new product they are planning to launch, that representative will explain everything about that product so their employees in that country will be ready to market it effectively. That sounds right, doesn't it?

Get a Glimpse of God's Perspective

God operates from a different perspective. Imagine His kingdom as the *company* that was launching the product and the church as the *product*. Jesus was teaching and training His disciples about the company and its method of operation more than about the product. He wanted them to become familiar with the company and its Owner before becoming too passionate about its product. Because only if an employee knew the purpose, values, and the mission of the company, would he understand why it was launching a particular product and then be able to explain it to others. The product represents the company and is intended to fulfill its vision and mission.

Jesus Taught about the Kingdom

Although the church was going to be the greatest enterprise God ever began, Jesus, who is the Head of the church, taught about it only twice in His entire recorded preaching and teaching. On the other hand, He mentioned His kingdom more than a hundred times in the four Gospels.

Jesus wanted His disciples to become familiar with how His kingdom operated. He wanted to create a kingdom mindset in them before they ever got to do anything with His church. Without it, the church won't be effective. Only when we understand a kingdom can we clearly understand the purpose of the church. The church is here to administer God's kingdom, but if its leaders don't know what the kingdom is and what it is made of, how can they administer it?

> **Only when we understand a kingdom can we clearly understand the purpose of the church.**

If Jesus' only intent for starting His church on the earth was to get a bunch of people saved and take them to heaven, then why did He spend so much time preaching and teaching about the kingdom of God rather than how to convert people? He could have just saved all that for when we got to heaven if there was no specific purpose or benefit to us knowing about His kingdom here on earth. If all He wanted was a choir in heaven, why would He create this planet Earth and put us here, allowing us to go through all this turmoil? Why would He allow His Son to endure what He endured? He could have just created us and put us in heaven in the first place! A religious spirit has deceived us for a very long time regarding our purpose personally and the purpose of the church as a whole.

I do not intend to condemn or diminish what the church is already doing today, but I would like to add an important missing and neglected element to its present program. Without it the church won't be as effective as it should be, regardless of what program, teaching, or even miracles we may have. God's purpose is to restore that kingdom mindset to His people who have been drenched in a church mentality for hundreds of years. There are many who are weary of it and can't wait to be part of a change.

Following are my intentions for writing this book:

◆ To train church members to be kingdom citizens

◆ To train believers to live as sons and daughters of God on this earth

◆ To equip kingdom citizens to exercise their rights and authority to administer His kingdom in the communities and the nations in which they are living

◆ To deliver the church from a religion, rapture, and revival mentality to a kingdom mindset

◆ To communicate that there is still hope for the West, but that hope is in the church

"I Will Build My *Ekklesia*"

The Greek word used for the church in the New Testament is *ekklesia*. What exactly does it mean? What picture came to the disciples' minds when Jesus mentioned the church to them for the first time? The word *ekklesia* in Greek means, "called out ones." [4] Called out from what and for what purpose?

When Jesus mentioned the church, the disciples were not surprised and did not take Him aside and ask Him for further direction like they did when He taught them how to pray. When we think of the church today, we think of a building with a cross on the top, or we picture a gathering of people singing or listening to a preacher. I wonder what came to the minds of the disciples when they heard the word *church* for the first time.

When Jesus referred to the church, He mentioned three things: (1) the fact that He would build it, (2) the idea that there was a battle going on, over which the church has the authority to prevail, and (3) that the church would reconcile relationships (Matthew 16:18-19; 18:15-18).

If the establishing of the church was such an important enterprise, why didn't He give more explanation about it? Why didn't He train the disciples about how to conduct a service or take an effective offering to meet their budget for different ministries? There are two reasons Jesus did not do that. First of all, He did not come with the purpose of revealing

---

4. Thayer and Smith. "Greek Lexicon entry for *ekklesia*," The NAS New Testament Greek Lexicon, 1999. Web.

the management of a church. Instead His message was about the kingdom of God. He came to reveal that kingdom and give back to us what we lost because of Adam's sin.

The second reason Jesus didn't teach about the church was that the revelation of the church that we are part of was to be given to Paul. It was through him that God chose to reveal the mystery of the New Testament church and how it is supposed to operate on the earth.

Some people think the concept of the church did not begin until Jesus' resurrection. That is not true. The church has been on this earth ever since the kingdom of God began to operate here. Every kingdom on this earth had a *church or ekklesia* that administered its policies and rules. Without a church, a kingdom cannot operate and without a kingdom, a church will not survive. I will show you that from the Scriptures in the following pages. The concept of the church was revealed in the Bible and throughout history in both the political and spiritual sense long before the New Testament church began. If anyone says they live in the kingdom and doesn't want to be a part of an *ekklesia*, it is because they lack a true understanding about a kingdom and how it operates.

> **Every kingdom on this earth had a *church* or *ekklesia* that administered its policies and rules.**

Called Out

> "This is he, that was *in the church in the wilderness* with the angel which spake to him in the Mount Sinai, and with our fathers: who received the lively oracles to give unto us" (Acts 7:38 KJV).

From this verse we understand that what might have come to the disciples' heart when Jesus mentioned the word *ekklesia* was a picture of the people of Israel in the wilderness; the same Greek word is used in the above verse to describe them. What was significant about the people of Israel in the wilderness? What did they do and how did they live as God's *ekklesia*, the called out ones? If we study their lives and the way God dealt with them, what He did through them, and how they functioned as a nation and handled their internal problems, we will get somewhat of an understanding about the church in the New Testament. Paul said that everything they went through was for our example (1 Corinthians 10:6, 11).

The Israelites were *called out* by God (from Egypt) to be a special kingdom, or a nation of kings and priests (Exodus 19:6) through whom He would accomplish His purpose on earth. The church today is also the called out ones, a royal priesthood and a holy nation (1 Peter 2:9). When we think of church today we should think of it as a nation ruled by a king. For many, what comes to their mind is that we don't belong here. We are waiting to fly away. That wasn't the way the Israelites functioned.

Imagine a nation divided into a million pieces: how effective can that nation be? That is what is happening to the body of Christ. Even though we are one body, we have been divided into a million pieces, so even a small enemy could easily conquer a local church. This needs to change and is about to change. A nation could be divided into states or provinces under one centralized governing authority and still function well. Unfortunately, the Spirit-filled body of Christ does not have the necessary unity and centralized governing system; that is our biggest weakness.

There is a church that is functioning as a nation on this earth today. They have more than a billion believers around the world and they all submit to one human leader. It really surprises me when I think about how they run their system. I have never seen one of their local leaders trying to do their own ministry and call it "So-and-So's International Ministry." They have their own economy, educational structure, and governing system. They function as a nation within the nation in which they exist—and that's how a church should operate.

The Israelites were different in every way from other nations around them. First of all, the people of Israel were a nation and God was their king. They had their own economy, educational, and governing system. They were different from all other nations in every way because they had a different operating system.

The Israelites depended on other nations only for trade and investment. They never borrowed money from other nations. They considered it as a curse or a defeat to borrow from the heathens. Whatever they experienced in the physical realm, we, the church, experience in the spiritual. Whatever power and authority they exercised in the physical world, we have over both the spiritual and the natural world.

When they came out of Egypt there was no one who was sick or poor. It was the same in the early church. There was no one sick or in need (Acts 2:45; 4:45; 5:16). All of their needs were met. When they reached the Promised Land, they had to defeat enemies to possess the land. The sad thing was they did not defeat and destroy the enemies that God told them to utterly destroy. In the future, those nations became a snare and a thorn in the flesh and drew them away from the one and only true God who brought them out of Egypt.

God is a king and He has a kingdom He wants to establish on the earth. That is His ultimate plan and objective. *Everything He does* is geared toward accomplishing that one purpose and nothing else. He wants to reveal His wisdom, glory, and power to the people on earth as well as to the principalities and powers in the heavenly places (Ephesians 3:10).

Another reason the disciples did not question Jesus about the church when He mentioned it was because they were familiar with the concept of kingdoms having an *ekklesia*, from a historic perspective (Israel was a kingdom) and from the political climate in which they were living. They knew Jesus was a King and that every king needed an *ekklesia*. It was a political term used in the Greek world and was never used to address a group of people who worshiped, preached, or sang. It was used to represent a group of men who were called out from among the people by a king or government to administer the political, judicial, economic, and social affairs of the people.

> **Jesus is the King and He has a kingdom so He needs an *ekklesia* to govern the affairs of His kingdom. That is why He started the church.**

Every king and kingdom had an *ekklesia* that governed its affairs. Jesus added a spiritual dimension to His kingdom and *ekklesia* when He said, "I will build my church" (Matthew 16:18), because His kingdom is a spiritual kingdom. Jesus is the King and He has a kingdom so He needs an *ekklesia* to govern the affairs of His kingdom. That is why He started the church.

The church is a multi-faceted organism and it has a very complex purpose and responsibility. Worship, preaching and teaching of the Word, reaching the lost, missions, prayer groups, praying for the sick, helping the poor and the widows, children's ministry, offerings, various types of ministries and classes, are all only various aspects and duties of a local church. But what is the main purpose of the church?

The Church Should Help You Solve Your Problems

When Jesus mentioned the church the first time, it was in the context of a political confrontation. It was a confrontation between two kingdoms: His church and the gates of hades. In this case the two kingdoms are spiritual kingdoms. They are the kingdom of God and the kingdom of darkness.

> "And I also say to you that you are Peter, and on this rock I will build My church, and the gates of Hades shall not prevail against it" (Matthew 16:18).

Jesus refers to the church as something He builds to withstand the operation of hades, or the powers of darkness. The above verse refers to a spiritual battle—one the church needs to be prepared to fight.

The second time Jesus mentioned the church, it was in reference to addressing or solving the relational (social) problems people have.

> "Moreover if your brother sins against you, go and tell him his fault between you and him alone. If he hears you, you have gained your brother. But if he will not hear, take with you one or two more, that 'by the mouth of two or three witnesses every word may be established.' And if he refuses to hear them, tell *it* to the church. But if he refuses even to hear the church, let him be to you like a heathen and a tax collector" (Matthew 18:15-17).

This verse refers to the church as a place where judicial or social problems are solved. When a person has an offense against another and they cannot find a solution by themselves, they are to bring it before the church to solve it. Jesus did not say when two people have problems, they need to go to church and worship. No, they are to *tell it to the ekklesia.* If the church was a building, could we tell our problem to a building? But the church is not a building; it is a group of people. And if the person refuses to *hear the church* (that group of people), let him be to you like a heathen and a tax collector.

The church needs to administer the kingdom of God and govern the affairs of men and women in society. When two people have problems that they cannot solve, Jesus did not say to go to the court system of the world, but to the church, a group of people appointed by God to administer His kingdom (Matthew 18:15-17). Even Paul admonished the Corinthian church to not go to a court of law against another believer. He asked the church to solve the issue.

> "Dare any of you, having a matter against another, go to law before the unrighteous, and not before the saints? *Do you not know that the saints will judge the world?* And if the world will be judged by you, are you unworthy to judge the smallest matters? Do you not know that we shall judge angels? *How much more, things that pertain to this life?"* (1 Corinthians 6:1-3).

When do you think we will be judging the world and angels? I was taught that we are going to heaven to sing. Paul is saying that we are going to judge the world and the angels, so how much more should we judge things that pertain to this life now? When the Israelites had a judicial, social, or spiritual problem they brought it before their elders. They did not go before the Gentiles to get help. That is the way the church is supposed to function too.

Each time Jesus mentioned the church He referred to a governing body, not a place of worship. He referred to a group of people who were assigned to exercise authority to solve problems both in *the spiritual* and in *the natural* world. In the political world of those days, the *ekklesia* was a group of people who were called out—or selected—from the general public to govern the affairs of a kingdom or a nation.

> **Each time Jesus mentioned the church He referred to a governing body, not a place of worship.**

The disciples knew that every king had an *ekklesia* in his kingdom that governed his affairs. That's why they kept asking Jesus when He was going to set up His kingdom on the earth. They wanted to sit and rule with Him (Matthew 20:21; Acts 1:6). When we read the gospel of Matthew, we notice that it was after Jesus said He will build His *ekklesia* that the mother of James and John came with the request for her sons to sit on His right and on His left in His kingdom (Matthew 20:20-21). They wanted to be part of His *ekklesia*, the governing body of His kingdom, but they only understood the natural aspect of the term. That's what they were familiar with at that time. The spiritual revelation of His kingdom or *ekklesia* came to them later.

Definitions for *Ekklesia*

Here are a series of definitions of the word *ekklesia* by respected Greek scholars. Please read them with an open mind.

> Liddell and Scott define *ekklesia* as "an assembly of citizens summoned by the crier, the legislative assembly."[5]

> Thayer's *Lexicon* says, "an assembly of the people convened at the public place of council for the purpose of deliberating."[6]

> Trench gives the meaning as, "the lawful assembly in a free Greek city of all those possessed of the rights of citizenship, for the transaction of public affairs."[7]

> Seyffert's *Dictionary* states "The assembly of the people, which in Greek cities had the power of final decision in public affairs."[8]

As you read this book, keep these definitions in your heart concerning the church. From here onward when you hear the word *church*, try to envision a "legislative assembly" instead of a building, people singing, or pastors preaching. The definition God gave me for the *church* is, "the governing body of the kingdom of God on this earth" or "a group of people who are called by God to administer the kingdom of God on this earth." Try to keep those definitions in your heart.

---

5. Liddell, Henry George, and Robert Scott. *A Greek-English Lexicon*. Oxford: University Press, 1855. 206.

6. Thayer, Joseph Henry, Carl Ludwig Wilibald Grimm, Christian Gottlob Wilke, and James Strong. Thayer's Greek-English Lexicon of the New Testament: Coded with the Numbering System from Strong's Exhaustive Concordance of the Bible. Peabody, MA: Hendrickson Publishers, 1896. 196.

7. Trench, Richard Chenevix. *Synonyms of the New Testament*. Grand Rapids: W.B. Eerdmans Pub., 1948. 1, 2.

8. Seyffert, Oskar, Henry Nettleship, and John Edwin Sandys. *A Dictionary of Classical Antiquities, Mythology, Religion, Literature, Art*. New York: Meridian Books, 1956. 202, 203.

THE EKKLESIA

In the modern day each country has a national leader and a governing body that helps him or her govern the affairs of that nation. In the United States, the governing body is called Congress. In the United Kingdom, it is called Parliament. In Israel, it is called the Knesset. The governing body of the kingdom of God is called *ekklesia*, or the church.

The picture that comes to your mind when you hear the word *church* is actually very important because that picture comes from the perception and understanding you have of the church. Our actions are subconsciously prompted and directed from those perceptions. So if our perception is not correct, our actions won't be either. Most of the time our understanding is not from a biblical perspective, but one formed by the religious culture or a particular tradition we grew up in. We say things like, "I grew up in church," or "I go to church," or "there was a special meeting in church." In the New Testament, people never used such terms. They used to go to the temple—not to church. The church *met* in the temple or houses. *They* were the church.

> **In the New Testament, people used to go to the temple—not to church. The church *met* in the temple or houses. *They* were the church.**

I want to make it very clear that the purpose of the church is not to be a charitable organization under any earthly government to take care of orphans and to feed the poor and widows. That's just one aspect of the ministry every local church must do; it's not the sole purpose. What do you think was in Jesus' mind when He used the word *church*? Was He thinking of a building where a group of people would come together to sing and hear someone preach on a Sunday morning? I don't think so.

The church is also not a non-profit organization that receives grants and subsidies from the government for its ministers or activities. It is not an entity to which you can donate money and claim it on your year-end tax return. The government allowed that because it was the church that was once entirely responsible for education and for taking care of the poor and the sick (hospitals) in our nation. But things have changed.

I will be using different phrases and words to express the concept of the church throughout this book. I will be using verses from the Bible multiple times to emphasize certain truths. When I refer to the church, I am never referring to a building or a particular denomination, sect, or group. The church is the body of Christ on the earth. I do not belong to any particular sect, group, or denomination. I belong to Christ and I am a member of His body and an ambassador of His kingdom to the earth. I have been sent to equip the body of Christ to administer His kingdom on the earth so that He can return.

If the church is here to administer God's kingdom, how do we do it in a practical sense? If God is making a "kingdom move" on the earth today, how does each believer take part in it? I am confident that as you read this book you will find the answers to those questions.

Additionally, I pray that God will open the eyes of your understanding to see everything He intended to do for His church and through His church on this earth. He is waiting for His body to catch up with His agenda and prioritize their lives according to His purpose. In Him we live and move and have our being (Acts 17:28).

Chapter 2: The Gospel of the Kingdom

Chapter 2: The Gospel of the Kingdom

"And this gospel of the kingdom will be preached in all the world as a witness to all the nations, and then the end will come" (Matthew 24:14).

What type of gospel did Jesus and the apostles preach in the first century? Have you ever wondered why God put the gospel of Matthew as the first book of the New Testament? He had a specific reason behind it. Each gospel is written to address a different group of people and to reveal a main character trait of Jesus and also a different aspect of His kingdom. Matthew wrote his gospel to prove to the world that Jesus is the king, to introduce us to His kingdom, and to show the Jewish people that He is the rightful heir to the throne of David. In it He revealed the kingdom mandate to us.

> **Matthew wrote his gospel to prove to the world that Jesus is the king, to introduce us to His kingdom.**

God wants the New Testament reader to know that with Jesus' coming, He started a new era of His kingdom here on earth. God wants us to look at the rest of the New Testament and this age with a kingdom mindset. Matthew talks about the gospel of the kingdom by saying, "Seek *first* the kingdom of God and His righteousness, and all these things shall be added to you" (Matthew 6:33). What did Jesus mean by telling us to seek His kingdom *first*?

Jesus knew that most people spend nearly all of their time working to provide shelter, clothing, and food for themselves and their families. Working means they are doing something other than what they were born to do and they are not happy. On the inside they know they are supposed to be doing something different.

Jesus commands us to seek His kingdom first—to find what His purpose and plan for our lives is *first*. Then all those other things (shelter, food, and clothing) will be given to us by God, so we will be free to do what we are called or born to do. This is so deep. Please don't skip over this until you really do understand it. You understand something when you know enough to take action based on what you know; otherwise it's just head knowledge.

What is mentioned in the above two paragraphs is enough for the body of Christ to make a U-turn from the direction we are going. Most Christians spend most of their lives doing a job they do not like to earn money for those three things, and they have little time left to do anything for the kingdom. Lord, have mercy! He said to look at the birds of the air, they do not work to earn their food, but our heavenly Father feeds them. Are you not more valuable than they? (Matthew 6:26).

Christians today hear more about worship, tongues, the coming rapture, revival, fire, hell, anointing, prosperity, grace, healing, miracles, and a lot of other things before they ever hear anything about the kingdom. I did not hear anything about the kingdom until I was twenty years into my Christian life and I was already in ministry. And I was a Pentecostal! Can you believe that? In the disciples' case, the first message and the last message (before His ascension) they heard from the mouth of Jesus was about the kingdom. It is because we have lost the kingdom as our focus that the church is not functioning the way it should.

Satan hates the message of the kingdom of God. He definitely does not want to see God's kingdom established on the earth, so he will do anything he can to deceive and blind us from understanding it. That is why we don't hear it preached much these days. As long as we preach about anything else, the devil is happy, but the moment you preach or touch the subject of the kingdom of God, you will see his reaction. That is the reason Jesus commanded us to seek His kingdom first before we do anything Christian.

Another reason Jesus told us to seek His kingdom first is because He knows that until we discover His kingdom we will not be fully satisfied. Man was created to live in His kingdom. Without His kingdom—even if we live in a mansion—we will feel like something is missing deep inside. We have this instinct in us to keep pursuing luxury and comfort, but luxury will not satisfy us—regardless of how much of it we have. It is the longing of our spirit to find its home in the kingdom, but many misunderstand this longing and run after the pleasures of this world instead. So the first thing He wants us to seek and find is His kingdom. Once we have it and learn to live in it, we have everything. In the natural we may have much or little, but our spirit will feel at home. The devil deceived us by causing us to pursue luxury, thinking that is God's kingdom. It is far from the truth.

How do we seek God's kingdom first? If God said to you, "Seek first the kingdom of Nebuchadnezzar," what would you do and where would you start? You would try to learn everything you could about how Nebuchadnezzar's kingdom operated, wouldn't you? Once you discover God's kingdom and learn to live in it, you will realize that everything you need is in His kingdom. There is joy in His kingdom. You may have lost your joy and depend on something of this world to bring happiness instead, but once you discover the kingdom you learn to tap into the joy that is in it. Kingdom joy is not based on what you possess or what you do; it comes from knowing the King, His kingdom, His love, and His plan for your life. God has made all of the resources, wealth, and wisdom that are in heaven available to us through Jesus Christ. We need to tap into them by faith. The only way to live in His kingdom is by faith and trusting in Him moment by moment.

The Gospel of the Kingdom

So many believers around the world are curious to know when Jesus is going to come and are wondering when this world is going to end, and the disciples of Jesus were just as curious. They asked Him very specifically, "Tell us, when will these things be? And what will be the sign of Your coming, and of the end of the age?" (Matthew 24:3b).

Jesus answered their question in Matthew 24 in detail and gave us a very specific clue to discern when this age is really going to end. He said, "And this gospel of the kingdom will be preached in all the world as a witness to all the nations, and then the end will come" (v. 14). He was very clear about when the end will come. He said, "When "this" gospel of the kingdom is preached." That means there are many other kinds of gospels that we could preach. Though no one can predict the day or the hour of His coming, we can speed up the process if we preach the gospel of the kingdom. Until that is done, the end is not going to come.

It is the book of Matthew that includes the twelve parables that reveal the mysteries of the kingdom of heaven. Matthew also talks about the culture, decrees, and laws of the kingdom of God. Among the four Gospels, it is only in the gospel of Matthew Jesus talks about the church. God wants us to see the entire age of the church and the New Testament through a kingdom lens.

Why the gospel of the kingdom? There are many types of gospels being preached today (2 Corinthians 11:4; Galatians 1:8); each denomination has their own version of the gospel message. I have not yet heard a group that preaches the gospel of the kingdom who has a full understanding about how a kingdom operates. That's why the world and the church are in the condition they are in today. We have been preaching every other kind of gospel: Pentecostal gospel, Baptist gospel, prosperity gospel, full gospel, half gospel, etc.: everything except the gospel of the kingdom. The following chart will show you some of the different kinds of gospels that are being preached today.

Humanistic Gospel/ Man-Centered Gospel	Religious Gospel/ Gospel of Salvation	Legalistic Gospel	Gospel of the Kingdom/Gospel of the Lord Jesus Christ
Focuses on self	Focuses on a self-made religious god and formed by the traditions of men	Worships the Law	Connected by an intimate relationship with Father, Son, and the Holy Spirit
Focuses on material blessings	Focuses on the power of God	Judges and criticizes one another/compares to see who is better	Focuses on love and relationships
It's all about what you can have now, no spiritual perception of what is happening around them	Focuses on what you will have in heaven and spiritualizes everything	There is nothing here and not much in heaven	Blessed to be a blessing
Preaches about all the blessed saints in the Bible	Enforces suffering for eternal glory and preaches about the suffering of the saints in the Bible	Believes all the people God used were perfect	Maintains balance between suffering and blessings on this earth

Humanistic Gospel/ Man-Centered Gospel	Religious Gospel/ Gospel of Salvation	Legalistic Gospel	Gospel of the Kingdom/Gospel of the Lord Jesus Christ
Cheap grace	Very little grace	No grace at all	Sound and balanced revelation of grace
Serves money/ mammon	Glorifies poverty	Nothing to enjoy on this side of heaven	All needs are met
Self-empowerment	Self-rejection	Self-deceived	Self-denial
Self-righteous	Righteousness by good works	Righteousness by obeying the law	Righteousness of God by faith
Personal success/achievements	Does not believe in success	Does not care about success	Doing and fulfilling the will/purpose of God is success
Focuses on prosperity	Focuses on salvation, heaven, and hell	Focuses on obeying the Ten Commandments	Focuses on God and His kingdom
Lives to make money	Lives to be religious	Lives to appear spiritual	Lives to glorify the Father
Thinks they are the best	Live with an 'I am nothing, just dust' attitude	Makes up and adds new rules	Lives to make Him great
Focuses on independence	Focuses on servitude	Lives to be served	Lives to serve others
Calls sin a weakness	Covers up sins	Slave to sin	Dead to sin
Gets rid of the cross	The cross is too heavy to carry	Adds more crosses	Carries the cross daily
Anything and everything goes	Lives in fear of being punished by God	Has no mercy at all—for self or others	Trusts in God's mercy and forgives from the heart
Propelled by perfectionism	Trying to be perfected in the flesh	Looks perfect outwardly	Focuses on the heart
Lives to do "big" things/ Dream "big" philosophy	Lives to preach	Lives to observe rules	Lives to administer the kingdom of God

Humanistic Gospel/ Man-Centered Gospel	Religious Gospel/ Gospel of Salvation	Legalistic Gospel	Gospel of the Kingdom/Gospel of the Lord Jesus Christ
Makes their own standard of holiness	Most holy people	Believes they are the only true saints and keepers of the faith	Trusts in Christ's holiness
Denies reality	Has zeal without knowledge	Has no power	No sickness, poverty, or curse
Exalts self	Is devoted to following the traditions of men	Focuses on being right	Led by the Spirit— moment by moment
"Will" worship	Follows form of religion	Worships in the flesh	Worships God in spirit and truth
Entertains and builds up the souls of men	Doesn't smile at church	It is a sin to be joyful. Uptight and spiritually bound	Joy of the Lord is our strength
Always buys the most expensive	Doesn't buy anything/ Lives with poverty mindset	Always buys the cheapest	Lives content with little or an abundance
Theme of most songs is, I, Me, and Mine	Theme of most songs is the coming of Jesus and life in heaven	Theme of most songs is suffering and the sweet by and by	Theme of most songs is exalting, magnifying, and worshiping the King
Gives the list to God and tells Him what to do	Always says, "If it is God's will."	Always has a condition to meet	Lives as a son to do the will of the Father, waits on His direction
Sees things in the light of the blessings they can get	Sees things in the light of hell	Sees things in the light of observing rituals	Sees things in the light of eternity
Joy based on circumstances	Looks forward to having joy in heaven	Can never do enough. Miserable day and night	Rejoices in the Lord always
Acceptance based on achievements	Acceptance based on religious works	Acceptance based on performance	Accepted based on love of Christ; adopted as His children

THE GOSPEL OF THE KINGDOM

Humanistic Gospel/ Man-Centered Gospel	Religious Gospel/ Gospel of Salvation	Legalistic Gospel	Gospel of the Kingdom/Gospel of the Lord Jesus Christ
Lives to please self	Lives by the fear of man	Lives to please people	God is already pleased with us; obeys Him out of love
Accumulates material wealth	Never has enough	Pretends to be blessed	Receives inheritance and manages it wisely
Man is the center of the universe	Traditions are the center of the universe	Everything centered around the Law	God is the center of the universe
Believes everything was created for *me*	Believes man was created to worship God	Believes man was created to obey God	Man was created to have fellowship with God, which leads to dominion
Believes in the great promises of the Bible that have personal benefits	Has Great Commission as priority	Has Ten Commandments as priority	Has Great Commandment as priority
You are the boss	Lives as a pilgrim/ orphan	Lives as a slave	Lives as a son and becomes a father to many
Everything is centered around having fun	Super- or hyper-spiritual	Not in touch with reality	Balances the natural and the spiritual
I can do it myself	Lives in the past or in a futuristic attitude	Only doom, gloom, and despair	Lives based on the revelation of "It is finished"
Seeks blessings	Seeks miracles	Seeks perfection	Seeks the kingdom

It is time to start doing what is right and what we are really called to do. We need to preach the gospel that Jesus preached and commanded us to preach.

> "Then Jesus went about all the cities and villages, teaching in their synagogues, preaching the gospel of the kingdom, and healing every sickness and every disease among the people" (Matthew 9:35).

> "Now after John was put in prison, Jesus came to Galilee, preaching the gospel of the kingdom of God" (Mark 1:14).

Seeing the World through a Kingdom Lens

Jesus wanted His disciples to have a kingdom perspective, a kingdom worldview. He wanted them to see the world through that kingdom paradigm before they got to do anything with the church. To prepare them, day and night He taught, preached, and trained them about the kingdom and how it operated. By the time the church started they had a kingdom mindset. That is why they were able to reach the whole known world with the gospel of the kingdom. Wherever they went and whatever they did they operated as a kingdom would operate. Therefore, God in His sovereignty ordained Matthew to be the first book in the New Testament.

Jesus knew that once people developed a *church mentality* or a *Christian mentality,* they would not be effective in administering His kingdom. He knew that a church without a kingdom mindset would be just another mediocre organization that would not bring any change in the community in which it existed. If a local church has lost its influence in its society, then that church has lost its kingdom purpose. That is why He made the comparison to salt that had lost its saltiness. What is it good for?

Jesus never asked us to pray for revival: He asked us to pray for His kingdom to come. I have never seen people crying for His kingdom to come, but I have seen people crying and wailing for revival. No wonder the world is in the shape it is!

> **Jesus never asked us to pray for revival: He asked us to pray for His kingdom to come.**

I believe His priority to see His kingdom established on the earth can be seen in everything He said and did. Every message was to reveal something of His kingdom and to see one aspect of His kingdom made manifest. Think about it: Jesus' first and last messages were about the kingdom of God (Matthew 4:17; Acts 1:3). The book of Acts also begins and ends with the kingdom message (Acts 1:3; 28:30-31).

"From that time Jesus began to preach and to say, 'Repent, for the kingdom of heaven is at hand' " (Matthew 4:17).

"To whom He [Jesus] also presented Himself alive after His suffering by many infallible proofs, being seen by them during forty days and speaking of the things pertaining to the kingdom of God" (Acts 1:3).

"Then Paul dwelt two whole years in his own rented house, and received all who came to him, preaching the kingdom of God and teaching the things which concern the Lord Jesus Christ with all confidence, no one forbidding him" (Acts 28:30-31).

Wherever I go, I see people seeking and hungering for miracles, signs, and wonders. They think that if we produce more miracles the world will come to Jesus. Jesus never asked us to *seek* miracles. There was one group of people in the Bible that were looking for signs: the religious leaders. They did that because of their unbelief, and Jesus did not commend them for it.

> **Jesus never asked us to *seek* miracles.**

Most people who saw and experienced miracles, both in the Old and New Testaments, did not remain faithful to God. The Israelites saw miracles as well as manifestations of the power of God in Egypt and in the wilderness. They saw more than all other people combined, but the majority of them perished in the wilderness. Did you ever wonder why the crowd that followed Jesus, who ate the bread He multiplied and saw miracles, were not there in the upper room?

Why does the Bible mention miracles and healings? They are "bait" to catch people to bring them into the kingdom. They are not the end but a means to get people attracted to the kingdom, or Jesus Himself. He told the disciples to go and heal the sick and to tell them that the kingdom of God has arrived (Luke 9:2).

Sadly, today we stop at the miracles rather than take people beyond them. We talk about them; we broadcast them; we even shout about them, and then we end the service. Not very many people go any further. When we seek His kingdom, we find everything we are looking for. Why should we seek just one or two aspects of His kingdom when we can have it all? God has made everything available to His children: everything He has in His kingdom.

What Do You Think about the Kingdom?

What comes to your mind when you hear the word *kingdom* is also important. Many Christians relate *kingdom* with the power of God. Others think of healing or miracles; still others think of helping the poor and those in need. These are all perceptions of the kingdom that have been distorted by the religious spirit.

What comes to your mind when you hear the phrase, "the kingdom of Alexander the Great" or "the kingdom of Persia"? Is it worship, healing, or helping the poor? What comes to your mind when you hear the phrase, "the kingdom of God"?

There has never been a kingdom on this earth that was just made of power or healings. In fact, no kingdom can exist on just power, regardless of what kind of power it is. A kingdom has many components. The most important component of a kingdom is its king. A kingdom is like any other nation except it is ruled by a king. The most important components of a kingdom are the king and the government that administers the king's kingdom.

If we are supposed to seek the kingdom first and the church is here to administer the kingdom of God, then we need to know what comprises a kingdom. A kingdom is made of twelve different components: 1) King, 2) Government/*Ekklesia*, 3) People, 4) Culture, 5) Decrees & Laws, 6) Army, 7) Territory, 8) Education/Teachings, 9) Economy/Treasury, 10) Business/Industry, 11) Media, and 12) Agriculture. In the Bible, twelve is the number of divine government.

> **If we are supposed to seek the kingdom first and the church is here to administer the kingdom of God, then we need to know what comprises a kingdom.**

When you hear the term "kingdom of God" I would like you to imagine all twelve ingredients, not just one or two of them, all working together to make a kingdom. There is a reason why there are twelve tribes of Israel and why Jesus selected twelve disciples. As I said earlier, everything God does has a kingdom flavor. The 120 in the upper room is also 12 x 10. The 3,000 souls that were saved on the day of Pentecost is 250 x 12, and the 24 elders around the throne in heaven is 12 x 2. These are just some of the examples to show that when God does something, He does it with a kingdom mindset.

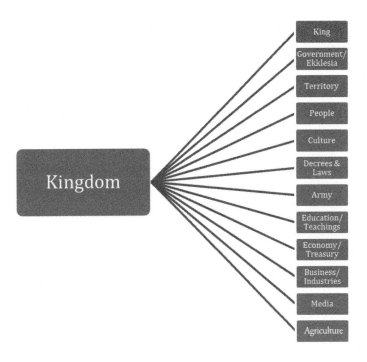

When Jesus taught us to pray, "Let Your kingdom come and Your will be done on earth as it is in heaven," it indicates God's will concerning each of those components by which a kingdom is made to manifest on earth as it is in heaven. Every nation on earth has these twelve components operating in them. Right now, in the nations the kingdom of darkness is occupying, it is through these components that the enemy operates. It does not take much wisdom to understand who is behind what is going on in the governments and educational systems of this world. When some pray, "Let Your kingdom come," they limit their thinking to only more miracles and healings taking place. When you think of heaven, think of it as a nation ruled by a King. Heaven has everything a nation has.

You might wonder why I did not mention miracles, tongues, faith, worship, grace, and other gifts of the Holy Spirit as being part of the kingdom. Some think the kingdom of God is only about power, healing, signs, and miracles. The gifts of the Holy Spirit are spiritual *tools* or *weapons* the army uses to accomplish certain tasks in the kingdom, but they are not the kingdom. No nation or kingdom can survive on its military or weapons alone. Others say the kingdom is all about love, righteousness, peace, and joy in the Holy Spirit. That is the *culture* of the kingdom, and again not the whole kingdom.

When we receive the kingdom as a whole and administer it effectively in our communities and nations, then the change we are looking for will happen. If we train our children to do the same, the ground we gain will be retained for generations to come. That is God's heart, and that is the mandate of the kingdom of God.

> **The gifts of the Holy Spirit are spiritual *tools* or *weapons* to accomplish certain tasks in the kingdom, but they are not the kingdom.**

The Kingdom of God and the Kingdom of Heaven

You might ask, "What is the difference between the kingdom of God and the kingdom of heaven?" I remember listening to an argument between some students at the Bible school where I studied. They were having a deep theological debate about those two different terms. I also wondered about it. Why did Jesus use both terms intermittently? One day the Holy Spirit illuminated this to me, "The phrase "kingdom of God" is talking about *who* the kingdom belongs to, like the kingdom of Nebuchadnezzar. The phrase "kingdom of heaven" is referring to *where,* or the place it belongs, like the kingdom of Babylon. It was that simple, and I said, "Thank You, Holy Spirit."

The Bible says the kingdom of God suffers violence and the violent take it by force (Matthew 11:12). As you know, God lives outside of time. His kingdom is an everlasting kingdom. From God's perspective, He has made available to us everything He has. He did not put any *time limit* on anything; He only put a *faith limit.* A couple of Old Testament saints—by faith—grabbed the grace we are enjoying now, brought it into reality, and lived in it. People like Abraham and David are examples. I asked the Lord how they did it. Jesus did not die until thousands of years later, but they enjoyed the grace and relationship with God we enjoy today. The Holy Spirit reminded me, saying, "The Lamb was slain from the foundation of the world" (Revelation 13:8). I said, "Wow!" They had a revelation of it. Through faith, anyone could have enjoyed His grace at any time.

A kingdom or nation is only as good as the *government* that leads it. There are many nations on this earth that are very rich in natural and human resources, but they remain poor for the lack of proper governance. The church is becoming ineffective and irrelevant in many parts of the world. It is not because it has lost its power or authority, but because we don't know how to administer the kingdom God has given us.

> "For he has rescued us out of the darkness and gloom of Satan's kingdom and brought us into the Kingdom of his dear Son" (Colossians 1:13 TLB).

> "Since we have a Kingdom nothing can destroy, let us please God by serving him with thankful hearts and with holy fear and awe" (Hebrews 12:28 TLB).

The above verse does not say that we are *going to have* a kingdom, but that we *have* a kingdom. If you are a Christian then you are in God's kingdom. Just like when you were born you became a citizen of your country, when you were born again you became a citizen of the kingdom of heaven. It is imperative for us to learn to think like people living in a kingdom. Otherwise, there is not much difference between us and the people in the world, other than the fact that we go to church on Sunday. That is pathetic.

> **It is imperative for us to learn to think like people living in a kingdom.**

If the church in any nation or city *used* its power and authority, then not even a little demon would move its pinky to do anything. It would be like Pharaoh told Joseph, "I *am* Pharaoh, and without your consent no man may lift his hand or foot in all the land of Egypt" (Genesis 41:44).

That is the kind of power and authority God wants His church to walk in. Joseph is a *type* of Jesus in the Old Testament. When Pharaoh (God) promoted Joseph in Egypt, he was made to ride on the second chariot and have people cry out before him, saying, "Bow the knee" (Genesis 41:43). You and I know that at the name of Jesus every knee shall bow and every tongue shall confess that He is Lord.

On the other side, there are many nations that used to be Christian and had many mighty revivals, but are now losing their Christian heritage. They consider themselves to be living in a post-Christian era. If we are not careful to learn from our past mistakes, many nations that God is moving in today and where the church is growing quickly will repeat the same pattern after one or two generations. Is there a solution to this problem? I believe there is. The solution is to train people to administer God's kingdom in their communities.

Designed for the Kingdom

It has been God's desire and design for us to dwell in His kingdom from the very beginning. We lost the kingdom because of the fall. We cannot function without a kingdom, good or evil. People were designed by God to live in kingdoms. It is a natural thing for the children of a king to live in their father's kingdom.

> We cannot function without a kingdom, good or evil. People were designed by God to live in kingdoms.

Though we sinned and disobeyed our Father, He did not forsake us forever. He had a plan of redemption in place beforehand to get us back into His kingdom. Sinful people cannot dwell in the kingdom of God and function properly. Sin is an operating system inherent to another kingdom, one that Satan introduced. An acronym for sin is Satanic Information Network. It is always misguided thoughts based on wrong information that produce sin.

The gospel of the kingdom offers man the "real thing" of all their heart longs for. The purpose, love, joy, peace, significance, provision, and eternal life that come from a relationship with the King of Kings and the Lord of Lords is found in His kingdom. Jesus is the door to His kingdom. No one can come to the Father except through Him. But to enter this kingdom, we will go through many tribulations (Acts 14:22).

There are three dimensions to the kingdom of God. The first dimension is the one we lost when Adam sinned. The second one is what God wants us to experience now in this life, which is made available through Jesus Christ. And the third is the one we will enter once we die.

There are three steps to experiencing the kingdom that has been made available to us right now. They are *seeing, entering,* and *inheriting* the kingdom. Many people misunderstand and think that if they are born again they have already inherited God's kingdom. The Bible does not teach that. It teaches that when you are born again you can *see* the kingdom.

"Jesus answered and said to him, 'Most assuredly, I say to you, unless one is born again, he cannot **see** the kingdom of God'" (John 3:3).

Just because you see it does not mean you will enter or inherit it. It's like when you go to buy a house or a new car. Just because you saw one, does not mean it's yours. If you enter a house, it does not mean you inherited it. Jesus explained the next step in the following verse.

"Jesus answered, 'Most assuredly, I say to you, unless one is born of water and the Spirit, he cannot **enter** the kingdom of God'" (John 3:5).

Jesus said that unless we are born of water (the Word) and the Spirit (Holy Spirit), we will not enter the kingdom. What does this mean? Man is a three-part being. When you receive Christ, your spirit is born again, and that is when you see the kingdom in your spirit. But you have a soul and a body that need to be born again too. How does our soul and body become born again? Our soul, which is made of our mind, intellect, will, and memory needs to be renewed by the Word on a daily basis. Until our thinking process is completely renewed and we reach a place where we naturally think according to the Word of God, we will keep going through trials. This is a process that takes time and it is not easily accomplished. The Bible calls it renewing our mind (Romans 12:2).

The moment we are born again in the spirit, God starts the process in us to have our soul and body born again too. Most people don't complete this process, in the same way that the majority that came out of Egypt did not inherit the Promised Land, but perished in the wilderness. They were saved but could not bring their soul and body under subjection to the will and plan of God. They saw the Promised Land (their destiny) in their spirit, but could not enter. It is easy to be born again in our spirit, all you have to do is to believe and confess that Jesus Christ is Lord. But for our soul and body to be born again, we have to die many deaths. We need to be crucified, as the Bible says (Romans 6:6; Galatians 2:20; 5:24; 6:14).

Our Promised Land is the dimension of the kingdom of God we enter and experience here on earth. That is why Paul said we must go through many tribulations to enter the kingdom of God. "Strengthening the souls of the disciples, exhorting *them* to continue in the faith, and *saying,* "We must through many tribulations enter the kingdom of God" (Acts 14:22).

Our body also needs to come under the total submission and leading of the Holy Spirit because our body is the temple of the Holy Spirit (1 Corinthians 3:16; 6:19). There are so many believers in our churches who are born again in the spirit, but their souls and bodies are still in captivity to the kingdom of darkness. I am sorry to say that they are not living in God's kingdom. It is not their fault; they were not taught correctly.

Just because you enter, doesn't mean you will inherit. Once our spirit, soul, and body are born again we will inherit the kingdom. You can make it to heaven by just being born again in your spirit, but that doesn't do any favors for you or for God and His kingdom on earth. Jesus did not save us so we can just make it to heaven. He wants us to make the place we possess on this earth, the place of our domain, like heaven before we leave here. He wants us to get a glimpse of heaven and make it a reality on earth. That is our mandate, God's will on earth as it is in heaven.

> "Do you not know that the unrighteous will not inherit the kingdom of God? Do not be deceived. Neither fornicators, nor idolaters, nor adulterers, nor homosexuals, nor sodomites, nor thieves, nor covetous, nor drunkards, nor revilers, nor extortioners will inherit the kingdom of God" (1 Corinthians 6:9-10).

> "Now the works of the flesh are evident, which are: adultery, fornication, uncleanness, lewdness, idolatry, sorcery, hatred, contentions, jealousies, outbursts of wrath, selfish ambitions, dissensions, heresies, envy, murders, drunkenness, revelries, and the like; of which I tell you beforehand, just as I also told you in time past, that those who practice such things will not inherit the kingdom of God" (Galatians 5:19-21).

There are two powerful books God gave me that deal with the above subject in detail. They are Seven Kinds of Believers: Why All God's Children Are Not Blessed Equally and Keys to Passing Your Spiritual Tests: Unlocking the Secrets to Spiritual Promotion. I would recommend you get a copy of each of these.

THE GOSPEL OF THE KINGDOM

For a person who is raised on this earth in the world system, it is not easy to change the way they have been trained to think. We will not learn it in any other way, so God allows us to go through challenges to train us to think differently. That is why when we go through trials and challenges and come out of it, we often say something like, "Oh, I didn't know it worked that way," or, "I didn't realize that before." That means you just learned something you did not know before, and as a result, you learned to think differently. That is the purpose of everything we go through after we receive our salvation. God is teaching us how to think differently and how life works in His kingdom.

Once we are trained to think for ourselves, become mature in the things of God, and understand how He operates, then He does not have to allow us to go through tribulations like we did when we began our walk with Him. Sadly, most people never learn and mature, and they die in the wilderness just like the people of Israel—without receiving the fulfillment of their promises. When you understand this, you will be able to count it all joy when you go through various trials and temptations like James tells us (James 1:2-4). They all work for our benefit, though we may sometimes feel like we are going to die.

From the moment Jesus began to preach, His passion was for people to rediscover His kingdom, not to take them to heaven. The first thing He preached was, "Repent, for the kingdom of heaven is at hand" (Matthew 4:17). We understood it to mean, "If you repent, I am going to take you to heaven when you die." That is not what He said. He said His kingdom is coming to this earth again; it's very close; and for us to receive and enter into it, we need to repent. Repent means to change the way we think. The kingdom way of thinking is opposite to the world's way of thinking.

Jesus brought the kingdom back to us and gave us one more opportunity to enter into His kingdom. "At hand" meant it was about to appear. It was very close. Jesus taught and demonstrated the kingdom to us through His life and ministry. He taught us everything we need to know about the kingdom and its mysteries, everything we need to be able to live in that kingdom instead of Satan's. Jesus' goal was that we would live in it and administer it on the earth.

Jesus came to reveal His kingdom and teach His people how it should operate. He taught about the qualities, culture, principles, mysteries, power, and authority of the kingdom. He came to establish His kingdom here. For a kingdom to function as a kingdom requires certain qualities and characteristics. First of all, a kingdom needs a king, then a territory, people, decrees and laws, an army, a working economy, and so on.

The Kingdom Is Inside of You

The kingdom of God is an invisible kingdom. We cannot see how it operates on the earth with our natural eyes. He put His kingdom inside us and it manifests to the world through the work we do. It is God's desire that His will is done *on this earth as it is in heaven.* This can only be done through human beings because the earth was given to us. The new era of the kingdom of God began to operate with the coming of the Holy Spirit on the day of Pentecost. The *ekklesia* of Jesus' kingdom began to operate from that day. We do not see anyone preaching that the kingdom is at hand after the day of Pentecost.

> **He put His kingdom inside us and it manifests to the world through the work we do.**

The kingdom of God belongs to God and He wants to give it to His children. Jesus said to cheer up, little flock, for it has been the Father's good pleasure to give us the kingdom (Luke 12:32). Only God's children can enter and dwell in His kingdom. God gave the authority to become a child of God to those who believe in Jesus and receive forgiveness of sins. The church's primary purpose is to see God's will accomplished on earth as it is in heaven.

When we come together as the church we are the governing body of the kingdom of God, His *ekklesia*. We need to listen to our King's directions for our region and partner with Him to accomplish that vision. Someone who sees the church should see the kingdom of God. Christ is the Head of the church, the King. We read in 1 Corinthians 14 how a body of believers should function and what should be done when an unbeliever comes in.

> "Therefore if the whole church comes together in one place, and all speak with tongues, and there come in those who are uninformed or unbelievers, will they not say that you are out of your mind? But if all prophesy, and an unbeliever or an uninformed person comes in, he is convinced by all, he is convicted by all. And thus the secrets of his heart are revealed;

and so, falling down on his face, he will worship God and report that God is truly among you" (1 Corinthians 14:23-25).

But didn't Jesus say He came to give us life and life more abundantly? Yes, there is no doubt, but sadly, the only thing that is hard to find on this earth today is abundant life. We confuse abundant life with having abundant stuff. There is abundant *stuff* all around us, but people are more miserable than ever before. Jesus was not talking about having abundant stuff, but abundant life—the very life that bubbles out of our inner being, regardless of our circumstances or the material things we possess. The Bible says this about Jesus: "In Him was life, and the life was the light of men" (John 1:4). Jesus was the most joyful person that ever lived. How many houses, donkeys, and fishing boats did He own? To my knowledge, none. He did not even have a place of His own to lie down and sleep. But He lived an abundant life. That is something to meditate on.

Most Christians do not live in God's kingdom. They were never taught properly so they live dependent on the world system as their source of joy and satisfaction. If a football team is playing on a Sunday, some Christians will

> **Most Christians do not live in God's kingdom.**

choose football over going to church that day. It's time for the church to prioritize and give the Lord His rightful place in our lives. Either accept Jesus as Lord and serve Him, or serve the god of this world. Please don't put one foot in the kingdom in an effort to possess its benefits and keep the other in the world. In the end, it will not work.

Kingdom Mindset

When we think of the church, we should think about it with a kingdom mindset. Before Jesus gave the revelation of the church to Paul, He came to reveal the kingdom of God to His disciples. For three-and-a-half years they were trained and equipped with a kingdom mindset. That's why twelve men were able to reach the entire known world with the gospel of the kingdom in their lifetime. There are three main reasons Jesus taught about the kingdom more than about the church.

The first reason is that before the *ekklesia* can operate there has to be a kingdom. If there is no kingdom then there is no need of an *ekklesia* to govern it. That is why He came to give us the kingdom first and preached and taught about it more than anything else. The problem today is there are many so-called *ekklesias* out there operating without proper knowledge of the kingdom.

The second reason is because Jesus knew that Satan had a kingdom and that it is well organized and established on earth, and He came to confront it. Satan does not run a non-profit or charitable organization, as many may think. He has a kingdom. We cannot confront a kingdom with a charitable or non-profit mentality. We need to confront it with a kingdom mindset. Jesus is a King and He has a kingdom He wants to see established on earth. He defeated Satan on the cross and received all authority and gave it to the church to accomplish that task.

The third reason is humans cannot exist on earth without a kingdom. We are kings and carry the very DNA of the King of kings. Either we are part of God's kingdom or live in the kingdom of darkness. It is impossible to be neutral. It is an instinct in every man to rule and to govern, and because we lost our God-given dominion we are constantly trying to control something or someone.

Again, the most important components of a kingdom are the king and his government. If you go to England and learn the customs of the people there, that will not give you an understanding about the royal family and how they once ruled the world. If you buy one of the rifles the British palace guard uses, that won't make you a royal citizen either. You have to live with them for a long time, read their history, and allow their culture, their beliefs, and their language to permeate your being to have a British mindset. You have to become British. The same is true of every culture.

The reason the church doesn't accomplish much these days is because we don't have a kingdom mindset. How does one kingdom invade another kingdom? In our case, we belong to the kingdom of God and are called to invade the territories that are ruled by the powers of darkness. When a kingdom invades another kingdom, they don't start by defeating the poorest of the poor that are living outside the city walls. They are looking for the king and people in authority who hold key positions.

> When a kingdom invades another kingdom, they don't start by defeating the poorest of the poor that are living outside the city walls.

THE GOSPEL OF THE KINGDOM

A kingdom operates differently than most people who grew up in a democratic government think. When a kingdom plans to conquer another kingdom the main focus is to capture or kill the king of the enemy kingdom. When the king is captured or killed, practically, it means that kingdom is taken. When Jesus, the King of the kingdom of heaven, came to this earth to conquer the kingdom of darkness, He didn't go around the world defeating little demons. He went straight to Satan, the king, defeated him and took the keys of hell and death from him. Not only did He defeat Satan, but also the major power holders in his kingdom. The Bible calls them principalities, and He made them surrender their weapons and made a public show of them (Colossians 2:15). Then He left the task of dealing with those little demons to us, the church. That's why He told us to cast out demons, not pull down principalities or bind Satan.

This is why it is important to understand what a kingdom is made of. Whenever God used someone to reach a kingdom He always started at the top and went down from there. That's what kingdoms do. We see the same principle applied in the book of Acts. A person with a church mindset will always start at the bottom. When God sent Moses to save His people, He told him to go and speak to the elders of his people and Pharaoh, the king of Egypt, not to the leper colony that was outside the city walls.

When God used Joseph, He started with servants of the king to finally bring Joseph to the king himself. Esther, Mordecai, Nehemiah, and Daniel are more examples. Why did God mention all these in the Bible? He is showing us examples of how to reach a nation so we can learn from them. Unfortunately, instead of learning from these experiences and putting them into practice, most Christians are still waiting for God to do everything.

What do I mean by putting them into practice? The Bible is a book of patterns, examples, types, and principles. Whatever happened to the people of Israel is for our example (1 Corinthians 10:6-11). Instead of waiting for God to send a Joseph, we could train someone to be the Joseph of our day. Joseph did not have universities and law schools accessible to him so God did what He needed to do to prepare him. There are many people sitting in our churches that are interested in politics and starting new businesses, but they are being held back because of fear and wrong teaching. Today, everything we need is at the tip of our fingers, but few are making use of the opportunities we have.

People live these days to have fun and with an entitlement mentality. They have become lovers of pleasure rather than lovers of God (2 Timothy 3:1-4).

If someone wants to become a Daniel of our time, he or she has the opportunity to go to college and learn. Other religions like Islam and Mormon have this mindset. They don't come to a country to start orphanages and homes for widows. They come to take over or influence governments and key positions in society where the decisions are made and the mindsets of the people are being shaped. They start schools and buy multinational businesses and media channels that shape the culture and the mindset of the people because they know that if they are going to influence and occupy a society they have to take control of those areas by which a society is made and the people are influenced. I recently heard that after the holdings of the U.S. government, Mormons own the most land west of the Mississippi River.

We are busy arranging crusades or another healing rally and worship night, while these forces are taking over nations left and right. We don't see Muslims holding a crusade, or Mormons arranging an evangelistic meeting. They have a different concept of evangelism. The church needs *kingdom mindset evangelism*. You might have heard of *power evangelism* but not *kingdom evangelism*.

> **We are busy arranging crusades or another healing rally and worship night, while these forces are taking over nations left and right.**

The Mandate of the Kingdom

We have erred in our mission because of a lack of understanding about the mandate King Jesus gave us. If you study the four Gospels in depth, you will find that there is a divine mystery hidden in each gospel about the kingdom and how it is supposed to accomplish its goal. Only when we understand them and practice them, and train our people to do the same, will we see the kingdom of God advancing on the earth.

In each gospel, just before Jesus ascended to heaven He gave a different mandate to His disciples. At first, it was difficult for me to comprehend because they all sounded so diverse. I do not know the time frame of each mandate, whether He told them all at the same time or on different occasions, but they are all similar and were given to accomplish one single overarching mandate. They are all different with regard to kingdom perspective, but at the end they accomplish the same ultimate goal.

In Matthew, Jesus said to go and make disciples of all nations (Matthew 28:18-19). I call it the *Kingdom Mandate*. How do we disciple a nation? We have miserably failed at discipling the nations. We have been so focused on making converts that we've neglected the nations. This is because of our lack of understanding of what makes a nation and how it should be approached.

To execute the *Kingdom Mandate*, when we think of evangelism we should not only think of winning more souls into the kingdom. When we evangelize with a kingdom mindset, we need to think and plan how to win a city or nation to Christ so we can declare and establish the rule and reign of Christ over that city and nation instead of the rule and reign of the kingdom of darkness.

It is very important to notice that many people and churches mentioned in the New Testament are known by the city in which they lived: for example Jesus of Nazareth, Joseph of Arimathea, and Lazarus of Bethany. Kings were known by the nation they ruled, like Cyrus, king of Persia, Jehoiakim, king of Judah, etc. The epistles Paul wrote to the churches are named for their cities, and the seven churches mentioned in the book of Revelation are actually the names of seven cities.

In the gospel of Mark, Jesus gave a different mandate: To go into all the world and preach the gospel to all creatures and He who believes, signs (casting out demons, speaking in tongues, healing the sick, etc.) will follow (Mark 16:15-18). That is a *Personal Mandate* because it focuses on dealing with people individually, like casting out demons and laying hands on people. We have been practicing that effectively and have many converts because of it. However, we have not done well in discipling them. We have not discipled the nations well because we are not doing it with a kingdom mindset. We have not discipled converts well either. We have been concerned about taking more people to heaven instead of teaching disciples how to live in God's kingdom on earth.

To execute this *Personal Mandate*, we need to recognize that every individual on earth is struggling in one or more areas of their life. As God's children we need to learn to tap into the power and resources of God to meet our needs. One of the ways Jesus evangelized is by meeting the needs of the people.

In Luke, we read about yet another mandate. They are directed to preach repentance and the remission of sins in His name and then told to wait in Jerusalem for the promise of the Father, that they would be endued with power (Luke 24:46-49). This is the *Power Mandate*, which we have been practicing and preaching. As a result, we have a great many churches in various nations, but the soul and heart of those nations remain unaffected by the gospel. This is because the church did not understand its real purpose.

To execute the *Power Mandate*, we need to learn not to limit the manifestation of the power of God through us. Most limit the power of the Holy Spirit to healing the sick and casting out demons. But when we study the Holy Spirit we find He is the Architect of the universe. The same power that casts out demons can help us govern nations. The same power can help us to invent and manufacture products.

In the gospel of John, Jesus did not give a specific mandate like He did in the other three, but demonstrated it. John was the apostle of love. In it we read that God so loved the world that He gave His only begotten Son. His gospel ends with Jesus reconciling Peter to Himself and restoring his faith (John 21:15-18). Love brings reconciliation—it is the very essence of the kingdom. We have been given the ministry of reconciliation (2 Corinthians 5:18). We reconcile people back to God and to each other. I call it the *Love Mandate*. We have not been very effective in executing this mandate either. Unfortunately, we are known more for what we hate than what we love and appreciate.

To execute the *Love Mandate*, we need to understand that every human being is longing for acceptance, recognition, and love. Only God's love can satisfy the longing of our soul. That is why the greatest commandment in the Bible is to love God and to love our neighbor.

The time has come for us to pick up where we left off and to redeem the areas where we have not been effective. We need to start with the gospel of Matthew, because that is the first one that preaches the gospel of the kingdom. Every other gospel and their mandates are complementary. They are supposed to work together to accomplish the mandate that was given in Matthew. I strongly believe that the next move of God will be discipling nations by administering His kingdom. We are already in it but as with any new move it takes time for people to change their mindset from the old to the new. This book will help you do that.

When you look at the New Testament and the church, you need to look at them with a kingdom mindset. What comes to your mind when you think of the church? Compare that with what comes to your mind when you think of the kingdom. A kingdom-minded Christian thinks and functions differently than a church-minded Christian. We will look at the differences in detail in the next chapter.

> **A kingdom-minded Christian thinks and functions differently than a church-minded Christian.**

Chapter 3: The Church Mindset versus the Kingdom Mindset

Chapter 3: The Church Mindset versus the Kingdom Mindset

"And He said to them, 'To you it has been given to know the mystery of the kingdom of God'" (Mark 4:11).

In the following pages I would like to explain the difference between how the church as we know it operates and how a kingdom operates, which is the way the church *should* operate. It will help you understand the difference between having a church mindset and a kingdom mindset.

The Kingdom Is Focused on Influence

When we study the book of Acts and the people God reached, we see something significant. God did not reach just anyone. He handpicked people from different nations and languages. He chose people of influence who in turn influenced others and even whole nations. Whenever God does something, He intends to make the maximum impact. He will orchestrate events and circumstances so He can get the most leverage for His glory and the expansion of His kingdom.

God chose the day of Pentecost to send the Holy Spirit. Why would God choose that particular day? With such a large group of people present from every nation under heaven, He knew He could initiate reaching the entire world at that time with one incident.

Philip the evangelist was led by the Spirit to share the gospel with an Ethiopian eunuch. Why this eunuch? He was the treasurer for the

> Kings and kingdoms are always reached from the top to the bottom. The church, on the other hand, starts from the bottom and tries to reach the top, but that doesn't work.

queen of Ethiopia, a man of influence, through whom the entire nation was reached with the gospel.

Kings and kingdoms are always reached from the top to the bottom. The church, on the other hand, starts from the bottom and tries to reach the top, but that doesn't work. That is why we don't have the influence we should have. It is taking more than two thousand years to do what twelve men accomplished in their lifetime.

The Church Is Focused on Events

Many churches try to keep their people busy with programs and events. One of the intentions of this method is to keep the people attending that particular church, and encourage fellowship and community building.

The Kingdom Wants Effectiveness

In the kingdom, it is not numbers that matter, but effectiveness. Whenever God accomplished something, it was not the number that He was concerned with, but the quality and faith of the select few. It's not the size of the church that matters but its effectiveness in administering the kingdom of God in the community and the nation it is in.

The Church Wants Numbers

For some reason we believe that if there are more Christians in a nation, then things will be different. America has more Christians in number, but they don't necessarily have any influence. They aren't forming policy or part of making decisions. History shows that only a handful of people have really affected cultures and history. We don't need another church in America like the ones we have. We need kingdom-representing churches. We need believers who are thinking and acting like the ambassadors of God's kingdom.

> We don't need another church in America like the majority of the ones we have. We need kingdom-representing churches.

A small number of people have shaped culture and civilization. In his book, *To Change the World*, James Davison Hunter[9] summarizes it this way,

> "Even if we add the minor figures in all of the networks, in all of the civilizations, the total is only 2,700. In sum, between 150 and 3,000 people (a tiny fraction of the roughly 23 billion people living between 600 B.C. and A.D. 1900) framed the major contours of all world civilizations. Clearly, the transformations here were top-down."

The Kingdom Wants to Rule and Establish Dominion

Any time a kingdom comes into a new region, they are not planning to start orphanages or help the poor. They are thinking about how they can take over the new territory and rule it. The main focus is to establish or take over one of the pillars a kingdom or a nation stands upon, and gain influence. They want to set up an extension of their dominion in that new nation. They may eventually have programs that would help the poor and orphans but that is not their first priority. God is looking for people through whom He can administer His kingdom on this earth now.

The Church Is Waiting to Escape the Earth

There are two topics that excite most Christians today: rapture and revival. Neither of these two words is mentioned in the Bible. Why don't we talk more about what Jesus actually talked about? Why aren't we passionate about what Jesus is passionate about—His kingdom?

Jesus was not running around making converts. He did not tell every individual He met, "Hey, if you don't believe in Me and repent, you are going to hell." Instead, He was calm and relaxed. We don't see the apostles doing that either. Jesus was not interested in converts or large crowds. They were actually a distraction to His mission. There were big crowds around Jesus all the time, but they were not all committed to Him or His cause. In the end, there were only a hundred and twenty people who waited for the promise of the Father.

---

9. Hunter, James Davison. *To Change the World: The Irony, Tragedy, and Possibility of Christianity in the Late Modern World*. New York: Oxford University Press, 2010.

The Kingdom Is Looking for Citizens

Kingdoms don't look for converts to fill a space in a pew. A convert becomes a liability and does not add any value. They come with a mindset to receive rather than to give. Kingdoms are looking for active citizens who will represent the king, government, and culture wherever they go and through whatever they do.

The Church Wants Converts

On the other hand, the church is looking for converts. At least that's what we have been doing over the past few centuries. Jesus never asked us to go and make converts—He told us to make disciples. We are trying to populate heaven but that is not our mandate. Where did we get that idea? Our mission is not to populate heaven. Our mission is to help the Father and the Son to accomplish their mission on this earth, which is twofold: The Father wants the enemies of His Son brought to His footstool. In turn, the Son will submit all the kingdoms of this earth back to the Father (1 Corinthians 15:24; Revelation 11:15).

> **Jesus never asked us to go and make converts— He told us to make disciples.**

The Father gave all authority and power to the Son and the Son gave them to the church, which is you and me. They sent us the Holy Spirit to help us accomplish it. The devil stole the kingdoms of this world from the Father by deceiving us. The question is, are we going to honor the Father and the Son for all the love and mercy bestowed upon us?

The Kingdom Operates from a Producer Mentality

Kingdoms are looking to influence. One way to have influence is to have products. God filled this earth with His products. He introduced Himself as the Creator in Genesis 1:1. Because He indwells us it means that the most creative Person in the universe is living within us. The Architect of the planets and galaxies is living in us. We—the church—should be the most creative and productive people on earth.

> **We—the church— should be the most creative and productive people on earth.**

The Church Operates from a Consumer Mentality

There are two groups of people on this earth: producers and consumers. The producers have influence over the consumers because producers make decisions for the consumers. The church is the largest consuming agency on earth, but we are supposed to be the most productive agency. We have been robbed, lied to, deceived, and kept ineffective till now, but that time is changing.

In most parts of the western world, it is during the so-called Christian holidays that the retailers make most of their money, though they will neither say "Merry Christmas" nor acknowledge the birth of Jesus. How sad it is that gullible Christians throng into those stores to buy stuff they don't need and make the devil richer while they remain poor. In my opinion, we should boycott those stores and not buy anything from them at all. It is time for Christians to stand for what they believe. As the saying goes, "If you don't stand for something, you will fall for anything."

There is a reason for commercializing a holiday. At these times people are prone to spending more money. Even if they don't have the money, many people go into debt to celebrate. Jesus would not have us borrow money to "celebrate His birthday." We give our hard-earned money to the devil and his kingdom to accomplish his agenda while most Christians remain broke. It is totally against God's kingdom principles. His Word says a borrower is a slave to the lender and that we shall not borrow, but lend, to many nations.

I believe the preaching of the prosperity gospel has done more damage than good to the church in last fifty to seventy years. Instead of encouraging and empowering believers to discover their purpose, start businesses, and engage in politics, prosperity preachers have robbed innocent believers. If we had done what we were supposed to do, we would not be in the political or economic dilemmas we are in today.

The majority of believers are in survival mode financially: often their houses and cars are owned by the bank and their credit cards maxed out. That is not true prosperity, but slavery. It's time to start doing something different now and create a different future for the next generation. What do you think?

The Kingdom Wants to Mentor

One of the reasons the church is not effective today is because there is no effective mentoring on any level. Everyone is trying to be a superhero or a supermodel. If you cannot reproduce yourself or cannot impart to someone what you know, then you really don't know what you think you know. The reason people don't mentor is because they are afraid of losing what they have. If they are busy mentoring, they won't be able to build their own personal kingdoms. The purpose of kingdom mentoring is to restore the image and likeness of God in people, and in turn, to have dominion on the earth.

The Church Wants to Worship

Jesus did not start the church to worship Him. If worship meant singing, I find it interesting that He never asked anyone to sing to Him while He was here. The disciples did not rise early in the morning and sing, "This is the day. This is the day that Jesus made." No. That was not part of their training. The word *worship* appears seventy times in the New Testament in the New King James Version. But, *not even one time does it mean singing.* When I found that out, I said "Wow!"

> **The word *worship* appears seventy times in the New Testament in the New King James Version. But, *not even one time does it mean singing.***

So much time, effort, and resources are spent today on so-called worship. Its intent is more to entertain or impress people than to please the Lord. The Lord is already pleased with us. We don't need to sing for an hour to please Him or for Him to show up. There have been many services where the presence of the Lord showed up on the first line of the song. They could have started tapping into what the Lord had for them, but they kept on going for another twenty or forty minutes just to make noise and to make the people tired. When it is time to listen to the Word, many are sleepy. Jesus said, "For where two or three are *gathered* together in My name, I am there in the midst of them" (Matthew 18:20).

The Kingdom Is Looking to Give

One of the economic principles of the kingdom is that in order to receive, you first have to give. The good news is you will always have something to give. It may not always be money but you are equipped to bless someone in some way at all times.

The Church Wants to Receive

The church has created a negative impression that we are always trying to get something cheap or for free and then call it favor or a miracle. That's a poverty mindset. The church is supposed to be equipped with all grace so that we always have all sufficiency in all things and have an abundance for every good work (2 Corinthians 9:8).

> **The church has created a negative impression that we are always trying to get something cheap or for free and then call it favor or a miracle.**

The Kingdom Produces Kings

God is a king. He is King eternally (1 Timothy 1:17). His children are supposed to be princes and princesses. The first identity we have in the kingdom is that of kings. In relationship with God, we are His children. In His kingdom, we are kings. What does a king do? He takes dominion and reigns.

The Church Produces Christians

The world is going the way it is not because there aren't enough Christians on this planet, but because most Christians do not have a kingdom mindset. Twelve men in the first century reached almost the entire known world with the gospel. We have been trying to do this for more than a century with close to a billion Christians. Christianity is the name of a religion.

The Kingdom Is Comprised of Sons and Daughters

When you believe in Jesus Christ, God gives you the authority or right to become His child (John 1:12). Most people live in the "believing" stage and never move to the stage of sonship. Every Sunday and on special holidays, many come and renew their "believing" status, but never grow beyond it. Sons and daughters don't visit a few times a year; they are an integral part of the kingdom.

The Church Is Comprised of Believers

We have many believers, but few true sons and daughters. The whole world is waiting for the manifestation of the sons of God. What would happen to this earth if the entire body of Christ began to act and exercise their authority as children of God here and now?

You, as a son or a daughter of God, are anointed to set free a part of creation from its bondage. That is your purpose. All of creation came under bondage from the fall. We are like sculptors chiseling away part of a rock to set free a beautiful image. That image was always hidden in the rock, but it took the imagination, tools, and the creativity of an artist to bring that image to light. That is the job before each of us.

> We have many believers, but few true sons and daughters. The whole world is waiting for the manifestation of the sons of God.

The Kingdom Has an Eye for Advancement and Taking New Ground

Advancement comes by taking ground. How do we take ground? It's not just by getting people saved. It is through teaching and training those who come to Christ using kingdom principles. Every human being has at least one problem they are struggling with. Through God we have the solutions to those problems.

The Church Is Focused on Outreach

There are many outreach programs, but how effective are they? I have seen outreaches that feed people, but do nothing to help or train them to change their living conditions or mindsets.

> I have seen outreaches that feed people, but do nothing to help or train them to change their living conditions or mindsets.

That is not kingdom outreach. When a kingdom ministry goes into a neighborhood, they are looking for transformation. They are looking for the ways they can bring the will of God into that area *as it is in heaven*. It will take some serious prayer, planning, strategy, and hard work to train and bring people out of darkness (ignorance) to the light (knowledge) of the gospel. As the old saying goes, if you give a man a fish you will feed him for a day, but if you teach a man to fish you feed him for a lifetime. That is a kingdom mindset.

The Kingdom Is Equipping Its Citizens to Create and Manage Wealth

In Deuteronomy 8:18, God said that it is He who gives power to create wealth to establish His covenant on the earth. The power of God is available for creating wealth. We need to empower people with the proper teaching about how to tap into the power of God to create wealth and use it for kingdom purposes.

The Church Is Looking for Free Money

The church is known for its "free lunch" mentality. Churches are interested in how much money is coming in the offering because that's what sustains a church and keeps it going. It's not the pastor's fault, but it's the way the system works right now.

The Kingdom Is Looking for Ambassadors

The kingdom is looking for ambassadors to send on diplomatic and special assignment missions to preach the gospel of the kingdom. That is what Jesus told His disciples to preach. The King was commissioning His ambassadors to go and represent His kingdom.

The Church Is Looking for Good Preachers

We all like good preachers. We get excited and motivated when we hear a good sermon. Most of the time that excitement and motivation vanishes by five o'clock on Sunday afternoon.

The Kingdom Brings Change through Legislation

If we really want to change cities and nations we need to change the laws and culture. One of the ways this is done is by executing kingdom purposes through strategic prayer. This book will train you to do that.

The Church Likes to Have Gospel Crusades

We have been doing crusades for years. The more money and popularity a ministry has, the more people show up at their crusades. We will gain some converts as a result of crusades, but they will never save a country or a city. Recently, while I was in a particular country, my heart was grieved. I saw churches

> I saw churches on every street but there were kids dying of hunger on those same streets.

on every street but there were kids dying of hunger on those same streets. "International" churches were being established and everyone was doing "international" ministry focused on healing, miracles, and tent meetings, but no one was caring for the children in the streets. God spoke to me, saying, "A crusade will save souls but it will not save a nation."

The Kingdom Is Looking for Martyrs

The highest honor a citizen has in a kingdom is to give his or her life for the king. Many false religions make false promises to their adherents if they die for their faith. In the kingdom of Jesus, there is a special crown and honor for those who die for their faith.

The Church Is Looking for Goose Bumps

We limit our experience with God and church to having a good emotional feeling. In some circles they call these feelings "goose bumps." If people have goose bumps, they will say it was a great service. It's time to change.

The Citizens of the Kingdom Honor Their King

When a woman came and poured expensive, fragrant oil on Jesus even His disciples became upset, saying, "Why this waste? For this fragrant oil might have been sold for much and given to *the* poor." Jesus said, "For you have the poor with you always, but Me you do not have always" (Matthew 26:8, 11). Through whatever we do, our intention should be to honor God. The Bible says that if we honor Him, He will honor us (1 Samuel 2:30).

The Church Likes to Help the Poor

We have been good at reaching out to the poor. There are many ministries that focus on the poor and feeding the hungry. But how many ministries are there to reach out to the kings/leaders and professionals in our communities?

The Kingdom Wants to Influence Government and Culture

God always starts from the top when He does something or reaches someone: either a nation or family. He always goes to the place and person of influence first.

The Church Is Looking for Reports

Churches like to receive reports of how many people were reached, and how many people were fed, and so on. This is because their focus is on numbers, rather than effectiveness. They are all about quantity instead of quality, and feel that quantity reflects quality, but it does not.

Jesus began by preaching, "Repent, for the kingdom of heaven is at hand" (Matthew 4:17b). The prerequisite to entering the kingdom was to repent. Repent means to change the way we think. Jesus knew that most people on earth don't grow up with a kingdom mindset, so in His first message itself He emphasized His priority. Before His kingdom comes it is required of us to change the way we think. He knew that without the change of mindsets His kingdom would not have any effect. Unless we change the way we think, we won't receive any benefit though He gives us the whole kingdom. Unfortunately, that is what is happening today. He gave us His kingdom but many are not enjoying any benefits because they have not changed the way they think.

People everywhere are talking about problems: political, physical, racial, and economic. Is there a solution? The solution is not to initiate more government-regulated programs and not to start more charitable and social organizations. I believe there is a solution for all evil and every dilemma our world is facing. The solution is kingdom-minded churches. When there are kingdom-minded churches in every city and town, the equipped body of Christ can tackle those challenges and come up with solutions. That is God's heart and His agenda for this season. This book is to prepare the church to be kingdom minded instead of having a rapture or revival syndrome.

Chapter 4: Why the Church Is Not Effective

Chapter 4: Why the Church Is Not Effective

"You are the salt of the earth; but if the salt loses its flavor, how shall it be seasoned? It is then good for nothing but to be thrown out and trampled underfoot by men" (Matthew 5:13).

God first introduces Himself in the Bible as the Creator, not as a preacher, healer, prophet, or even a king. Why did God introduce Himself as the Creator? That is the first attribute He wants us to know about Him. Why? It's not only so we will know there is a Creator, but also that creating is the first attribute He wants us to manifest or imitate on this earth as His children. We should produce something.

As I usually say wherever I go to preach, people with products have influence. The Bible says the earth is full of His glory (Isaiah 6:3). How? The earth is full of His products. When I walk into a supermarket, I wonder how many products they carry in that store. There are thousands and thousands of them. When I look, I am amazed at some of the products people have come up with and the reason for them!

When I hear the news and read about what is going on in different parts of the world, I ask the Lord why His church does not have much influence. Why are we not effective at tackling and solving some of the problems our nations are facing? Instead, the church is busy with their programs and singing, while thousands of people are dying and going to hell every day.

In the Beginning

The Lord told me something powerful that changed my life and perspective. He said the reason we are not effective is because we don't understand Genesis 1:1. I was shocked! I have known that verse since I was three years old. I recited it back to Him. It didn't seem like He was impressed with my recitation. He told me to go back and read it again. I did. I went and read the verse again. Then He began to speak to me from that one verse things I did not know before.

That one single verse from the Bible contains almost everything we need to know to be successful in our life. I have read that verse hundreds of times but never fully understood the depth of wisdom and revelation contained in it. If one verse from God's Word contains such wisdom and knowledge to transform our life, what would it be like if He opened up the rest of it?

God made all things beautiful and simple, but we have turned things into a complicated mess. Anytime God gave me solutions to the biggest problems I have faced in my life, they were always simple. His wisdom and understanding are unsearchable.

The Bible begins with, "In the beginning God created the heavens and the earth."

This is some of what God told me about Genesis 1:1. When the Bible says, "In the beginning," it does not mean six thousand years ago. It could have been millions or billions of years ago because God existed prior to creating the heavens and the earth. He created the heavens for His throne and the earth as His footstool. The heavens and the earth were created at the same time, which was in the beginning. The earth we live on is as old as the heavens above us. How do I know that?

> Many believe the earth was created during the six-day account of creation, but it was not. God only remodeled it and brought it back into order for man to occupy at that time.

When God began His six days of creation in Genesis 1:3 (actually, it was restoration), we see that the dark earth covered with water existed prior to that. We do not see God creating the earth or water during the six days of creation. How long has the earth existed? We do not know. We only know it has existed as long as the heavens. There is plenty of evidence in the scientific world that shows our planet earth is millions of years old. Many believe the earth was created during the six-day account of creation, but it was not. God only remodeled it and brought it back into order for man to occupy at that time.

Unseen and Supernatural

Heaven represents the spiritual or the unseen realm. Believe it or not, there is a spirit world out there that controls the natural. Spiritual does not mean weird, spooky, or ignorant. Some people cannot believe anything they cannot reason or see. Spiritual means supernatural. Spirits are not limited to time and space. You are a spirit. Right now you are limited because of your physical body. The mind of your spirit however is unlimited. It can travel anywhere or imagine anything.

Your life is regulated by the spirit world. You did not choose to be born. You did not choose your family or the country of your birth. Who made that choice for you? God did. You also do not choose the day of your death. I recently read in the news about the tragic loss of life because of an airplane that crashed into the sea. 165 perished. They were not planning for their death that day. They were travelling for different purposes: some for vacation, others for business, and others to meet family and friends. Death can come and knock on our door at an unexpected time.

Heaven represents the unseen. The Bible says that the things we see were created by things that are not visible. "By faith we understand that the entire universe was formed at God's command, that what we now see did not come from anything that can be seen" (Hebrews 11:3 NLT). Wow! Did you understand what you just read? Every material thing that you see around you, everything that you touch and feel, was made of things that were unseen. That means the matter by which everything was created was invisible "matter." It may not make any sense to your natural mind when you read that material things were created by invisible substance, but it's the truth. You cannot see an atom with your natural eyes.

> **You came from the invisible to the visible to accomplish a purpose and you existed before you came to this earth.**

You came from the invisible to the visible to accomplish a purpose and you existed before you came to this earth. There are hundreds of millions of planets outside of our solar system. The sun can hold more than a million Earth-size planets. The moon and the stars all have influence over this earth and life on this earth. This all has been proven biblically and scientifically, so I am not talking about anything spooky or weird here.

Genesis 1:1 also teaches us three very important principles which are imperative for life on this earth. The first principle is the relationship between heaven and earth and the balance between the spiritual and natural realms. Heaven represents the spiritual, or unseen, and the earth represents the natural, or what is seen. Human beings are both spiritual and natural at the same time. We are a spirit being living in a physical body. We need to know how to relate to both realms and manage them effectively.

Many people I know are so heaven bound they have no clue how the natural things work on this earth. Others are so earthly-minded they are not aware of the spirit world or even their own spirit. God has put everything we need for our life on, or in, this earth. Wise people will know how to tap into those resources and their lives will prosper.

> **Many people I know are so heaven bound they have no clue how the natural things work on this earth.**

The second principle is that heaven is mentioned first and is above the earth. We need to give priority to spiritual things. Life on this earth depends on—and is ruled by—heaven above us. The weather, different seasons, the rain, and much more are all regulated by the atmosphere. The sky above us functions like a thermostat that controls the temperature, just like the one we have in our home. That means we need to look at the earth and our life with heaven's perspective. When a person or society loses their spiritual perspective, life becomes chaotic and meaningless.

Everything in Life Operates According to Laws

The third principle is that the spiritual and natural worlds are both governed by laws established by God. When we discover those laws and operate our life accordingly, we will be successful. People have been discovering these laws throughout the centuries and human lives have never been the same.

> "Do you know the laws of the heavens? Can you make them to rule over the earth? (Job 38:33 NLV).

Another translation says:

> "Do you know the laws of the heavens? Can you regulate their authority over the earth?" (Job 38:33 ISV).

"You made the earth, and it still stands. All things continue
to this day because of your laws, because all things serve you"
(Psalm 119:90b-91 NCV).

For example, gravity is a law that has been in operation since the creation of
the earth but no one discovered it until the time of Sir Isaac Newton. He did
not *invent* the law of gravity, but he *discovered* it. He observed how apples fell
and was the first one who could prove how it worked.

The law of aerodynamics had been in operation since creation but no one
knew how it really worked until the Wright brothers invented an airplane and
made the discovery. Travel has never been the same since.

You have probably heard about positive thinking. It's actually a law. When you
apply that law and practice it, you will receive the benefit of it. When I say
law, I am not talking about the ceremonial laws of the Old Testament. A law
is a system of operation established by God, by which every aspect of your life
is supposed to function. When an area of your
life is not in accordance with God's system of
operation (or laws), then you will have trouble
in that area. He has a system of operation for
everything: family, money, success, weather,
night and day, sowing and reaping, seasons,
and so on. No one can change His system. If
we do not obey those laws we are asking for
trouble.

> When an area of your
> life is not in accordance
> with God's system of
> operation (or laws),
> then you will have
> trouble in that area.

Everything on Earth, and in this universe, functions according to laws. The
engine of your car operates by a law. There are laws yet to be discovered.
I believe there are laws that exist that make material things disappear or
transport them at the speed of light.

Understanding Breeds Influence

If you are having challenges in any area of your life, it is because you are not
functioning according to God's system. Discover it; then you will prosper. As
kingdom citizens we need to get involved with the natural aspects of the nation
and country we are living in because we have been sent by heaven to influence
them. The church has neglected the natural aspect of nations for so long and

blamed the devil and bad politicians for the problems. They complain about what is going on, but they do not have much influence over anything.

Before we can influence our nation for the kingdom of God, we need to understand the nation itself. Other religions, cults, and groups who are minorities have more influence than the majority because they have people in high places. Some major corporations and enterprises are owned and operated by them. Therefore they exert influence in those areas.

> Before we can influence our nation for the kingdom of God, we need to understand the nation itself.

As an individual you are both a spiritual and natural being and have natural and spiritual talents. We need to develop both of these talents to prosper. We need to train our children in the spirit and in the natural so they will excel in both areas.

The earth represents the natural realm and science is based on this realm. The earth that we live on is amazing. Studies that are being done on different subjects related to the earth are innumerable. There are branches of study about animals, birds, plants, the sea, sea creatures, insects, precious stones, oil, gas, and much more. The earth is governed by natural laws. Everything God established operates according to a system. That's why we have different seasons at particular times of the year. We can walk and live here because of the law of gravity. Everything we need for our natural body comes from the earth. Everything you eat and wear and use comes from the resources of the earth. Every product you use, the water you drink, and the fruits you enjoy are all products of the earth.

Why Some May Not See Miracles

Some people take care of their body, but totally ignore their spirit. There are others I know who focused only on their spirit, totally ignored their body, and died before their time. Many people are in need of various miracles and people across the globe are crying out because of unmet needs. Does God care about those people and their needs? Why does it seem that God chooses and answers one person's need and seems to pass by others who have the same problem? Is God partial?

No, God is not partial. He is willing to help anyone who operates in accordance with His laws. Faith is a spiritual law established by God (Romans 3:27). Whether Christian or non-Christian, when anyone on this earth applies that law, God moves on their behalf. That's why many non-believing people came and received miracles from Jesus when many religious people died in their sickness, even though they might have prayed to God.

God will never do for us what we are supposed to do for ourselves. He has given us the natural world to govern and to exercise dominion. It is our responsibility to discover those laws that govern our natural and spiritual life. When we do what we are supposed to do in the natural, God moves in and does a miracle. If we study the miracles in the Bible in detail, we see that every miracle required something done in the natural (natural law) before God moved in the supernatural (spiritual law).

> If we study the miracles in the Bible in detail, we see that every miracle required something done in the natural (natural law) before God moved in the supernatural (spiritual law).

Neglecting the Natural

Some believers don't appreciate the natural or do things with excellence. Meanwhile the ungodly do things in the natural with excellence and prosper. Why? Because they are following God's principles whether they realize it or not. We are a natural and spirit being at the same time. Some people give more importance to spiritual things. Some people give more importance to natural things. Just like a bird needs two wings to fly, we need to excel in both spiritual and natural things in order to be effective on this earth. There must be a balance. God began to show me all the miracles He did in the Bible and the natural laws people operated which caused God to apply His spiritual laws.

For many years the church has been neglecting the natural. We have been super- or even hyper-spiritual and have lost touch with the planet that was given to us. The devil deceived us, saying the earth didn't belong to us, that it was evil and belonged to him. We believed that lie and did nothing while the ungodly prospered, using the resources that have been put here by our God for us to use.

Some denominations, like the Baptists and Catholics, are good at natural and practical things. They excel in areas of life where other denominations don't. There is something to be learned from them. If we can marry the spiritual and the natural, instead of saying either/or, we will win this world for Christ in no time.

Miracles Operate by Laws

The first miracle Jesus did was to turn water into wine. I wondered for many years why Jesus asked the people to fill the jars with water when He could have just done it all. But, He wouldn't because He knew that laws govern the natural world and people needed to apply those laws. He is not a magician. Magicians don't submit to the laws God created. They manipulate those laws and deceive us by their tricks. God does not make things appear out of nowhere. If you study His ways and everything He does, you will see that He always follows the laws He established. He will not violate His own laws and principles.

> God does not make things appear out of nowhere. If you study His ways and everything He does, you will see that He always follows the laws He established.

When Jesus saw the man by the pool of Bethesda who had been sick for thirty-eight years, He asked the man, "Do you want to be healed?" If so, then he needed to apply a law that God established. Jesus said, "Rise, take up your bed and walk" (John 5:8). There are two laws that were applied in that command. One is spiritual, which is faith. He was telling the man to exercise his faith. Then He told him to put into operation another law in the natural, to take up his bed and walk. The man had to *do* something: the law of work, which is a natural law. Work and faith are two different laws, one natural and the other spiritual, that cooperate in God's kingdom.

> "Where *is* boasting then? It is excluded. By what law? Of works? No, but by the law of faith" (Romans 3:27).

Sin and death are spiritual laws that the enemy uses to keep all humanity under bondage. Isn't it interesting to notice that even the enemy operates by laws? As I said earlier, everything in this universe functions by laws that were established by God. God had to institute another superior law to break those laws and to set us free: the law of the Spirit of life.

> "For the law of the Spirit of life in Christ Jesus has made me free from the law of sin and death" (Romans 8:2).

Did you know that righteousness is also a law?

> "But Israel, pursuing the law of righteousness, has not attained to the law of righteousness. Why? Because *they did* not *seek it* by faith, but as it were, by the works of the law. For they stumbled at that stumbling stone" (Romans 9:31-32).

God, through the death and resurrection of Jesus Christ, made known to humanity the laws that will set them free from the law of sin and death. But many remain under the law of sin and death because of ignorance.

God Is Not a Magician

Another example is the woman that came to Elisha, complaining about her creditors. Her husband died, leaving behind a huge debt. This sounds like it could be a present-day situation. In most families, if the main breadwinner dies, a mountain of debt is left behind. Elisha asked this woman what she had in her house. She replied that she had a small jar of oil. It is amazing to me to see that Elisha understood how things work in the natural and in the spirit. He knew it took something in the natural to create a miracle. He told her to go and borrow as many vessels as she could, bring them all into her house, and shut the door and start pouring the oil into those jars. It did not matter how big or small the jars were, nor did he put any limit on the number of jars. The oil flowed until they were all filled.

It was up to her how many jars she collected. She could have had as many jars as she could find. The man of God did not put any limit on his word. It was up to the size of her faith that she borrowed vessels and jars. She filled her house with empty jars. What was she doing? She was activating a natural law. You cannot pour oil into air and hope it will get stuck; that is magic. As I said, God is not a magician. He operates by the laws He established.

That is why when people came to Jesus for help, even though their need was evident He still asked them what they wanted Him to do for them. He did that not because He was unaware of their need, but because He wanted them to apply the natural law first, which was to "ask" before He could activate the spiritual law.

Every miracle requires an action in the natural: an action according to the laws God established for the earth. The next time you read about a miracle in the Bible, please study the laws that were in operation instead of just the story. Discover which natural and spiritual laws were applied in that miracle. Try to practice them in your own life. Find out which law in the natural that person operated so God could move in the supernatural. Then you can have the same miracles in your life.

> **Every miracle requires an action in the natural: an action according to the laws God established for the earth.**

What was the natural law the widow and her son were walking in? It is the law of preparation, which is a natural law. God will move on your behalf to the level of your preparation. He will not do for you what you are supposed to do in the natural. He will not come and clean your house or cars for you. We have the authority to rule the natural world. When we discover and put those laws that govern the natural world into operation, we will see God moving on our behalf.

Every law—both spiritual and natural—that we need to know pertaining to every aspect of our life is mentioned in the Bible. We need to discover them and teach our kids about them at home and in Sunday school. That is kingdom education. We have Christian education in many places but little or no kingdom education. Every study and discovery that has been done on this earth throughout the years is a discovery of the laws God established. That is why the Bible says there is nothing new under the sun.

For a long time, the church has been focusing on only spiritual aspects. They are running around trying to get people saved, but not training them to seek the kingdom first or discover the laws God has established. The result is that most people remain poor and sick even though they are saved. They limit their salvation to reaching heaven. That is not the gospel Jesus preached.

Manifest the Wisdom of God

As I said earlier, the church was a mystery hidden in the heart of God. One of the purposes of the church is to demonstrate the manifold wisdom of God to the principalities and powers in heavenly places. When we do this, we will see miracles.

> "To me, who am less than the least of all the saints, this grace was given, that I should preach among the Gentiles the unsearchable riches of Christ, and to make all see what is the fellowship of the mystery, which from the beginning of the ages has been hidden in God who created all things through Jesus Christ; to the intent that now the *manifold wisdom of God* might be made known by the church to the principalities and powers in the heavenly places" (Ephesians 3:8-10).

Churches today give more importance to the power of God than the wisdom of God. The above Scripture does not say, "That now the power of God may be manifest to the principalities and powers"; it is talking about the *wisdom* of God. The purpose of a church to the needy is to demonstrate the love of God to people who do not know Him. The purpose of the church to the governments and the spirit world is to demonstrate the wisdom of God.

Jesus healed the sick and fed the hungry, not only because He had the power to do it but because He loved them and had compassion on them. We look for the power of God without being willing to manifest the love of God. Power comes as the result of the compassion and love we have for the people. If we really want to make an impact for God, we need the wisdom of God—not just the anointing or power of God. Throughout the centuries people who made a difference, made it through the wisdom of God. We will not win this world through the power of God alone.

> "See, I have called by name Bezalel the son of Uri, the son of Hur, of the tribe of Judah. And I have filled him with the Spirit of God, in wisdom, in understanding, in knowledge, and in all manner of workmanship" (Exodus 31:2-3).

Joshua had the wisdom of God: "Now Joshua the son of Nun was full of the spirit of wisdom, for Moses had laid his hands on him; so the children of Israel heeded him, and did as the Lord had commanded Moses" (Deuteronomy 34:9). Joshua received the spirit of wisdom because Moses laid his hands on him. Moses had the wisdom of God in Him. Joshua accomplished in six years what Moses could not do in forty years.

Psalm 105 says Joseph had the wisdom of God:

> "He sent a man before them—Joseph—who was sold as a slave. They hurt his feet with fetters, he was laid in irons.…He made him lord of his house, and ruler of all his possessions, to bind his princes at his pleasure, and teach his elders wisdom" (Psalm 105:17-18; 21-22).

Daniel made a difference in Babylon through the wisdom of God. Daniel 1:17 says, "As for these four young men, God gave them knowledge and skill in all literature and wisdom; and Daniel had understanding in all visions and dreams."

Jesus grew in wisdom and stature long before the power of God came upon Him (Luke 2:52). The manifold wisdom of God should be demonstrated through the church in business, the arts, science, music, education, economics, politics, and in every discipline on earth. We have been waiting for the rapture to take place when Jesus told us to go into all the world and preach the gospel of the kingdom.

We have left the natural aspect to some particular denominations or to the ungodly. They start excellent schools, colleges, universities, hospitals, and businesses, and get involved in government while the evangelical churches remain on the side, asking for something for free. Unless we properly balance the spiritual and the natural in our lives, we will be like a bird that is trying to fly with just one wing! The bird can work hard but won't cover much distance, it will keep going in circles. Likewise, the church has been trying hard but not covering much distance. To a bird, its wings are the natural aspect and the air is the supernatural aspect. When the church excels in both the natural and in the spirit, watch out! Nothing will be impossible for us. There is one more reason the church remains ineffective: We have misunderstood why God created us.

> **When the church excels in both the natural and in the spirit, watch out! Nothing will be impossible for us.**

96

Chapter 5: God's Purpose in Creating Man

Chapter 5: God's Purpose in Creating Man

"The heaven, even the heavens, are the Lord's; but the earth He has given to the children of men" (Psalm 115:16).

Before I explain the power and authority of the church, it is important to touch on the subject of the purpose of human beings. I have heard that only three percent of people know exactly what they are supposed to do with their life. That means 97% of people do not know why they are here on earth. The church is made of people. If people don't know their purpose, then it is certain the church will not accomplish its purpose either. The majority of the population on this earth does not know why they are here. That is scary. Now we know the reason for all the chaos around us!

> Only three percent of people know exactly what they are supposed to do with their life. That means 97% of people do not know why they are here on earth.

This is why the church is not effective today. Ninety-seven percent of the people coming together every Sunday do not know their purpose! How effective can that body be? I have written a book called *The Three Most Important Decisions of Your Life* to help people discover their purpose.

Before we can recognize our individual purposes, we need to understand the corporate purpose God had for creating human beings. Our individual purposes must fit into the corporate purpose of God for the entire species. Traditionally, I was taught that man was created to worship God. I found that everywhere I went, people all over the world are taught the same thing. If we were created to worship God and if worship means singing some songs, then how many hours a day do we worship? Why do only a few people on this earth have the real ability to sing? Did God make a mistake by not giving most people the ability to sing? Or were we misled?

I began to search the Bible to find out where it says man was created to worship God. To tell you the truth, I could not find it. I found the place where it says everything that has breath praises the Lord. Everything God created praises Him (Psalm 148). But that is not their purpose. An apple tree was created to produce apples. The sun was created to rule the day. Birds were created to fly. A cow was created to give milk and meat. This is how they praise Him.

Why Do We Worship?

The greatest commandment in the Bible is to love God. Worship is one of the ways we can express our love to God, but it is not the purpose for which we were created. Worship deals with the posture and attitude of the heart more than singing. I love anointed worship where the presence of the Lord shows up. I have experienced the power of true worship in many areas of my life.

Today, many consider the song service to be worship, but the word *worship* appears seventy times in the New Testament and not even one time does it have anything to do with singing. It means to fall prostrate before God. The kind of worship that we know of today did not start until almost a thousand years after man was created. God created millions of angels to sing to Him, and they are doing it in heaven non-stop.

> **The kind of worship that we know of today did not start until almost a thousand years after man was created.**

Jesus did not come to teach us how to sing and never asked any person to sing to Him. The disciples did not sit around Jesus every morning singing to Him. Neither did Jesus sing songs to the Father while He was on this earth. There is no record of it in the Gospels other than after the Passover when they sang a hymn (Matthew 26:30). He was teaching and showing them how to live in His kingdom. Jesus said at the end of His ministry, "I have glorified You on the earth. I have finished the work which You have given Me to do" (John 17:4). I believe the greatest form of worship is discovering and fulfilling our God-given purpose here on earth.

Another thing I was taught by church tradition was that when we get to heaven, we will be worshiping God day and night. We will be flying around like angels and singing hallelujah for all eternity. Is there proof of that in the Bible? I began to read the book of Revelation and it says the same thing about man that the book of Genesis says. The first chapter of Genesis says man was created to have dominion (reign) on the earth and the last chapter of Revelation says we will be reigning with Christ forever and ever on the earth.

> "There shall be no night there: They need no lamp nor light of the sun, for the Lord God gives them light. *And they shall reign forever and ever*" (Revelation 22:5).

Another interesting thing I found in the book of Revelation is that the song the living creatures and the twenty-four elders in heaven sing is about us reigning on this earth.

> "Now when He had taken the scroll, the four living creatures and the twenty-four elders fell down before the Lamb, each having a harp, and golden bowls full of incense, which are the prayers of the saints. And they sang a new song, saying: 'You are worthy to take the scroll, and to open its seals; for You were slain, and have redeemed us to God by Your blood out of every tribe and tongue and people and nation, and have made us kings and priests to our God; and *we shall reign on the earth*'" (Revelation 5:8-10).

Prayer Precedes Worship

The person from the Bible that most people use as an example for worship is David. He wrote songs and danced before the ark of God. But have you ever wondered what David's purpose was? What did he do with his life? His purpose was to be the king of Israel. In fact, he was the greatest king of Israel and God said that his throne shall endure forever. It's great to sing or dance like David danced, but be sure to fulfill your purpose like David did as well. Reign in life!

There are a few verses and incidents in the Bible that people use as an example for worship and to defend the reason for all the lengthy singing that goes on in some churches. Again, I am not against singing; I am all for it, but we need something to praise and shout about before we start singing. Most people have no motivation to sing. They are doing it as part of the tradition or by compulsion.

One example used about singing in church is the story of Jehoshaphat in 2 Chronicles. He appointed singers to go in front of the army to the battle. But if we study that incident in detail, we see that when the enemy came against him he declared a fast and decided to seek the Lord with all his heart. He prayed a powerful prayer before God and all the people of Israel.

> "And Jehoshaphat feared, and set himself to seek the Lord, and proclaimed a fast throughout all Judah. So Judah gathered together to ask *help* from the Lord; and from all the cities of Judah they came to seek the Lord" (2 Chronicles 20:3-4).

As a result of prayer and fasting, the Lord told him to send Judah first in the battle against his enemies. He didn't do this every time he went into battle. How absurd is it that we copy his experience without following the principles he applied before he started singing, and expect the same result? Both the Old and New Testament give more importance to prayer than singing.

Another major incident people use is in the New Testament when Paul and Silas were put in prison. Preachers usually use this incident and say they sang praises and God sent an earthquake. But, again, if we read the Bible carefully, we see that they prayed before they praised God. I believe they prayed so earnestly that when they received the assurance that God was going to answer their prayers, they began to sing praises to Him for that answer. When there is a reason in your life to praise God, praise goes to a whole new level.

> **When there is a reason in your life to praise God, praise goes to a whole new level.**

First of all, Paul and Silas were put in prison because they cast a demon out of a girl who had the spirit of divination. The Bible says in Acts 16:16, "Now it happened, as we went to *prayer,* that a certain slave girl possessed with a spirit of divination met us." Paul and Silas were going to pray when they met this girl.

> "But at midnight Paul and Silas *were praying* and singing hymns to God, and the prisoners were listening to them" (Acts 16:25).

We see in the above Scriptures that they prayed before they sang. As you know, if two of us agree on earth and ask anything in Jesus' name, He will do it. Paul and Silas prayed in agreement and God answered their prayer. There are three other primary Scriptures people use to support their worship-as-singing theology. The first is when Jesus said, "If I be lifted up I will draw all men unto me." They use that verse to support worship. This is a perfect example of using a verse out of context. If you read the next verse, you will see this particular verse has nothing to do with lifting His name in worship. Instead, He was talking about His death and being lifted up on the cross.

> " 'Now is the judgment of this world; now the ruler of this world will be cast out. And I, if I am lifted up from the earth, will draw all *peoples* to Myself.' This He said, signifying by what death He would die" (John 12:31-33).

I pray that churches would remove songs from their praise and worship list that do not lift or praise Jesus or do not mention the name of Jesus, Christ, God, or any of His names. Humanism is creeping into our contemporary praise and worship songs. Many of the modern songs we sing are about I, me, and mine.

True Worship

The second verse people use to support their worship services is when Jesus told the Samaritan woman that the Father seeks true worshipers who will worship Him in spirit and in truth:

> "But the hour is coming, and now is, when the true worshipers will worship the Father in spirit and truth; for the Father is seeking such to worship Him. God *is* Spirit, and those who worship Him must worship in spirit and truth" (John 4:23-24).

We cannot use the above verse and declare the whole human race is created to sing to God. I have seen very few people who understand the meaning of this verse. Jesus was explaining this to a woman who believed God must be worshiped only on a particular mountain, or at a certain place, in a certain way and time. Jesus was saying the hour is coming when people would worship the Father from every known place, not just on one mountain or in a particular building.

Worship in the spirit means two things. Old Testament worship did not include the spirit of man; it was an outward (body) worship that included dancing, shouting, and other movement. In the New Testament, because our spirit is born again, God wants us to worship Him with our spirit (Romans 1:9; Philippians 3:3). Notice the small "s" used for the word *spirit* in these verses, which represents our spirit. "I will sing with the spirit, and I will also sing with the understanding" (1 Corinthians 14:15b).

> "Speaking to one another in psalms and hymns and spiritual songs, singing and making melody in your heart to the Lord, giving thanks always for all things to God the Father in the name of our Lord Jesus Christ" (Ephesians 5:19-20).

The second meaning of that verse is to worship without limit. Today, people can worship God anytime, anywhere. It was not the case in the Old Testament; they were allowed to worship only in the place chosen by God and only at the times appointed by Him. Now that He indwells us with His Spirit, we are no longer limited in this way.

The third and most popular reference used to support today's stance on worship is the Scripture that says our God dwells in the praises of His people. "But thou art holy, O thou that inhabitest the praises of Israel" (Psalm 22:3 KJV). This is an Old Testament concept because He could not dwell in people then, though it has always been His desire. There had to be praises all the time to sustain the presence of God among the people.

In the New Testament we are the temple of God and the Holy Spirit (1 Corinthians 3:16; 6:19; Romans 8:11). What would be the result if each believer lives in the revelation that God and His Spirit lives in them 24/7? How would

> **We do not need to sing to sustain God in our lives. He lives in us.**

our attitude and response to situations in life change if we knew that God lives in us? Because He lives in us, He goes with us wherever we go. We do not need to sing to sustain God in our lives. He lives in us. That is why Paul said to make melody in our hearts, singing to the Lord with our spirit (Ephesians 5:19).

It would be beneficial to do a Bible study on the word *worship* in the New Testament and see how many times it means singing. You may be surprised at what you find. Most of us today think of singing right away when we think of worship.

In Matthew 8:2 we see that a leper came and worshiped Jesus and said, "Lord, if You are willing, You can make me clean." He did not sing to Jesus. It actually means "to bow down or to fall prostrate." His worship was evident in the attitude of his heart and had nothing to do with singing.

Most churches have full-time worship leaders or worship pastors as staff, but I haven't seen very many prayer coordinators as full-time staff members in churches. That's why I said we are majoring on the minors and minoring on the major subjects of New Testament theology.

An Overemphasis on Singing

Once we lost our original purpose and the purpose of the church, we had to invent other ways or programs to busy ourselves and keep people interested and coming back to church. So we brought entertainment to our churches with music, drama, dance, and other programs.

> Once we lost our original purpose and the purpose of the church, we had to invent other ways to keep people interested and coming back to church.

Jesus did not start His church to sing to Him. If He did, He would have taken at least a day to train His disciples about singing and vocal techniques. Imagine having Peter and Judas as members of the same choir or as choir leaders! Again, while He was on this earth, he never asked anyone to sing to Him. Why? Because He knew the *singing* dispensation ended with His coming and the *living inside of us* dispensation was getting ready to begin.

The kind of church that we see today did not exist in the New Testament. The one-hour fast-food-type services prevalent in our times were not part of the early church. The New Testament gives more importance to prayer than worship, but we have reversed the emphasis and we now have more singing in the church than prayer. That is why we do not see the same results they saw in the first century.

Most of the songs and the style of music we have today in the church are just a copy of the style of music that is in the world of entertainment. We have not been taught the difference between the world and the church. Most people think they are all the same, especially the younger generation. Jesus said, "They are not of the world, just as I am not of the world" (John 17:16). In His High Priestly prayer, Jesus clearly differentiated the world and people that believe in Him to the extent that He said, "I do not pray for the world" (John 17:9).

Why Did the Old Testament Put More Emphasis on Singing?

We do not see as many references to praise and worship in the New Testament as we see in the Old Testament. That was not the primary focus of Jesus, or Paul when he established or wrote letters to the churches. There is a reason for this. The reason we see more references to worship in the Old Testament is because at that time God could not dwell in people. They were not redeemed—or born again—as we are by the blood of Jesus. He dwelt (His presence) in a tent (tabernacle), in a temple, or in the praises of His people (Psalm 22:3).

David was a man who loved God and His presence very much. He did not like the idea of the Spirit of God coming and leaving. He wanted something that remained or was constant. He had a revelation, an idea, to keep the presence of God continually around him. The idea was to implement non-stop praise and worship. Constant praises and singing were arranged to sustain His presence (1 Chronicles 9:33; 23:5; 25:1, 6).

The more time we spend with God, the more aware we become of His presence in our lives. The trouble is that we are busy doing so many things that our priorities are messed up. When we put God first in our life and spend time with Him first thing in the morning, our lives will be much better in every way.

The New Testament gives more importance to prayer than praise. If we spent as much time praying as we spend singing, this world would not be in the shape it is in. It would be different. God's house (us) is supposed to be a house of prayer for all nations (Mark 11:17). Paul exhorted believers to pray (not praise) without ceasing (1 Thessalonians 5:17). When the church discovers her original mission on this earth, then the change and transformation we want to see will begin to happen.

Worship Is Not Our Main Purpose

Everyone God used in the Bible was a worshiper, but that was not their *main* purpose. Moses was a deliverer; Joseph was a prime minister; Job was a businessman; Daniel was a statesman; Paul was an apostle; Esther was a queen; Luke was a doctor. They all accomplished their primary calling first. What about you?

We are created in the image and likeness of God. The DNA of our spirit is of God. God likes to create and rule because that is His nature. Whatever comes from God bears His nature and attributes. Everything that God created rules over something. He created the sun to rule the day. He created the moon and stars to rule the night (Psalm 136:8-9). Birds rule the sky and animals rule the forest, and fish rule in the oceans. Dogs rule over cats and cats rule over mice and mice over cheese. You and I—created in His image and likeness—are supposed to do the same thing God does.

The Bible says God surrounds us with songs of deliverance (Psalm 32:7). Just because He sings does not mean that is His purpose. He is a King and His kingdom rules heaven and earth. A kingdom has music, songs, worship, and dance, but that is not the primary function of a kingdom. We are His children. Let's find our true purpose!

All of creation is waiting for the manifestation of the sons of God to be set free from bondage (Romans 8:19). Unfortunately, most sons and daughters of God are busy singing inside a four-walled building that we call a church. If God did not create us to worship Him, then why did He create us? Let's look at our purpose, but first let's look at why purpose is even important.

Why is Purpose Important?

Discovering your purpose is important for the following reasons.

Your provision is connected to your purpose.

For most people on earth, not having enough money is their limiting factor. Your financial blessing is attached to your purpose. The reason for poverty on this earth is because people do not know their purpose. Many nations think population is their problem, and the reason for poverty. Population is not a problem. People not knowing their purpose is the real problem. Many developed nations do not have enough people to do the work so they allow people from other nations to migrate to their countries.

Your provision is in the place of your purpose.
Your purpose is also connected to a place. Once you discover your purpose, you need to know where you are supposed to fulfill that purpose. Each person has a specific place and nation where they are supposed to fulfill their purpose.

Purpose gives you freedom.
We all like the freedom to do what is really important to us. We like to see places and help other people. When you are doing what you were created to do, it frees you up from being a slave to a system or being tied to a mundane schedule.

Purpose gives you fulfillment.
Nothing else gives you more satisfaction and fulfillment than when you do what you were created to do. Many are not satisfied and feel unfulfilled so they try to find fulfillment in the wrong places. Or they need a hobby to make them happy.

Purpose gives you direction and focus.
Many people do many jobs, but they do not do them well because they do not have focus. Every journey has a destination. Your life has a destination, which is the accomplishment of your purpose. When you know what you are supposed to do, you can really focus on it. Knowing your purpose also gives you direction about where to go with your life.

Purpose gives you boundaries.
Everything God created has a boundary. Jesus said the path to life is narrow and difficult (Matthew 7:14). He meant that living a life dedicated to your purpose, single-heartedly, is not easy. Purpose keeps you focused and on a narrow path.

Purpose gives you hope.
Everyone needs hope for tomorrow. Purpose gives us a reason to be alive. If we have no hope, we will not have any motivation to do anything. In that state, we are alive, but not really living. There are millions of people

on this earth who do not have hope for their future because they have not yet discovered their purpose.

Both the Old and New Testaments Say the Same Thing about the Purpose of Man

In Genesis 1, God said that we are created to rule on the earth, and in Revelation 22:5, we read that we will be reigning on this earth forever and ever. He did not change His mind in between. In Romans 5:17 we read that we are supposed to reign in life. Paul says in 2 Timothy 2:12 that if we endure with Him, we shall reign with Him. The questions to ask are: "How should each of us reign," and "Why, then, should we worship God?"

There has been much teaching about praise and worship, but I never heard anyone teaching about *how to reign* in this life. There are some who teach that we are created to reign, but I never heard the "how" part until the Holy Spirit revealed it to me from the first chapter of Genesis. I will share that with you in this book.

Man Was Created to Have Dominion over the Earth

"Then God said, 'Let Us make man in Our image, according to Our likeness; *let them* have *dominion* over the fish of the sea, over the birds of the air, and over the cattle, over all the earth and over every creeping thing that creeps on the earth.' So God created man in His own image; in the image of God He created him; male and female He created them. Then God *blessed* them, and God said to them, 'Be *fruitful* and *multiply; fill the earth* and *subdue it;* have *dominion* over the fish of the sea, over the birds of the air, and over every living thing that moves on the earth'" (Genesis 1:26-28).

In the above verses, God the Creator reveals His purpose for creating man and how it is to be fulfilled. *Only the manufacturer knows the purpose of a product.* It is very important that we understand this. We all have preconceived notions in our heart and mind that we were taught by the religious spirit in the world today. Because of this, when we read that Scripture we assume we know what it means, but truthfully, very few people on this earth fully understand its meaning.

In order to understand our individual purpose, we need to understand why God created the human race. The above verses tell us how and why God created us. God is a king and He has a kingdom. He decided to extend His dominion to a planet called Earth. He needed someone to exercise His dominion on that planet, so He decided to create a very unique species in His own likeness and image called humans. Then He gave the dominion of the earth to them. *That is the reason we are here.*

We are created in the image and likeness of God to have dominion over the earth. Each of us is created to have dominion over a particular area of life and God has equipped each human being with the capacity and ability to accomplish their task. We could call this purpose, vision, a product, or a calling. He deposited our purpose into us in seed form. When we discover that seed and follow the principles, or the steps He laid out in verse 28, we will prosper.

> **Each of us is created to have dominion over a particular area of life and God has equipped each human being with the capacity and ability to accomplish their task.**

There is no one born on this earth without that seed. The problem is that many of us have not discovered it yet. We call the seed *potential* or *talent*. Each seed needs a particular environment in order to grow and be fruitful.

Man's eternal purpose is to be a king on this earth. Kings have kingdoms and kingdoms have dominion. But, because of the fall, God added two other dimensions to man's life: priest and prophet. Those two dimensions are temporary until we are redeemed from this present life. Once we are redeemed, we will reign again on the new earth forever and ever (Revelation 5:10; 22:5). Adam was a king. At the end of time, there will only be kings as it was in the beginning.

Let "Us" and Let "them"

One of the age-old questions man has been asking is, "If God is good and powerful, then why does He allow evil to happen on this earth?" Or, "Why doesn't He intervene to stop a catastrophe or help people who are going through bad times?" One thing to notice very carefully is that when God created man, He said, "Let *Us* make man." When it came to delegating the dominion and authority over the earth, He said, "Let *them*." God did not include Himself in the exercise of dominion.

God created the earth for man and gave it to him as an inheritance. It was up to man to decide what he wanted to do on the earth. God will not interfere with the affairs of man unless man asks Him for help. Until the creation of man, God did everything on the earth. After creating man, God did everything on earth *through human partnership*. God is just and holy and will not violate His own Word. That is one of the reasons evil takes place on this earth and God does not intervene to stop it. Man was created with a will—he has a choice to either work *with* God or to work independently of Him.

Why Subdue and Take Dominion over the Creatures?

God specifically told man to take dominion over the fish of the sea and over the fowl of the air, over the cattle and over every living thing that moves upon the earth (Genesis 1:28). Why does man need to subdue and take dominion over these creatures? How could they be dangerous to man in any way? The reason is this: Satan and evil spirits were on the earth before God created Adam. They had access and permission to enter the earth realm and the animal kingdom before the fall of man. They are the second reason for the evil happening on the earth.

As a loving Father, God was preparing Adam for a possible uprising from the enemy's kingdom—one that would most likely use one of those four sectors of the animal kingdom. Satan and demons are spirit beings, so they need a physical body to operate on the earth. They were not allowed to enter Adam and Eve, so they had to use either the fish of the sea, birds of the air, cattle of the earth, or the creeping things. Satan chose the serpent because it was more cunning than any other creature God had made on the earth. Even in our world today, in many cultures, creatures from those four categories God told man to subdue are worshiped or considered gods. In India, rats and snakes are worshiped as gods. In America, worldly success is an idol. The devil is the same everywhere, but he puts together a different package for each culture. In other cultures, his idols might look radically different.

God wanted Adam to subdue (to make submit by force) any rebellion or attempt to usurp his authority. He was to put it out immediately. It was man's duty to keep them where they belonged. Unfortunately, Adam did not do it, but listened to the serpent and willfully disobeyed God.

Kings and Priests

There is a teaching across the body of Christ that says you are either a king *or* a priest. People who are in ministry are called priests, and people who work in the secular world or run businesses are called kings. The New Testament does not advocate this teaching. Christ is King, Priest, and Prophet all at the same time. Each believer is also supposed to function in all of these dimensions. Abraham, David, and other Old Testament saints, who lived in the revelation of life in Jesus, functioned in these three roles. The Hebrew word for dominion is *radah*, which means "to rule, have dominion, dominate, tread down."[10]

> Christ is King, Priest, and Prophet all at the same time. Each believer is also supposed to function in all of these dimensions.

When I first heard that Jesus is King of Kings, I thought He was the King of all kings of all kingdoms that had ever ruled the earth. But God opened my eyes to see that it really means He is the king of all who have been made kings and priests by His Father. He is talking about us.

From Genesis to Revelation, it is God's plan to establish His kingdom *on earth as it is in heaven*, and for man to have dominion over the work of His hands. God is a king and we are His children. Whatever He does from Genesis to Revelation has a kingdom thread. Kings rule over a territory and that territory is called a kingdom. That is why whenever God mentions the position of man, He always put the kingship or royalty first and not the priesthood. Please read the following verses and you will see what I am talking about.

Right now everyone in the body of Christ is a king and priest at the same time. When God brought the people of Israel out of Egypt, He said He wanted them to be a kingdom of priests: " 'And you shall be to Me a *kingdom of priests* and a holy nation.' These are the words which you shall speak to the children of Israel" (Exodus 19:6).

---

10. Strong, James. *Strong's Exhaustive Concordance*. Peabody, MA: Hendrickson Publishers, 2007. #H07287.

We see the same thing in the New Testament:

> "But you *are* a chosen generation, a *royal priesthood*, a holy nation, His own special people, that you may proclaim the praises of Him who called you out of darkness into His marvelous light" (1 Peter 2:9).

> "And from Jesus Christ, the faithful witness, the firstborn from the dead, and the ruler over the kings of the earth. To Him who loved us and washed us from our sins in His own blood, and has *made us kings and priests* to His God and Father, to Him *be* glory and dominion forever and ever. Amen" (Revelation 1:5-6).

> "And have *made us kings and priests* to our God; and we shall reign on the earth" (Revelation 5:10).

> "There will never be night again. They will not need the light of a lamp or the light of the sun, because the Lord God will give them light. And they will rule as kings forever and ever" (Revelation 22:5, NCV).

None of the above Scriptures say that God made some kings and others priests. Instead, it says He made us kings *and* priests. That includes everyone. Revelation 22 mentions only kings. That is the finale.

God wants each of us to exercise our royalty first—before we move into any other capacity He created us for. Royalty is our identity and when we exercise our kingship (our dominion) over an area of life, we will have provision for our living.

> **Royalty is our identity and when we exercise our kingship (our dominion) over an area of life, we will have provision for our living.**

Jesus is King, Prophet, and Priest. When the wise men from the east came to see Him, they came to see a king, not a prophet or a priest (Matthew 2:1). He was born a king. During His ministry time, He functioned as a prophet and a priest – and not as king. At His death He was recognized as a king again. When He comes back the second time, He is coming as king, but not just any king, but the King of Kings.

The enemy knows that if he can keep us busy singing songs inside a building, we will not bother him with the dominion or resources of the earth. He and his cohorts will have the whole planet to themselves. We will stay inside our homes and church buildings, singing songs. God did not ask Adam to sing to Him either. He did not give Adam a guitar or a violin and tell him to sit in the garden and sing to Him on the seventh day! Neither did Jesus.

Throughout the Bible God says we are created to reign on the earth. What if a cow stays in its stall and sings all day long? Will it fulfill its purpose? No. A fig tree is created to produce figs. When Jesus saw a fig tree and it did not have any fruit, He cursed it. He did not say, "Well, at least it is praising me, so let it remain fruitless." He said that no one would eat fruit from it ever again (Mark 11:14).

David had a passion for praising God, but his primary purpose was to be a king. There is a familiar song we sing, "When the Spirit of the Lord comes upon my heart, I will dance like David danced." Well, let us not only dance like David danced, but reign like he reigned. It is easy to dance, but not so easy to reign. To reign, you need to discover your purpose and master at least one area of life.

Another big deception the enemy has used is to make people believe that God created us primarily to live in heaven. I do not see that anywhere in the book of Genesis or in the book of Revelation. The devil knows that if he can keep us ignorant of the fact that the earth belongs to us, then he can freely misuse the whole earth and its resources for his purpose, and the church will not bother him. The church will not try to get back what originally belonged to us. God created man to live on this earth and gave him the earth to manage. We are going to reign with Christ on the new earth, not in heaven. Only if we learn how to reign in this life will we know how to reign with Him in the next.

> **Another big deception the enemy has used is to make people believe that God created us primarily to live in heaven.**

Steps to Having Dominion

After God created man, He blessed them and gave them dominion over all the earth and all He made. That is your purpose, my friend, to have dominion over the earth, but not people. He explains the steps to dominion in verse 28.

The first thing He said was to be *fruitful*. Man is made of spirit, soul, and body. For many years I believed that when God said to be fruitful, He was only talking about us having children. That is true, because children are the fruit of our body. But there are two other parts, spirit and soul, that need to bear fruit. What is the fruit of the spirit and the soul?

We know the fruit of the spirit from Galatians 5:22-23: love, joy, peace, patience, kindness, goodness, faithfulness, gentleness, self-control. There is another kind of fruit of the spirit: spiritual children. Just like we have physical children when we have matured and married, we need to give birth to our spiritual children. That is one of the signs of spiritual maturity.

What is the fruit of our soul? Our soul is our mind and is comprised of our will, intellect, imagination, emotions, and memory. How do we bear fruit in our mind? Every product you see is the fruit of someone's imagination. We need to come up with products and services that help humanity. Once you have a product, you need to apply the steps mentioned in verse 28 to prosper.

Every living thing God created multiplies or reproduces itself. God wants us to be fruitful, so He put a seed in our spirit. A seed is something that has unlimited potential to reproduce its own kind. That seed could be ability, talent, skill, passion, creativity, an idea, a product, an invention, or a dream. He wants you to focus your life on that seed, plant it, nurture it, and use it to solve a problem other people have. When you possess a quality that others do not have, they will pay to reap the benefits of what you have. That is your purpose. That is the key to your prosperity.

> When you possess a quality that others do not have, they will pay to reap the benefits of what you have. That is your purpose. That is the key to your prosperity.

The second step to having dominion is to *multiply*. Once you know what you are supposed to be doing, your purpose, and your product (fruit), you need to multiply it. To multiply means to mass-produce. If it is a book, or a song, you produce copies of that book or CD to reach the whole world.

The third step to having dominion is to *fill the earth*. To fill the earth means to distribute or market your product, service, idea, talent, so that others can benefit from it.

The fourth step to having dominion is to *subdue*. Subdue means to do what you do like no one else does, and bring that sphere of life under your subjection. That means you become an expert in that particular field and present it in a way that others need what you have to increase their quality of life. To subdue means to take authority over and master something. You are created to subdue and master an area of life on this earth.

The fifth step is *dominion*. When you subdue an area of life, you will have dominion. This is the secret of all prosperity and of fulfilling your purpose. Every successful business uses these principles as their foundation for growth, whether they realize it or not. God set that in motion in the first chapter of the Bible. Whatever God does has the potential for growth.

The Good News

Before God decided to create you, He first saw a need on this earth and then decided your purpose—which is to meet that need. He designed your physical body and form and prepared all the resources it would take for you to fulfill that purpose. Finally, He released your birthplace and time and you were born. There is no instance in the Bible when God called someone to do something but they could not do it because they did not have access to money or other resources. It does not exist. Be encouraged: However big your purpose is, there is provision for it. Your provision is in your purpose.

> There is no instance in the Bible when God called someone to do something but they could not do it because they did not have access to money or other resources.

I have been told that in Third World countries the two major problems are population and poverty. There is no such thing as a population problem, only a purpose problem. There are millions of people in the Third World countries who do not yet know their purpose. There is no such problem as a poverty problem, but there is a productivity problem. People do not produce anything, so they remain poor. They don't produce anything because they don't recognize the resources God put in their mind and on the earth for them, and don't know how to put these to use.

Paradigm Shift

Jesus was very intentional, but very careful when it came to presenting new revelations that required an absolute change in the way people thought or did things. If you tell someone outright that what they are doing is wrong, and if they think that what they believe and do is the truth and the right thing, they will oppose or even rebel against it. That is why He did not give them the whole truth in one shot. He only gave them what they could handle a little at a time. He changed their mindset step by step. One of those elements that required change was about the temple in Jerusalem.

Jesus knew that for a Jew the temple was the center of all their spiritual and political affairs. They revered the temple as much as they revered God Himself. But He knew by His coming, the temple was not going to continue to have the same significance because God was more interested in *living temples* than a building made of mortar and bricks. He wanted to live in people.

Jesus had to find a way to present that truth to the people without offending them. If He just told them not to go to the temple anymore because the veil was going to be torn and His blood was going to be offered as a once and forever sacrifice, the people would not have received it well. They might have even tried to kill Him for saying that. Their temple was a sacred place for them.

In Matthew 12:6 He said, "Yet I say to you that in this place there is One greater than the temple."

Jesus made a whip and cleansed the temple from all the money changers and people who sold things inside. When the Jews questioned why He was doing such things, He answered them, saying, "Destroy this temple, and in three days I will raise it up" (John 2:19). They mocked Him because they did not understand what He was talking about. They thought He referred to the physical temple in Jerusalem that was made with stones, which had taken forty-six years to build. They did not understand His language. He was not talking about rebuilding the physical temple when He said He would raise it up in three days.

> "Then the Jews said, 'It has taken forty-six years to build this temple, and will You raise it up in three days?' " (John 2:20).

Jesus was talking about His physical body, which is the *real* temple of God. With His arrival God would no longer dwell in a temple or a house made with hands. His intent has always been to dwell in us, who were created in His image and likeness. Our physical body is the only temple God has here on earth now. There is a big difference between the two ideas.

After Jesus' resurrection, the disciples understood what Jesus meant by destroying the temple and how He would raise it up in three days. They had a revelation.

> "But He was speaking of the temple of His body. Therefore, when He had risen from the dead, His disciples remembered that He had said this to them; and they believed the Scripture and the word which Jesus had said" (John 2:21-22).

In Matthew 24 we read the conclusion of the revelation about the temple. When the disciples showed Him the workmanship of the temple, He said the entire place would be torn down and not even one stone would remain upon another. It was a total shock for them because they thought Jesus was going to establish His kingdom on earth and the temple would be the logical place for His kingdom's spiritual capital.

> "God, who made the world and everything in it, since He is Lord of heaven and earth, does not dwell in temples made with hands" (Acts 17:24).

The reason He told them this was to create a paradigm shift because He was talking to a group of people who were stuck with the temple worship idea. They had limited God to a man-made building for their spiritual experience for hundreds of years. God was doing a new thing and they would miss it if they did not change their way of thinking.

In the New Testament, those who are born again are the temple of God and He dwells in us permanently (1 Corinthians 3:16; 6:19; Ephesians 2:21-22; 1 Peter 2:5). Wherever we go, God goes with us. Whether we praise or sing or not, He is always with us and in us. That is why Jesus did not ask anyone to sing to Him. Instead, He wanted them to stop singing and not limit Him to only dwelling in their praises, but allow Him to live in and with them forever.

I will explain more about the house of God in another chapter. Now, because we know our purpose is to have dominion and God wants to exercise His dominion through us, we can delve into the subject of the church and why Jesus started it by paying such a huge price.

Chapter 6: "I Will Build My Church"

Chapter 6: "I Will Build My Church"

"And I also say to you that you are Peter, and on this rock I will build My church, and the gates of Hades shall not prevail against it. And I will give you the keys of the kingdom of heaven, and whatever you bind on earth will be bound in heaven, and whatever you loose on earth will be loosed in heaven" (Matthew 16:18-19).

Why is Matthew the only one to mention the church? The church is the embassy of the kingdom of God here on earth. The verse above may be the most important verse regarding the church in the New Testament because it answers the who, what, why, where, and how questions about the church.

Who Is Building the Church?

Let's start with "who" is building the church: "And I also say to you that you are Peter, and on this rock I will build My church." Jesus is the builder of the church. Who is Jesus? Foremost He is a king and He has a kingdom. I explain in detail about who Jesus is in a later chapter. There are two applications to this truth. Who is the rock Jesus was talking about? We know from the Old and New Testaments that Jesus is the Rock that followed the people of Israel in the wilderness (1 Corinthians 10:4). The name *Peter* also means a rock or a stone.

The word *build* represents building a house or a building. Whenever you build something, it is done progressively and starts with the foundation. Jesus is speaking prophetically here. When He finishes the building process, what does it look like? He is building a temple with living stones where He can dwell. That is His ultimate purpose (Ephesians 2:21-22; 1 Peter 2:5).

THE POWER AND AUTHORITY OF THE CHURCH

The church is a group of people called to govern the spiritual and the natural affairs of God's kingdom on earth. Here Jesus is speaking to Peter, one of His prominent apostles. Many look at this verse from a natural perspective when it says, "You are Peter and on this rock I will build my church." It was not on Peter, the natural man, on which Jesus was going to build His church, but on who he was in the spirit.

Who was Peter in the spirit? He was an apostle. *Jesus was saying upon that apostolic anointing and foundation He would build His church.* Although it is Jesus who builds the church, it was the apostles that He would use to accomplish that task. How do I know that?

> **Jesus was saying upon that apostolic anointing and foundation He would build His church.**

The book of Acts contains many examples of Jesus using His apostles to build His church. It was the necessary next step. They were the foundation He built upon.

> "Now, therefore, you are no longer strangers and foreigners, but fellow citizens with the saints and members of the household of God, *having been built on the foundation of the apostles and prophets, Jesus Christ Himself being the chief cornerstone,* in whom the whole building, being fitted together, grows into a holy temple in the Lord, in whom you also are being built together for a dwelling place of God in the Spirit" (Ephesians 2:19-22).

> "And God has appointed these in the church: first *apostles,* second *prophets,* third teachers, after that miracles, then gifts of healings, helps, administrations, varieties of tongues" (1 Corinthians 12:28).

If there had been no apostolic or prophetic anointing, there would not have been a foundation for that church. When Jesus said, "On this rock I will build my church," He meant the apostolic anointing Peter was carrying. It was Peter who preached the first message on the day of Pentecost when three thousand people were saved. The New Testament church was birthed on that day. The New Testament church was established on the apostolic anointing.

When the church in a nation loses the apostolic and the prophetic anointing, it loses the power and the purpose for its existence. Then people have to invent all sorts of programs and events or systems to keep the church alive and interesting. We see that all around us these days. What I mean by a system is man-made religious rules, clergy, and programs.

The mystery of the church and Christ was revealed to the apostles and the prophets.

> "For this reason I, Paul, the prisoner of Christ Jesus for you Gentiles—if indeed you have heard of the dispensation of the grace of God which was given to me for you, how that by revelation He made known to me the mystery (as I have briefly written already, by which, when you read, you may understand my knowledge in the mystery of Christ), *which in other ages was not made known to the sons of men, as it has now been revealed by the Spirit to His holy apostles and prophets:* that the Gentiles should be fellow heirs, of the same body, and partakers of His promise in Christ through the gospel" (Ephesians 3:1-6).

What is Jesus Building?

Now let's look at the "what." Jesus was building His church. Again, it is important to keep in mind the church is not a building. It's a group of people. Jesus wanted to establish His kingdom on this earth so He chose a group of people to accomplish that task. Whatever you do, your foremost purpose is to partner with Jesus in establishing His kingdom and executing His will on the earth today.

That is the will of the Father as well. When Jesus taught us to pray, He told us to pray for His kingdom to come and for His will to be done *on earth as it is in heaven*. What is Jesus trying to accomplish through the church? His intent is to establish His kingdom here. When a church loses that intent, it loses its purpose.

I am not talking about establishing a natural kingdom now. It's a spiritual kingdom and it is to bring the rule and dominion of God into our communities and nations. When a believer in Christ is in charge of a business, school, or a hospital and runs them based on kingdom principles, that particular business, school, or hospital is under the dominion of God. This means God can accomplish His will through that business, school, or hospital here and now.

When Daniel was in the position next to the king in Babylon, he became not only a witness for God, but through him God could accomplish His will in Babylon and all the other regions Babylon was ruling at that time. We need people like that in government in every nation on earth. We need to train our children and our generation to occupy key places in every sphere of society so the devil will have no chance to put his finger on anything.

Possessing the Gates

And "why" is Jesus doing this? He said, "I will build My church, and the gates of Hades shall not prevail against it." As you know, there is a kingdom of darkness operating on earth. Its intention is to eliminate anything that is godly or that belongs to God. There is a power struggle that has been going on for ages in the spirit world. The gates of hades are trying to prevail against the purposes and the principles of God. He is building His church to withstand and destroy its evil purposes.

What are the "gates of Hades" and what do they have to do with the church? The gates of hades represent the portals of the governing body of the kingdom of darkness. In Bible days, cities and nations were controlled and protected by gates and were guarded by soldiers who opened and closed the gates. It was at the gate of a city or a town where judgments were pronounced and justice was implemented for the people of that city or town. Gates represent power, legal and political authority, control, access, identity, influence, and government. Gates represent a place of authority where decisions are made.

> Gates represent power, legal and political authority, control, access, identity, influence, and government.

> "And Hamor and Shechem his son came to the gate of their city, and spoke with the men of their city" (Genesis 34:20).

> "And all the people that were in the gate, and the elders, said, 'We are witnesses'" (Ruth 4:11a).

There were two types of gates: one was the physical gate that was on the border or wall that actually controlled access to the city, and the other was spiritual, the seat of legal authority. Jesus meant the second kind of gate when He was talking about the gates of hades. There are many cities and countries that have a gate in the middle of the city or capital. For example, in New Delhi, India, close to the capital building, there is huge gate called the India Gate. It is a historic monument and a tourist attraction. This gate has nothing to do with controlling the border of India. It is a monument that represents the government and the army of India.

The city gates controlled access and they were the city's best protection against the enemy. These gates represented a place of authority as well. At the gate, business transactions were completed and social problems were solved by the elders of the city. Representatives of the government/kingdom called elders sat at the gate to administer the judicial and social affairs of the people.

It is also important to notice that Jesus said gates, the plural form of the word. This means there is more than one gate of hades operating on the earth today. I believe there are seven gates through which the kingdom of darkness operates that correlate with the seven components of the world system. Keep in mind, as I mentioned earlier, the kingdom of darkness has twelve components as the kingdom of God. These components operate through a system called "the world," which has seven gates. I will explain this more.

Jesus knows all about the kingdom of darkness and how it operates. He said in Matthew 12:26, "If Satan casts out Satan, he is divided against himself. How then will his kingdom stand?"

When He said the gates of hades would not stand against the church, He was talking about the kingdom of darkness and the power it represents. Any assault the kingdom of darkness brings against His church will not prevail. The church has power and authority to cancel or make void any plans or decisions the kingdom of darkness makes against the church or the nations in which the church exists.

> It is our assignment to possess the gates of our enemies and to cancel their agendas before they manifest in the earthly realm.

God promised Abraham that his descendants would possess the gates of their enemies (Genesis 22:17). Why didn't God say they would possess the land, houses, or businesses of their enemies? It is because in those days the one who controlled the gate controlled the whole city or nation. We are the seed of Abraham by faith in Jesus Christ (Galatians 3:29). It is our assignment to possess the gates of our enemies and to cancel their agendas before they manifest in the earthly realm.

Power in the Body

Every day, thousands of people are being brutally murdered all over the world. These souls who do not believe in Jesus will go to hell. Some of those being murdered are Christians. Why does Jesus want to build His church? Only through the church can He destroy the works of darkness here. The church is also called the body of Christ. Christ is the Head of His church. The Head has given a very clear command to the body about what we are supposed to be doing. Unfortunately, in many cases the body is telling the Head what to do.

If my head gave the order for my feet to move and begin walking, my feet would have to obey my head. Otherwise, I will not get anywhere. But the church body does not want to do anything, so it remains ineffective. Every Sunday we come and ask the Head to walk, to heal, to touch, to comfort, to give, and much more. My head cannot do any of those things. It can only give the order. *My* feet have to walk. *I* need to pray and heal the sickness. *My* hands have to touch and give. *My* words have to comfort.

The physical strength of a person is in his body, not in his head. The church, the body of Christ, carries the power and authority of Christ. Whatever power or authority Christ has now, His body carries the same power and authority because God has put everything under the feet of Jesus Christ.

Most governments are instruments of the kingdom of darkness that execute the will of Satan. The church needs to cancel those plans by executing God's will on this earth. I talk more about this in the Kingdom Legislation chapter.

Why does it look like evil is prevailing on this earth? It is because the church is not doing what it is supposed to be doing. If you visit most churches today, especially those places where evil seems to prevail, the church is afraid or they do not know what to do. So they do all sorts of funny things when they come together except what they are supposed to be doing. They have no understanding of the authority and power that has been made available to them through Jesus Christ.

All Authority

For the church to understand who we are and what has been made available to us, the eyes of our understanding need to be opened. The god of this world has blinded our spiritual eyes so we only see what we can see with our natural eyes. For the eyes of our understanding to be opened, God has to give us the spirit of wisdom and revelation. For God to give us the spirit of wisdom and revelation we need

> For the church to understand who we are and what has been made available to us, the eyes of our understanding need to be opened.

to pray and ask Him. That is how the apostle Paul prayed for the church in Ephesus in a powerful prayer. To me this is the most powerful prayer next to the Lord's Prayer in the whole Bible.

> "Therefore I also, after I heard of your faith in the Lord Jesus and your love for all the saints, do not cease to give thanks for you, making mention of you in my prayers: that the God of our Lord Jesus Christ, the Father of glory, may give to you the spirit of wisdom and revelation in the knowledge of Him, the eyes of your understanding being enlightened; that you may know what is the hope of His calling, what are the riches of the glory of His inheritance in the saints, *and what is the exceeding greatness of His power toward us who believe, according to the working of His mighty power* which He worked in Christ when He raised Him from the dead and seated *Him* at His right hand in the heavenly *places,* far above all principality and power and might and dominion, and every name that is named, not only in this age but also in that which is to come. And He put all *things* under His feet, and gave Him *to be* head over all *things* to the church, which is His body, the fullness of Him who fills all in all" (Ephesians 1:15-23).

Listen to how the New Living Translation puts this passage:

> "I also pray that you will understand the incredible greatness of God's power for us who believe him. This is the same mighty power that raised Christ from the dead and seated him in the place of honor at God's right hand in the heavenly

realms. Now he is far above any ruler or authority or power or leader or anything else—not only in this world but also in the world to come. God has put all things under the authority of Christ and has made him head over all things for the benefit of the church. And the church is his body; it is made full and complete by Christ, who fills all things everywhere with himself" (Ephesians 1:19-23, NLT).

When Jesus rose from the dead He made a statement that the demonic world does not want the church to grasp. He said, "All authority has been given to me in heaven and on earth. Go therefore" (Matthew 28:18b-19a).

I believe you understand the meaning of the word *all*. If Jesus Christ has received all authority in heaven and earth, how much authority is left for the devil? None. The difference between power and authority is that power is the physical strength or might to do something; authority is the right to exercise that power.

As a church, we have received both power and authority. Why then do we not see the manifestation of much of it in and through the church today? It is because there are only a few who believe it. Some believe this power is only good for healing sicknesses and casting out demons. No, it is not. This power will work anywhere and over anything. If we can get two people in agreement over anything according to God's will, this power will work for them.

Why Don't We Exercise Our Authority?

In the Gospels, Jesus gave this power to the disciples to exercise over sicknesses and demons. That is the base level. When I went to buy a car, there were different models available for the same product. There is a base level, then there is a luxury model, then there is the limited edition, and so on. People buy different models based on their financial capacity, but that does not mean other levels do not exist.

It is the same in the church. There are many who exercise this power over sickness and demons, but they never venture out into the higher levels. There are a lot of people who do not even believe they have authority over a simple flu or even a fly.

> There are a lot of people who do not even believe they have authority over a simple flu or even a fly.

There is a reason why Jesus gave only the power and authority over sickness and demons to the disciples before His death. It is because only after He died and resurrected did He receive *all* authority once again over the heaven and earth, over every kingdom and rule, dominions and principalities, and every name that is named in heaven and earth. The name of Jesus is exalted higher than any other name.

Again, we must take note of the term "heaven and the earth." The Bible began with the statement, "In the beginning God created the heavens and the earth." Heaven represents the spirit or the unseen world and the earth represents the natural or the physical world.

Once Jesus was resurrected, His children, the church have not only power over sicknesses and diseases, but over everything that is in the physical realm and the spirit world. The church has to believe it and exercise this power by faith. This revelation does not manifest itself by feelings; it manifests by faith. If you wait until you feel the authority, then it might never happen. But the more you begin to speak it, the more you will see the manifestation of it.

> **The reason many churches are closing and memberships are dwindling is because they do not understand what is going on in the spirit world.**

Many times I have gone to church and get to my car and wonder, "What did I do? Did I learn anything? Did I exercise my spiritual gifts or authority today?" I often go home thinking I never want to go back to church again.

You might be one of those people who are tired of the church. You might be fed up with the things that are going on in the so-called church today. Many mature believers do not have an outlet to exercise their gifts or the spiritual authority God gave them. Many of today's leaders lack the revelation to train and equip the saints for the work of the ministry.

The reason many churches are closing and memberships are dwindling is because they do not understand what is going on in the spirit world. I see people who were once on fire for God no longer active in church or serving God. Many leave altogether. They are like neutralized horses or lions. They are discouraged and disappointed.

The Word Is Our Example

The Bible is written and given to us for a reason. It is not just to read and preach about its stories, but for us to understand what is available to us, what we are able to do through faith in our God.

When we study the Old Testament, we see God's people using their authority over kings and kingdoms. No one was able to stop them, even in the times when they were outnumbered by their enemies.

A few years ago I visited a country in Europe. The Muslims in that particular nation were trying to legislate their rule into the government and there was a vote in the parliament for it the following Monday. I was preaching on that Sunday and I asked the church to pray. We prayed and cancelled the vote and declared the Muslim rule would not take effect in that country. The next day the vote was taken and the legislation did not go through because it did not receive enough votes.

If we only knew the things the church could have stopped or changed if we had prayed when we got together. I have not yet seen a church that fully understands and exercises its authority on a regular basis. Jesus' heart is to see the will of God done on this earth as it is in heaven. How is that going to take place if the church has no understanding about heaven and how heaven has authority over the earth?

The power that is available to us has no limit because God has not given any limit to His church. The verse in Ephesians says, "the exceeding greatness of His power toward us who believe." Another translation says, "the immeasurable greatness of his power in us who believe." Why would God give such power to His church if all He planned for us to do is sing, attend Bible studies, die, and go to heaven?

I don't believe the church has tapped into even a small portion of that power yet. God is waiting for His church to arise in all the nations of the world, storm the gates of hell, and declare the victory of our King, Lord, and Savior, Jesus Christ. The church should be in the forefront of all that, attesting to the fact that Jesus is victorious over the world system and the demonic forces that have taken their positions against Him.

"In whom are hidden all the treasures of wisdom and knowledge." It means all the treasures of wisdom and knowledge that are out there are hidden like treasure in Christ Jesus. That same Christ lives in each believer. We need to learn to tap into that wisdom and knowledge and solve the problems people and nations are facing today (Colossians 2:3). Let the sons of God manifest all over the world in Jesus' name!"

The "Where" of the Church

Now let us look at the "where" of the church. Jesus said, "And I will give you the keys of the kingdom of heaven, and whatever you bind on earth will be bound in heaven, and whatever you loose on earth will be loosed in heaven."

Jesus did not just say He is going to build His church and everything is going to be wonderful. No, He has given us the tools to accomplish a task. He gave us the keys of the kingdom of heaven and whatever we bind on this earth will be bound in heaven. Whatever we do on this earth, heaven will respond to it.

All the things mentioned above take place on the earth where the church exists, not in heaven. Many believers are more concerned about what is going on in heaven than on the earth. They are more concerned about what is going to happen after they die than fulfilling their mission here. They seem uninterested in why God put them on the earth in the first place.

> Many believers are more concerned about what is going to happen after they die than fulfilling their mission here.

This happens because people do not understand their purpose. Before the year 2000, if you turned on Christian television the main topic of discussion was the end times and the Antichrist. Praise God, we don't hear much of that stuff anymore. My calling and anointing is to equip you, the church, to accomplish all that God has planned for us. That's my main focus.

The "How"

The next part is the "how" of the church. How is the church going to accomplish this task? Whatever the church binds on this earth will be bound in heaven and whatever the church looses will be loosed in heaven.

As a church there are things we need to bind or stop here on earth and there are things we need to loose or permit. Unless the church does its part, heaven is not going to do anything. Stop praying prayers that do no good and start praying to bind and loose things using the authority Christ has given us. We have been binding demons for a long time, and there is no lack of demons out there. Jesus gave us the keys of His kingdom to bind and to loose. We are supposed to use the keys to lock the gates of hell and prevent them from operating in our cities and region.

> Unless the church does its part, heaven is not going to do anything.

Chapter 7: The Function of the Church

Chapter 7: The Function of the Church

"Now you are the body of Christ, and members individually"
(1 Corinthians 12:27).

The Church—Not a Building

This is not a book on the doctrine of the church, but I feel it is imperative to briefly mention the system by which the church functions. The New Testament church has nothing to do with a building other than the fact that having a building makes it convenient for the *church* to assemble as a body.

The church is a mystery hidden in the heart of God for eternity, which He decided to reveal at this age. The mystery God had in mind was not to build a beautiful cathedral with steeples reaching to the sky. Those are man-made reflections of God's eternal plan to show their pride and pomp; they are also one of the devil's distractions to deviate the church from its real mission. In Paul's letters to the church, we do not see him talking about a building fund or how to manage a church's material assets. The greatest asset a church has is not its physical substance, but the souls that come to worship the Lord.

> **The New Testament church has nothing to do with a building other than the fact that having a building makes it convenient for the *church* to assemble as a body.**

As mentioned before, *church* comes from the Greek word *ekklesia*, which means "called-out ones." When God saw us in eternity He chose us in Christ to be part of His plan. He called us out before we knew Him. The church is not an individual; it is made up of many individuals. It takes at least two people to make a church.

A Look at the Church through the Ages

In the Old Testament, God chose the nation of Israel to accomplish His plan. Whatever He did on the earth was based on the covenant He made with Abraham, Isaac, and Jacob. Then He anointed different individuals to be in leadership and to be His spokesmen for the rest of the people in the world.

Next, God decided to extend His grace and the covenantal promises and blessings to the rest of the world, the Gentiles. He did not reject the people of Israel; He kept them aside for a season because they had rejected Him. In turn, they fell and He gave them up for disobedience until the time and number of the Gentiles are completed. In truth, God caused all these to happen.

Today, a believer in Christ can enjoy the same blessings and promises God made to Abraham and become his seed through faith in Jesus Christ. The Bible says in Romans 9:25-26, "As He says also in Hosea: 'I will call them My people, who were not My people, and her beloved, who was not beloved. And it shall come to pass in the place where it was said to them, "You are not My people," there they shall be called sons of the living God.'"

> "For I do not desire, brethren, that you should be ignorant of this mystery, lest you should be wise in your own opinion, that blindness in part has happened to Israel until the fullness of the Gentiles has come in" (Romans 11:25).

> "Concerning the gospel they are enemies for your sake, but concerning the election they are beloved for the sake of the fathers. For the gifts and the calling of God are irrevocable. For as you were once disobedient to God, yet have now obtained mercy through their disobedience, even so these also have now been disobedient, that through the mercy shown you they also may obtain mercy. *For God has committed them all to disobedience, that He might have mercy on all.* Oh, the depth of the riches both of the wisdom and knowledge of God! How unsearchable are His judgments and His ways past finding out!" (Romans 11:28-33).

God did not replace the people of Israel with the church, but extended His love to the rest of the world through them. He created *one new man* by joining both the Jew and the Gentile (Ephesians 2:14-19). Whatever God does on the earth He intends to do through His church. The destiny of a nation depends on its church, not its political government.

The Church Determines the Future of a Nation

A church that is in a nation that blames its political government for where the nation is going or what is happening in that nation does so because the believers in that nation do not understand the power and authority God gave them. Where the church goes, a nation goes. The future of any nation depends on the body of Christ in that particular nation.

In the previous chapter we learned that Jesus received all authority in heaven and on earth. What did Jesus do with all the authority and power He received? Did He take that to heaven? The Bible says, "According to the working of His mighty power which He worked in Christ when He raised Him from the dead and seated Him at His right hand in the heavenly places, far above all principality and power and might and dominion, and every name that is named, not only in this age but also in that which is to come. And He put all things under His feet, and gave Him to be head over all things to the church, which is His body, the fullness of Him who fills all in all" (Ephesians 1:19-23).

> When we ask a government to fix our problems that are the result of spiritual causes, we are asking the physical world to rule the spiritual world. That is against spiritual law.

According to that Scripture Jesus received all power and authority. That means there is nothing left for anyone else, and He gave all the authority and power He received to the church, which is His body. God put all things under Jesus' feet, things on this earth and things in heaven. All principalities, powers, and dominions remain subject to Him. If they are under Jesus' feet, they are under our feet because we are Jesus' body, the church.

He did not give all the power and authority to a government or to a king. Governments and rulers have temporary and limited authority over certain geographical areas. The Bible says all authority is given from God. Their authority is limited to the natural world and they do not have any authority over the spirit world.

The spiritual world rules over the physical world, not the other way around. When we ask a government to fix our problems that are the result of spiritual causes, we are asking the physical world to rule the spiritual world. That is against spiritual law. The physical world functions in subjection to the spiritual world. The kingdom of God rules over the kingdoms of men. God appoints kings and presidents and removes them when He wants (Daniel 4:17).

God did not give His authority and power to an individual, but to a body—the church. Christ is the head of the church and whatever the Head plans to do, He does it through the body. The church is not effective today because different individuals are trying to do different things on their own. They act like they have all the power and authority, but they are not subject to the Head.

A body of believers needs to receive this revelation and come into agreement about the mission of the church. Then we will see all God intended for the church. The world has yet to see all God has intended *for* the church and *through* the church. Christ is not manifesting in His fullness through the church because the body is fragmented into hundreds of pieces with each piece trying to do what the entire body is supposed to do together. It is like one part of our body trying to do the function of the whole body. How would that work? If my hand tries to do the function of my whole body, the result will be total dysfunction.

> Christ is not manifesting in His fullness through the church because the body is fragmented into hundreds of pieces with each piece trying to do what the entire body is supposed to do together.

What Is the Church?

Finally, the question is, "What is the church?" Though I explained the definition of the word ekklesia in an earlier chapter, I can never fully explain the function, power, and the essence of the church using words. Since the church is made up of people it is important to know how to function together with all of our differences of opinions, and problems. The Bible uses object lessons that are familiar to us to explain the function, power, and the essence of the church. God always uses images, types, parables, and symbols of the natural world that we are familiar with to explain a spiritual truth. We are going to explore a few of them.

God used Paul to reveal the mystery of the church in his letters. Throughout the Bible and through multiple writers, different object lessons are used to explain its function.

- Paul uses the human body to explain the function of the church (1 Corinthians 12:27).

- Paul compares the church to an army to explain its power (2 Timothy 2:4).

- Jesus compared us to salt and light to explain the duty and responsibility of the church (Matthew 5:13-16).

- The church is compared to a race to explain the necessary discipline and commitment (Hebrews 12:1).

- Paul compares the relationship between the church and Jesus to a marriage (Ephesians 5:22-32).

- James uses farming to explain the rewards and productivity the church should expect (James 5:7).

- Paul compares the existence of the church to a kingdom (Colossians 1:13).

- Peter and Paul compare the relationship and position between believers in the church to the construction of a building, calling each member a living stone (1 Corinthians 3:9; 2 Timothy 2:20-21; 1 Peter 2:5).

- The daily life of a believer is compared to a battlefield (2 Corinthians 10:3-5; Ephesians 6:12).

- The character of the church is pictured as that of sheep among wolves (Matthew 10:16).

The Church Is a Body

The simplest way to understand the church is to understand the function of a human body. A body is made up of many parts, or members, instead of a single unit. Paul uses our body as an example to explain the function of the church.

Whoever believes in Jesus as the Son of God is a member of His church, the body of Christ. Paul compares the church with a human body. As our body has different members, the body of Christ is made up of many members. Each member (part) of our body has a specific function. Each part needs to work in harmony with the other parts to accomplish any task. It works the same way in the body of Christ.

> "For as we have many members in one body, but all the members do not have the same function, so we, being many, are one body in Christ, and individually members of one another" (Romans 12:4-5).

Each part of our body is fixed into a particular place in our body with a specific purpose and function. What the eye can do the ear cannot do, and what the ear can do the eye cannot do. But they need each other. They both need the brain to process their function. In the same way, the body of Christ (the church) has to work in harmony to accomplish God's will on the earth. To do that each member has to know his place and his function.

> **Unless each believer understands his or her place and function that church will not grow to accomplish God's purpose.**

Unless each believer understands his or her place and function that church will not grow to accomplish God's purpose.

Each member has to supply his or her gift for the benefit of the rest of the body for the proper growth and function of the whole. One member cannot dominate another; the eye cannot dominate the ear. They both have a unique role and both are necessary. There is no need for competition because each one has a unique task to accomplish and no one can do another's job, no matter how hard they try.

Unfortunately, because of ignorance and a lack of understanding about one's gift and its function, some members fight for another's position. But the eye cannot take the ear's position, or the leg cannot take the mouth's position; in the church one person cannot function in the place of another.

There is too much jealousy, envy, and competition going on in the body of Christ. This happens because people do not understand which part of the body they are and what their exact function is. Either they are afraid someone else will take their place or they are trying to copy others. Once they understand their position and their function, then schisms will disappear. To remedy this problem, we need proper teaching to equip the saints so they know where they belong and what they should be doing.

Not walking in God's Spirit is another reason for division among believers. We try to do God's will in our flesh and to fulfill fleshly ambitions; this creates division. In our body each member has to function in submission to the other parts; one cannot work independently of the other.

> "For as the body is one and has many members, but all the members of that one body, being many, are one body, so also is Christ. For by one Spirit we were all baptized into one body— whether Jews or Greeks, whether slaves or free—and have all been made to drink into one Spirit. For in fact the body is not one member but many" (1 Corinthians 12:12-14).

None of our body parts are unnecessary. God put them together with great wisdom and precision and they all need each other. Though sometimes some parts may give us pain, or we wish that they looked different, we need all of them to live well.

Finally, all the parts are connected (by nerves) to the brain, which controls all the bodily functions. Christ is the Head of the church. Churches require spiritual leadership appointed by God, which I will mention briefly later. Without the brain no part of our body can function. It does not matter how strong our arms are or how clear our eye can see, they need to be connected to the brain. Another part of our body, which is essential for the function of the entire body, is the heart. The heart supplies blood into each part of the body including the brain, and they are all connected to each other by nerves and veins that are not visible.

> **Though sometimes some parts may give us pain, or we wish that they looked different, we need all of them to live well.**

There is no fight between these parts of our body to do one another's task. The heart is not trying to do the job of the brain and the brain is not trying to be a heart. They work with complete unity. There needs to be total unity between the members of the body of Christ as well.

To accomplish that purpose, God gave ministry gifts to the church. They are called the five-fold ministry gifts and are mentioned in Ephesians 4:11-14: apostles, prophets, evangelists, pastors, and teachers. Their job is to equip the believers to do the work of the ministry until we all come to unity of faith and maturity in Christ. The Bible says each believer is given gifts from God so the church can function properly. Through these gifts, we serve one another.

> "But the manifestation of the Spirit is given to *each one* for the profit of all" (1 Corinthians 12:7).

> "But to *each one of us* grace was given according to the measure of Christ's gift" (Ephesians 4:7).

> "As *each one has received a gift,* minister it to one another, as good stewards of the manifold grace of God" (1 Peter 4:10).

> "For I say, through the *grace given to me,* to everyone who is among you, not to think of himself more highly than he ought to think, but to think soberly, as *God has dealt to each one a measure of faith.* For as we have many members in one body, but all the members do not have the same function, so we, being many, are one body in Christ, and individually members of one another. *Having then gifts differing according to the grace that is given to us, let us use them"* (Romans 12:3-6).

Each member of the body of Christ has received a gift, an ability, a measure of grace, a measure of faith from God. When each member discovers their particular gift and begins to use it with maturity and under the guidance of the Holy Spirit, the church will grow properly.

In Romans 12, Paul says each of us should not think more highly than we ought to think. What does that mean? It means each one should find out what their exact gift is, not what they wish it to be, or assume in their heart it should be, could be, or ought to be. I have seen believers who *think* they are an apostle, but there are no signs of this calling in their lives. I have also seen believers who *think* they can do a better job than their pastor but they are not called to be a pastor.

We need to think soberly. God has given each one of us a measure of faith. We should use that faith, gift, or grace in submission to other members in the body in the same way our human body functions. Only then will there be proper edification in the body and each member will be built up into a spiritual house and a dwelling place for God.

One of the problems we have is that no one wants to submit to another and each of us is trying to operate in our gifts independently and wants everyone else to submit to us. Many think that one person's gift is better than other gifts. Which part of our body is insignificant? This happens because of the lack of apostolic teaching in the church. Paul said those parts that are less honorable were blessed by God with greater gifts or honor. This point is critical to our understanding of church life.

> "For in fact the body is not one member but many. If the foot should say, 'Because I am not a hand, I am not of the body,' is it therefore not of the body? And if the ear should say, 'Because I am not an eye, I am not of the body,' is it therefore not of the body? If the whole body were an eye, where would be the hearing? If the whole were hearing, where would be the smelling? But now God has set the members, each one of them, in the body just as He pleased. And if they were all one member, where would the body be?

> "But now indeed there are many members, yet one body. And the eye cannot say to the hand, 'I have no need of you'; nor again the head to the feet, 'I have no need of you.' No, much rather, those members of the body which seem to be weaker are necessary. And those members of the body which we think to be less honorable, on these we bestow greater honor; and our un-presentable parts have greater modesty, but our presentable parts have no need. But God composed the body, having given greater honor to that part which lacks it, that there should be no schism in the body, but that the members should have the same care for one another. And if one member suffers, all the members suffer with it; or if one member is honored, all the members rejoice with it. Now you are the body of Christ, and members individually" (1 Corinthians 12:14-27).

THE POWER AND AUTHORITY OF THE CHURCH

This is followed by: "And God has appointed these in the church: *first apostles, second prophets, third teachers,* after that miracles, then gifts of healings, helps, administrations, varieties of tongues" (1 Corinthians 12:28).

God has prioritized the gifts so the church can function properly. That does not mean these gifts have the right to dictate to others what they should do or how they should live. The apostle's job is to connect the believer with their Shepherd and the believer should hear from their Shepherd Jesus regarding their personal function and direction. It is not a hierarchy of positions, but a responsibility of function. Apostles cannot function without the rest of the body, and the rest of the body cannot function without the apostle.

Our brain, heart, liver, and kidney are critical for our health. Without one of them a person cannot stay alive. A person can function without ears, eyes, or even legs or arms. In such a case, one part of the body has to try to fill in for the missing parts. It is the same in the church. The apostles and prophets are the necessary foundation.

Our feet are on the bottom part of our body, but that does not mean other parts are superior to them. Without the feet, we could not walk. Our hands are made for multitasking and they help almost all the other parts of the body. Hands represent the ministry of helps and giving. Our hands write, play instruments, wash the other parts, do various tasks, bless others; it's almost impossible to list everything our hands can do. That means the ministry of helps and giving is very important. It may be that more people are called to do that than any other function. We need a revelation of the balance of the body. We only need a few prophets and teachers, but many, many more in the ministry of helps and giving if the body is to handle all its needs and outreach. The one gift is not better than the other, just different.

At times, our pride and egocentric thinking make us feel like we are more important than others in the church, but we need to deliberately disarm those feelings and gain the mind of Christ (1 Corinthians 2:16) about how we serve the rest of the body. Just as each part is important for the function of the body so each person is important for the proper functioning of the church. God is bringing His divine order back into His church. We have been functioning without it for a long time and are not as effective as we should be as a result. To many, the purpose of the church has been reduced to singing, preaching, offerings, buildings, and material things. But He has so much more for us.

Unless we are called into full-time ministry, God's will for us in church is different than His will for us in other spheres of our lives. You may be working at a local supermarket or running a business, or you may be a leader in the community, but when you come to church you have a different function than when you are working outside.

Each believer has a vocational call and a spiritual call. In other words, natural and spiritual gifts. Your vocational call is to support yourself and your family financially and your spiritual call is to serve the body of Christ. Paul was a tentmaker by vocation, but an apostle by his spiritual call. The Bible clearly mentions some of the ministries believers must do in church, each one according to their call. Grace is given to them to fulfill their call. They exercise the manifold wisdom of God as faithful stewards within their measure of faith.

There is a misconception in some circles of believers that when a person discovers their gift then that person needs to be in full-time ministry. That is a grave mistake and one of the main reasons churches are not thriving in many cultures. Instead of yielding to one another and working in harmony, we separate ourselves from the fold we are in to start yet another local church or ministry. Even if we're called to be pastors, that does not mean we have to have our own church. Healthy churches have many people who are operating as pastors.

> There is a misconception in some circles of believers that when a person discovers their gift then that person needs to be in full-time ministry.

As far as I can see, most local churches are unhealthy in their function because of a lack of mature believers. The Bible describes no parachurch ministries or mission organizations like we have today. In the early church, every ministry flowed out of a local church, often a home. It is time for churches to unite together in cities and towns. Instead of building our own little kingdoms, let us join our hearts and hands to build His kingdom.

It is also very unfortunate that people had to leave a local church to express their gifts and calling. Many talented people left the church to express their gifts and fell prey to the enemy. Local churches need to make room for believers to express their gifts. We should not limit people or their gift but help them maximize it. Though our God has no limit, there is an unseen limitation that is upon the body of Christ. I believe it came because of religion and the tradition of men. It is time break them.

Jesus directly calls and appoints those appointed to the five-fold ministry. And those who operate in the five-fold ministry gifts are not better than the rest of the body. Each part of the body is valuable and unique. But we have been trained that it is only worthwhile to be a pastor or a prophet. On top of that, we assume that if someone prophesies (delivers a message from God), he or she is a prophet. And if you win souls, you are an evangelist. That is not so. We need to listen carefully to the call of God and happily serve Him in whatever capacity He has called us. Just because you have a heart for people and are good with them does not mean you are a full-time pastor. But it may mean you are to help the full-time pastor with discipling others.

> Just because you have a heart for people and are good with them does not mean you are a full-time pastor. But it may mean you are to help the full-time pastor with discipling others.

In Mark 16, Jesus said certain signs would follow those who believe. What did He say? Who do those signs follow? Not only the apostles or prophets or evangelists, but anyone who believes in Jesus! Every believer has the authority to pray for the sick, cast out demons, and to speak in tongues. That does not mean all those who operate in the gifts of the Holy Spirit should be in full-time ministry though. If that were so, every believer should be in full-time ministry because every believer has a gift.

The more a believer faithfully uses his gift, the more he matures in it. As a result, God increases his or her influence in a local body of believers. That believer may eventually spend more and more time ministering than doing his vocational job, but he is still not expected to give up his job and go into the ministry full-time.

There are two different types of gifts and calling. One is for full-time ministry and the other is to serve in a local church. When you serve in a local church, you will be used in various capacities. You may pray for the sick and they will get healed. God may give you messages to tell others, or you may bring unbelievers to the church. You may teach children or youth. You may take meals to the sick or serve on a leadership team to help with administration. All of these are vital to the working of the body.

Another misconception some ministers have is that once they are in ministry, they should not be doing any other form of work, like running a business or any other paid venture. That is not true according to the Bible. Paul supported himself. He made tents and either sold or rented them (Acts 18:2-3). Many of the Old Testament saints we adore were also businessmen and women. God's covenant name is the God of Abraham, Isaac, and Jacob (Exodus 3:6). These three patriarchs of our faith were shrewd businessmen. They lived well and became wealthy by trade, animal stock, and agriculture. But making money (or more money) was never their main objective in life!

> Another misconception some ministers have is that once they are in ministry, they should not be doing any other form of work, like running a business or any other paid venture.

The Church Is the Embassy of the Kingdom of God

An embassy is a representation of a country in a foreign country. For international relationships and bilateral ties, each nation sends their representatives—called ambassadors—to different nations. The office in which they function is called an embassy. America has an embassy in India and the American government has sent an ambassador to represent America in India. Whatever America does in India, it does it through its embassy. When the president of America wants to communicate a message to the Indian government, he does it through the American ambassador there.

God has a kingdom called the kingdom of heaven. His kingdom rules the whole universe. The earth belongs to the Lord and its fullness. God wants to see His will accomplished on the earth as it is in heaven. The church is the embassy—or the extension—of the kingdom of heaven here, and whatever God wants to do, He will do through His church. At least that is His intention. If He cannot use the church, then He will find someone else outside the church that He can use. The mission of the church is to function as His embassy. The church is the only visible form of the invisible kingdom of God.

The church has become everything but what God intended it to be. We have made the churches into entertainment, worship, and Christian outreach centers. We forget that whatever the King wants to do in a region He wants to do through His church there.

> "Now then, *we are ambassadors for Christ*, as though God were pleading through us: we implore you on Christ's behalf, be reconciled to God" (2 Corinthians 5:20).

As an ambassador of the kingdom of heaven, Paul is speaking on behalf of Christ to other people and telling them to be reconciled with God. Whatever God wants to speak to a region, He says through His ambassadors; when they speak, it is the same as if God had spoken. Each believer in Christ is an ambassador of Christ. You cannot be an ambassador in your own country. An ambassador has to be a citizen of a foreign country. The Bible says we are citizens of heaven (Hebrews 11:16).

I was born and brought up in India, which was ruled by Britain for over a hundred years. Queen Elizabeth I of England sent a small group of people to establish a business relationship with India. They reached a little coastal village in the west and received permission from the king of that region to set up a small business center. Gradually, they began to spread and took over the whole country in a short time. They either entered into agreements with the kings that were ruling different regions of India or fought with them and killed them. India eventually became a colony of Britain. The kings and queens of England never came to India, but sent their representatives, governors, businessmen, and soldiers to accomplish their will in India.

God sent the Holy Spirit as the Governor of His kingdom and the church because God wants to accomplish His will on earth through the church—His embassy—here.

The Church Is a Training Center

Jesus did not teach the disciples how to conduct a worship service or train them as a choir, but He was constantly teaching and training them about the principles that govern the kingdom of God. He selected twelve disciples out of the crowd and spent most of His time with them. Out of the twelve He had three disciples that were close to Him, and John was the closest. He spent very little time with the crowd.

148

THE FUNCTION OF THE CHURCH

It is the will of God for us to live in His kingdom. The world is a counterfeit of the kingdom of God. The church is the visible form of God's invisible kingdom, and the world system is the visible form of the invisible kingdom of darkness. One of the main duties of the church and the ministry gifts is to train believers; this process is called discipleship.

Believers must be trained to discover their natural and spiritual gifts. After that, they must be instructed in how to use their gifts with integrity and wisdom so they develop into the most productive people in society. Manuals should be produced for children, youth, and adults that train them in every aspect of life. When the people of the world look at the people of the church, they should wonder why we are so prosperous and happy and content.

> When the people of the world look at the people of the church, they should wonder why we are so prosperous and happy and content.

We need to train believers to be business owners and the best employees they can be. Companies should be fighting to hire Christians because they know they are the most honest and fruitful employees they could ever have. Today, the situation is just the opposite. Believers are some of the laziest, most ignorant people on earth. They lie and cheat just like the people in the world. Instead of being productive, they are busybodies who don't think twice about slandering their neighbor. They give no thought to the effect of their words on our society. This needs to change.

Old Testament believers made a great impact on governments, with some holding highly influential positions. Many of them were promoted because of the wisdom and knowledge God had given them. The church today (especially the evangelical churches) has mastered the trade of preaching or proclaiming the gospel with words, but many are not demonstrating it through their actions. The Roman Catholic Church has picked up where we left off and started educational institutions and hospitals in every culture under heaven. They do not preach as much as the evangelicals but demonstrate the kingdom by their works. Meanwhile, the universities that were begun by the church in America and Europe have been taken over by non-believers.

You Have Natural and Spiritual Gifts

Each believer has both natural and spiritual gifts. Every human being has at least one natural gift they received at birth. God put these in each individual for them to develop and use to make a living. We are not supposed to suppress or bury our natural gift but use it for the benefit of the kingdom. Because of ignorance, many have been taught to suppress their natural gifts, forgetting that it was God who gave them. Then they go around begging for money and say they are suffering for Christ. God might have put abilities in you to write, draw, sing, act, or manage great businesses. It is not sinful to use your gifts to make money; it actually glorifies the Lord when you do. He is grieved when our gifts are buried and wasted.

> **It is not sinful to use your gifts to make money; it actually glorifies the Lord when you do.**

The apostle Paul had a business. He was an apostle called by God but he did not deny his natural ability. He used that to support himself and his ministry, and he asked his followers to do the same. He was a tentmaker by trade (Acts 18:1-3). As believers we need to be sure of our call and our vocation.

The church should teach people to discover their natural gift(s) and encourage them to develop them through further training. Then they should be sent out into the world. Your trade or skill is the tool through which you influence the world by using kingdom principles. It is also the method God has ordained for you to meet the material needs of your family. That is your natural gift. Your calling is the tool by which you meet the spiritual needs of the people. That is your spiritual gift.

The Bible refers to our natural gift, trade, or occupation as good works. "For we are His workmanship, created in Christ Jesus for *good works*, which God prepared beforehand that we should walk in them" (Ephesians 2:10). The phrase "good works" appears twenty-eight times in the New Testament. The Greek word for "work" is *ergon*, which means "to work, business, employment, that with which anyone is occupied. Any product whatever, anything accomplished by hand, art, industry, or mind."[11]

---

11. Thayer, and Smith. *New Testament Greek Lexicon.* #2401.

We have limited good works to things like helping orphans, feeding the poor, or visiting nursing homes and prisons. That's not the only meaning of good works. *Anything* you do that is productive and fruitful on this earth is a good work. Any work that God gave you to do is a good work. That means that a mother caring for her children is doing a good work and pleasing to God. Similarly, the person who works and develops his talents in any field is pleasing God. Jesus and Paul tell believers again and again to engage themselves in good works.

You Have a Ministry

Every believer has a calling or ministry. They also have one or more natural gifts that God has given them. Though only a few are called into five-fold ministry, each believer is a king and a priest. As a king, you demonstrate and exercise your dominion over the natural realm. As a priest, you demonstrate and exercise your dominion over the spiritual realm. As a king, you use your trade to bring the spoils, the wealth of the world, into the kingdom. As a priest, you use your spiritual gifts to minister to God, to one another, and to bring souls into the kingdom.

> "But you are a chosen generation, a royal priesthood, a holy nation, His own special people, that you may proclaim the praises of Him who called you out of darkness into His marvelous light" (1 Peter 2:9).

> "And has made us kings and priests to His God and Father, to Him be glory and dominion forever and ever. Amen" (Revelation 1:6).

These Scriptures address every believer in Christ. In 1 Peter 2:9 the Greek word used for praise is *aretas* which means "any excellence of a person (in body or mind) or of a thing, an eminent endowment, property or quality, a virtuous course of thought, feeling and action; virtue, moral goodness or any particular moral excellence, as modesty, purity."[12]

Any time you do something with a spirit of excellence you are *proclaiming* the praises of your God to the people around you, whether at home or the workplace. It is sad that many believe that our proclamation of His praise is done only through singing.

---

12. Thayer, and Smith. *New Testament Greek Lexicon.* #703.

Very few are called to do ministry without using their trade or skill. It was not necessary for Paul to make tents to support his ministry: It was his personal decision to not become a financial burden on the people and churches to whom he was ministering. We see the opposite today where many ministers are accumulating and hoarding personal wealth taken from their flocks. They milk their sheep until they bleed. I believe ministers should live well, but there must be a balance.

Some believers think that if a person is called into full-time ministry, they should not do any other job or business. That is not biblical. If God specifically told you not to do any other job then don't do it; otherwise God commands us to work with our own hands for our livelihood.

> **Many ministers are accumulating and hoarding personal wealth taken from their flocks. They milk their sheep until they bleed.**

Go *Into* the World

If we are to preach the gospel effectively, we need to learn how to penetrate the systems of the world. It takes wisdom, skill, and enormous training to equip someone to go into the world because people in the world are already doing things with excellence. Jesus told His disciples to be wise as serpents and harmless as doves. He also said He was sending them out as sheep among wolves.

When Jesus trained His disciples He not only trained them in what to preach, He taught them how to deal with the people of their day. The modern church has been doing just the opposite. They have been teaching believers to stay away from the world because the Bible says we are not of the world and not to love the world and its lusts. That is true: Once we are saved we do not belong to the world, we are part of the kingdom of God. But the kingdom of God operates on this earth to the extent that we practice and administer it on the earth.

The result is that believers stay inside the four walls of their church because it is safe and they are afraid to go out where the people are. We should not love the world and its lusts but we are commanded to go into the world and make an impact for Jesus. We should understand how things work in the world and not be ignorant of it, but we do not need to marry the world to do that. Instead, we need to take people from the world and train them, then send them back into the world to make an impact for God. We need to go into the world and train people how to live in the kingdom. Our job will not be finished until everything in this world functions according to the principles of His kingdom.

Whenever a believer tries to penetrate one of the systems of this world, he will face enormous opposition from the enemy. Satan will not give up easily. One of the reasons Christians are not able to penetrate the kingdom of darkness is because they try to do it alone. Jesus did not give His power and authority to an individual, but to His church. The church is made up of more than one individual. It takes at least two to be the church. If two of us agree on earth and ask anything in Jesus' name, we will get an answer. It is difficult for two people to come into agreement about anything, but this is our goal.

> Believers stay inside the four walls of their church because it is safe and they are afraid to go out where the people are.

If you are part of a business or ministry, it is imperative that you have another person with you in agreement in what you are doing. It could be a coworker or your spouse. When two people work together in agreement, they become an undefeatable force for the kingdom of God.

Most people are slaves to their culture. When we come into the kingdom, we need to get free from our own culture and submit to the culture of the kingdom. In every nation we need godly people who run the education system; that means the best schools, colleges, and universities should be run by born-again, spirit-filled Christians who are trained with a kingdom mindset.

It should be the same with the economy, government, entertainment, scientific, and religious worlds. We need Christian politicians, educators, economists, entertainers, scientists and theologians with kingdom mindsets. Then the earth will be filled with the knowledge of God as the waters cover the sea. Jesus will come back for such a glorious church. He is waiting for His enemies to be made His footstool.

> "But this Man [Jesus], after He had offered one sacrifice for sins forever, sat down at the right hand of God, *from that time waiting till His enemies are made His footstool*" (Hebrews 10:12-13).

The Church Is an Army

Every nation or kingdom has an army to protect its territory and citizens, and to advance its dominion beyond its borders. The church is the army of God commissioned to advance His kingdom. We have an enemy who claims to be the god of this world. As a church, our purpose is to reclaim the earth and its citizens for God.

We are in the middle of an age-old battle between the kingdoms of darkness and light. Every single human being alive on this earth is part of one of these kingdoms; there is no neutral ground. Just because someone is an atheist does not mean they are not influenced by one of these kingdoms. In fact, according to Scripture they are a slave of the demons of the kingdom of darkness called ignorance and foolishness. The Bible says, "The fool has said in his heart 'there is no God' " (Psalm 14:1).

> **We are in the middle of an age-old battle between the kingdoms of darkness and light. Every single human being alive on this earth is part of one of these kingdoms; there is no neutral ground.**

The battle we are in is not a physical battle. It is psychological and spiritual warfare. We do not fight against other humans. We fight against spiritual forces, strongholds, imaginations, arguments, philosophies, ideologies, demons, and thoughts that control people. Jesus defeated the king of the kingdom of darkness and disarmed its generals (principalities and powers) on the cross. He has left the little demons for us to take care of (Colossians 2:15; Mark 16:17).

The kingdom of darkness is organized and works in particular ranks: Satan runs it and under him work principalities that rule over nations and cities and under those come powers, under those come rulers of darkness and under those come spiritual hosts of wickedness.

> "For we do not wrestle against flesh and blood, but against principalities, against powers, against the rulers of the darkness of this age, against spiritual hosts of wickedness in the heavenly places" (Ephesians 6:12).

Originally, principalities, powers, and dominions, were created by Jesus and for Him (Colossians 1:16). Lucifer and his hosts occupy these places for the time being until God brings all His enemies under Jesus' footstool (Hebrews 10:12-13). When Jesus died on the cross, He defeated Satan and disarmed all principalities and powers. Through His death, He defeated the one who formerly had power over death.

> "Having disarmed principalities and powers, He made a public spectacle of them, triumphing over them in it" (Colossians 2:15).

> "Inasmuch then as the children have partaken of flesh and blood, He Himself likewise shared in the same, that through death He might destroy him who had the power of death, that is, the devil" (Hebrews 2:14).

Satan has two generals working under him: death and hell, or hades. Under these two generals work all principalities and the rest. Jesus defeated death and hell and took their keys from them. Death and hades are demonic beings that will be cast into the lake of fire.

> "Then Death and Hades were cast into the lake of fire. This is the second death" (Revelation 20:14).

> "Then comes the end, when He delivers the kingdom to God the Father, when He puts an end to all rule and all authority and power. For He must reign till He has put all enemies under His feet. The last enemy that will be destroyed is death. For 'He has put all things under His feet.' But when He says 'all things are put under Him,' it is evident that He who put all things under Him is excepted" (1 Corinthians 15:24-27).

> "Who has gone into heaven and is at the right hand of God, angels and authorities and powers having been made subject to Him" (1 Peter 3:22).

There are different kinds of armed forces in the natural. They are the army, navy, air force, marines, and covert intelligence branches. In the spirit, there are different kinds of warfare too. The air force consists of those who fight the enemy through prayer and intercession. The navy are those who speak the Word (water represents the Word) and attack the enemy forces. Army soldiers are apostles and evangelists who go into the enemy's territories to preach the gospel and establish new churches. Prophets and intercessors are the spies, or those who collect intelligence reports of the enemy's moves and plans, and thwart them before they can happen. God has given us armor and weapons to fight against the enemy.

> "Therefore take up the whole armor of God, that you may be able to withstand in the evil day, and having done all, to stand. Stand therefore, having girded your waist with truth, having put on the breastplate of righteousness, and having shod your feet with the preparation of the gospel of peace; above all, taking the shield of faith with which you will be able to quench all the fiery darts of the wicked one. And take the helmet of salvation, and the sword of the Spirit, which is the word of God; praying always with all prayer and supplication in the Spirit, being watchful to this end with all perseverance and supplication for all the saints" (Ephesians 6:13-18).

> "For though we walk in the flesh, we do not war according to the flesh. For the weapons of our warfare are not carnal but mighty in God for pulling down strongholds, casting down arguments and every high thing that exalts itself against the knowledge of God, bringing every thought into captivity to the obedience of Christ, and being ready to punish all disobedience when your obedience is fulfilled" (2 Corinthians 10:3-6).

The devil's major assault against a believer is psychological. Psychological means mental or emotional warfare. Through imaginations, arguments, and thoughts, the enemy attacks our mind to bring fear and doubt. We need to resist the enemy and cast those arguments and imaginations down and bring every thought into captivity to the obedience of Christ.

It is the thoughts that are generated through demonic strongholds that keep people in bondage. A stronghold is a fortress made up of thoughts in our mind that make us think a particular way about a particular subject, circumstance, or person. We behave according to the way we think. If we are to change our actions we need to change the way we think. That is called repentance in the Bible. We need to pull down those strongholds in Jesus' name and cast out the demon that is ruling that particular area of our life through a particular way of thinking.

THE FUNCTION OF THE CHURCH

It is possible for a believer to have a stronghold in their mind. Any area of our life that does not line up with the Word of God is under the influence of demonic strongholds or thoughts. Our enemy works through deception and lies. A person who is deceived will not know he is deceived. That is why it is called deception. If we know we are being deceived, then it is not deception. Others can recognize it and that is why we need the help of other believers to fight against the enemy. This accountability is one of our greatest assets.

> **A person who is deceived will not know he is deceived. That is why it is called deception.**

Even though God gives us victory over areas, circumstances, or relationships, sometimes we are struggling because of a stronghold that was formed in our mind. While we may be battling that issue and thinking in a certain way about those areas, we will not feel the victory until we deal with that stronghold. Instead, we will keep fighting the same battle over and over out of ignorance and deception when the victory was already won. In that case, once we realize the victory is won, we need to renew our mind purposely and intentionally.

An army is organized into different ranks and order for its proper function. God has empowered each believer with a particular gift and a measure of faith for the proper function of the church. The church is not functioning the way it should because people are not abiding in the rank and order where God has placed them. Though we are all part of the same body of Christ, we do not all have the same function and responsibility. God has a specific call and specific gift for each of us according to the grace that is given to us. That's why it is so important that each believer discovers that gift and grace that is given to him or her.

> "Don't you realize that your bodies are actually parts and members of Christ?" (1 Corinthians 6:15 TLB)

> "But as God has distributed to each one, as the Lord has called each one, so let him walk. And so I ordain in all the churches" (1 Corinthians 7:17).

> "Let each one remain in the same calling in which he was called" (1 Corinthians 7:20).

The apostle Paul admonished his young protégé, Timothy, to endure hardship as a good soldier of Jesus Christ.

> "You therefore must endure hardship as a good soldier of Jesus Christ. No one engaged in warfare entangles himself with the affairs of this life, that he may please him who enlisted him as a soldier" (2 Timothy 2:3-4).

Armies have generals, majors, colonels, captains, sergeants, and so on. God put five generals in the church: apostles, prophets, evangelists, pastors, and teachers. In 1 Corinthians 12:27-28, God has put an order for some gifts and functions: "Now you are the body of Christ, and members individually. And God has appointed these in the church: first apostles, second prophets, third teachers, after that miracles, then gifts of healings, helps, administrations, varieties of tongues."

The Church Is a Family

Family is a God-ordained institution. The enemy fights against everything that is God-ordained. There is nothing that has been more attacked by the enemy in the last twenty to thirty years than family life. The enemy knows that family life is the foundation of all society and the church. If he can destroy the family, he can destroy a society and eventually, a nation. Paul used the relationship between husbands and wives to teach us about the relationship between Christ and the church.

> There is nothing that has been more attacked by the enemy in the last twenty to thirty years than family life.

> "Wives, submit to your own husbands, as to the Lord. For the husband is head of the wife, as also Christ is head of the church; and He is the Savior of the body. Therefore, just as the church is subject to Christ, so let the wives be to their own husbands in everything. Husbands, love your wives, just as Christ also loved the church and gave Himself for her, that He might sanctify and cleanse her with the washing of water by the word, that He might present her to Himself a glorious church, not having spot or wrinkle or any such thing, but that she should be holy and without blemish. So husbands ought

158

to love their own wives as their own bodies; he who loves his wife loves himself. For no one ever hated his own flesh, but nourishes and cherishes it, just as the Lord does the church. For we are members of His body, of His flesh and of His bones. 'For this reason a man shall leave his father and mother and be joined to his wife, and the two shall become one flesh.' This is a great mystery, but I speak concerning Christ and the church. Nevertheless let each one of you in particular so love his own wife as himself, and let the wife see that she respects her husband" (Ephesians 5:22-33).

Christ is the Head of the church just as the husband is the head of the family. Christ does not rule through power and subjugation or by force but through love and patience. Through the centuries the church has made enormous errors and backslid often, but Christ has dealt with the church as a faithful husband, continually bringing her back to Himself. Though He corrects her, He will never divorce her, no matter how much the church rebels against Him. He washes her with the Word and pours out His love and blessings to prepare her for His coming. That is the same attitude we should have in our family life.

The Church Is the House of God

It has always been the plan of God to dwell in human beings. Since the fall, God could not dwell in man and He dwelt in temporary tents and temples made by man instead. In the New Testament, a born-again believer became the temple of Holy Spirit. No longer did God live in any building. Now He lives within us instead. Of course, one human being cannot manifest the fullness of God. God is infinite in His wisdom, power, and glory. But when we join together, God can move through us.

God wants to manifest Himself to the world through us. He chose the church as the vehicle to do that. When we come together as a church body with each of us manifesting the grace and gifts given to us by God, and minister to each other and the world, we are manifesting the manifold wisdom of God. We can do this anywhere we meet.

"Now, therefore, you are no longer strangers and foreigners, but fellow citizens with the saints and members of the household of God, having been built on the foundation of

159

the apostles and prophets, Jesus Christ Himself being the chief cornerstone, in whom the whole building, being fitted together, grows into a holy temple in the Lord, in whom you also are being built together for a dwelling place of God in the Spirit" (Ephesians 2:19-22).

"Coming to Him as to a living stone, rejected indeed by men, but chosen by God and precious, you also, as living stones, are being built up a spiritual house, a holy priesthood, to offer up spiritual sacrifices acceptable to God through Jesus Christ" (1 Peter 2:4-5).

In India, most buildings are made of bricks or stones. A building is made up of hundreds or thousands of bricks. The more efficient and useful a building, the more bricks we need to use. Each believer is a living stone by which the Holy Spirit builds a spiritual house for the habitation of God. No one can build a building with only a hundred stones or bricks. The reason the devil has split churches into so many fragments is to reduce the effectiveness of the body. We fight with each other over doctrinal and other issues while he is devouring unsaved souls. The more a church is divided the less effective that church becomes.

> The reason the devil has split churches into so many fragments is to reduce the effectiveness of the body.

In one American city I visited, I was surprised to see a different church at almost every intersection. These churches do not talk to each other or work together. Each one is trying to build their own little kingdom. How can we tell the world we worship the same God and preach the same gospel when we cannot even talk to each other? Why do we need so many different types of churches?

We are living stones, not dead ones. A stone needs to be shaped according to the place it needs to fit. Sometimes the mason needs to chip away the corners and sharp edges before he will lay the brick. A stone cannot build itself into a building; it has to be pliable in the hands of the builder. We need to be pliable so that God can shape us through the spiritual leadership we are called to be under. I will go into more on this in the House of Prayer for All Nations chapter.

Chapter 8: Binding and Loosing

Chapter 8: Binding and Loosing

"And I will give you the keys of the kingdom of heaven, and whatever you bind on earth will be bound in heaven, and whatever you loose on earth will be loosed in heaven" (Matthew 16:19).

What Have You Been Binding?

One of the most misused phrases in the New Testament is "binding and loosing."

In Pentecostal and Charismatic circles this phrase is used mostly to bind or loose demons. Are we supposed to bind evil spirits and the devil himself? When Jesus talked about binding, did He say anything about demons or Satan? Today, the most popular commanding word used against the devil is *bind*. Is there any evidence in the Bible of Jesus or the apostles binding a demon or Satan?

The church has been binding demons for centuries and there is still no shortage of them. Do we have other Scriptures that support a believer in Christ binding the devil? Did Jesus or the apostles ever in their public ministry bind evil spirits or principalities? To my knowledge, they did not.

> The church has been binding demons for centuries and there is still no shortage of them.

If we bind an evil spirit, what happens to it, and by what means do we bind them? If a person comes to us possessed with an evil spirit, he is already *bound* by that spirit. Are we supposed to bind that demon again or loose him from the hold of that spirit? If someone comes to us with a sickness that is caused by demons, do we cast that demon out or bind that demon and sickness in him again?

When a person is bound by a demon of sickness, if we bind that demon again in that person aren't we making the situation worse than before? If someone binds you with a rope, you will be unable to move or walk. Therefore, if we bind the spirit of infirmity in a person, we make that infirmity stronger. Is that the ministry Jesus gave us?

There is no evidence in the Bible that Jesus or the apostles ever bound a demon or principality. Instead, they loosed their hold on people to set them free. If a person is bound and put in prison, we don't bind him again to free him, but we loose him from that prison. We have been binding demons for a long time with few results. Can it be that we have been binding what we should loose and loosing what we should bind?

> **There is no evidence in the Bible that Jesus or the apostles ever bound a demon or principality. Instead, they loosed their hold on people to set them free.**

Anytime Jesus or the apostles had an encounter with a person who was demon-possessed, they always cast the demon out of that person. If a person was bound by Satan, they loosed him from his bondage. The command Jesus gave to us in relation to demons is to "cast them out." He said, "In My name they will cast out demons" (Mark 16:17a).

Today, believers are trying to bind principalities over nations. Most nations that I know of are going from bad to worse in sin and wickedness. It appears that these principalities and powers are too strong for the church to overcome. According to the above verse, both binding and loosing are done on the earth. There is nothing for us to bind or loose in the heavenly realm. Heaven belongs to God and He has given us the earth (Psalm 115:16). Heaven responds to what we do on this earth.

Is there any Scripture in the Bible that supports binding principalities and powers over nations? How did Jesus, our example, deal with the devil?

Jesus Never Bound Satan

When Jesus died and rose again He defeated and disarmed the enemy. "Having disarmed principalities and powers, He made a public spectacle of them, triumphing over them in it" (Colossians 2:15). Jesus defeated Satan and his kingdom on the cross and disarmed principalities and powers, making them surrender their weapons. He did not direct us to bind them or pull them down. We need to believe this and walk in it by faith daily.

> "When evening had come, they brought to Him many who were demon-possessed. And *He cast out the spirits with a word,* and healed all who were sick, that it might be fulfilled which was spoken by Isaiah the prophet, saying: 'He Himself took our infirmities and bore our sicknesses' " (Matthew 8:16-17).

It does not say Jesus bound any spirits or sicknesses or principalities. Instead, He cast them out. He loosed people from the hold of those unclean spirits. When Jesus set the man in Gadarenes free, the demons begged Jesus, saying, "If You cast us out, permit us to go away into the herd of swine" (Matthew 8:31). Why did He not just bind all those demons?

Demons know what should be done to them—whether they should be cast out or bound. But sadly, today many Christians and ministers don't know what to do with them. There is no verse that says we need to destroy any evil spirit or send them to hell. As I mentioned earlier, we need to send them to be the footstool of Jesus. That's where they belong.

In Mark 1:23-26 we read that while Jesus was teaching the Word in a synagogue, an evil spirit manifested in a person. He rebuked it by saying, "Be quiet, and come out of him!" We don't see Him binding that evil spirit, but loosing its hold over the person. In Mark 3:14-15, Jesus called His twelve disciples and gave them power and authority to heal sicknesses and cast out demons. He did not tell them to cast them *in* or bind them, but to cast them *out.* You always cast evil spirits out of a person; you never bind them in. Again, in Luke 4:33-35 we see Jesus commanding an evil spirit to come out of a person.

In Luke 13:11-16 we see one of the main accounts of deliverance in the New Testament. A woman who had a spirit of infirmity for eighteen years and was bowed down and could in no wise lift herself up. How does Jesus deal with this situation? When Jesus saw her, He called her to Him and said to

THE POWER AND AUTHORITY OF THE CHURCH

her, "Woman, you are loosed from your infirmity." He loosed her instead of binding those demons in her again.

When the ruler of the synagogue questioned Jesus in verse 16, He replied, "So ought not this woman, being a daughter of Abraham, whom Satan has *bound*—think of it—for eighteen years, be loosed from this bond on the Sabbath?" Here Jesus is revealing a key to becoming free from demonic oppression. Satan is in the *binding* ministry; he will try to bind anyone, even a daughter of Abraham, with sickness, addiction, infirmity, whatever he can use. Jesus is in the *loosing* ministry. His purpose is to loose people from the hold of the devil. He came to set the captives free (Luke 4:18).

> **Satan is in the *binding* ministry; Jesus is in the *loosing* ministry.**

The Church Got It Wrong

Anytime you see anyone binding anything in Scripture, it was always the enemy or kingdoms binding God's people. Both Old and New Testaments prove the same. If there was anyone loosing anything, it was God loosing His people from the bondage or captivity of the enemy and the chains that bound them.

You may ask, "Why can't we bind the demon and loose the person?" If a person is bound by sickness or curse, he is already bound by demonic forces. Why should we bind those demons again? Nowhere in Scripture does Jesus tell His disciples to bind an evil spirit. We should do what Jesus did, what He told us to do: cast out demons. It's that simple.

If those verses are not about binding and loosing demons, then what did Jesus mean when He said it? For many years the church has been binding Satan and demons, but we are not being effective. Could it be true that the devil deceived the church from knowing what Jesus really meant, so that he can go on creating havoc on the earth?

I went on a search to find out what Jesus really meant in that verse. I began to read different translations of the Bible and one day it hit me like a lightning bolt. When I realized what Jesus really meant by what He said, I understood why the church and the world are the way they are.

BINDING AND LOOSING

Why does evil seem to be prevailing in our culture, in our government, and in our school systems? Because the one force that God put on this earth to stop it is not doing its job. The church is not exercising her authority as she is supposed to be. Jesus gave us the keys of His kingdom. A key is used mainly for opening and closing, to begin or to end, to allow or not allow something. We open and lock doors with a key. We start our car and shut the car off with a key.

There are many literal and figurative uses of a key. Keys represent authority. If the key is yours, you have the right to use that key. Figuratively, we use the word *key* for understanding something, like the key to unlock a mystery. Now let us see from the Word what that verse really means. Look and see how these different translations render this verse:

> "And I will give you the keys of the kingdom of Heaven. Whatever *you forbid* on earth will be *forbidden* in heaven, and whatever *you permit* on earth will be *permitted* in heaven" (Matthew 16:19, NLT).

> "I will give you the keys of the kingdom of heaven; the things you don't *allow* on earth will be the things that God does not allow, and the things you allow on earth will be the things that God allows" (Matthew 16:19, NCV).

> "I will give you the keys of the holy nation of heaven. Whatever *you do not allow* on earth will not have been allowed in heaven. Whatever you allow on earth will have been allowed in heaven" (Matthew 16:19, NLV).

> "And I will give you the keys of the Kingdom of Heaven; whatever doors you *lock* on earth shall be *locked* in heaven; and whatever doors you *open* on earth shall be *open* in heaven!" (Matthew 16:19, TLB).

Whatever the church allows on this earth, heaven will allow. Whatever the church does not allow, heaven will not allow. So who is really responsible for all the evil that is being permitted in our nations: The devil, God, or the church?

> **Whatever the church allows on this earth, heaven will allow. Whatever the church does not allow, heaven will not allow.**

THE POWER AND AUTHORITY OF THE CHURCH

What if the church really exercised her God-given dominion based on Matthew 18:18? What if we regularly forbid the agendas of the enemy before they manifested in our nations? *What if we were that involved?* There is only one agency that can stop what the devil and his kingdom is doing on this earth and that agency is the church. But how many churches really exercise that right?

Jesus was saying to the church, "Whatever you forbid on this earth, heaven will forbid, whatever you allow on this earth, heaven will allow." In other words, whatever we allow on this earth will be allowed by heaven and whatever we don't allow on this earth, heaven will not allow.

Who is to blame for all the evil that is going on around the world today? It is happening because the church is not doing anything about it. The one agency that is supposed to stop the enemy is busy singing songs while he executes his plans and agendas through governments and other agencies of this world system. And he is taking millions of souls to hell with him along the way.

How should we exercise our authority as kingdom citizens to bring about change to our communities and nations? I am convinced that unless the church does this, there will not be any positive change in the nations of the world; instead, the situation will get still worse. It does not matter how many so-called churches or Christians there are in a nation or city. *What matters is whether or not they exercise God's power and authority in that nation and city.*

We are going to look through the Bible at some people who really administered God's kingdom on the earth. They were the spokesmen for God. From Genesis to Revelation we see that God and His people had authority over kingdoms of men, regardless of how powerful they were. When they spoke something on behalf of God, it literally happened as they said. Whatever they permitted on this earth, heaven permitted; and whatever they did not allow, heaven did not allow.

I am not saying everything they flippantly said happened. They were in tune with God and were in one spirit with Him. They worked in partnership with God and God worked in partnership with them. Let's look at some incidents from the Old Testament where God and man worked together to accomplish His purpose.

God and Man—Working Together

There are many times God did according to what a man had spoken or asked. One example is Moses. God made him as a god to Pharaoh; whatever Moses said over Pharaoh and Egypt happened as he spoke because Moses was speaking and acting in obedience to what the Lord had told him.

> "Moses and Aaron went out from Pharaoh, and Moses cried out to the Lord concerning the frogs which he had brought against Pharaoh. *Then the Lord did according to the word of Moses.* And the frogs died out of the houses, the villages, and out of the fields" (Exodus 8:12-13).

We see that highlighted phrase many times in relation to Moses, where the Lord did something according to what Moses had spoken (Exodus 8:31; Numbers 14:20). Moses was a man who was committed to obey God at any cost.

> "So when the Syrians came down to him, Elisha prayed to the LORD, AND SAID, 'STRIKE THIS PEOPLE, I PRAY, WITH BLINDNESS.' AND HE STRUCK THEM WITH BLINDNESS *according to the word of Elisha*" (2 Kings 6:18).

> "And Elijah the Tishbite, of the inhabitants of Gilead, said to Ahab, '*As* the Lord God of Israel lives, before whom I stand, there shall not be dew nor rain these years, *except at my word*'" (1 Kings 17:1).

> "Then Joshua spoke to the Lord in the day when the Lord delivered up the Amorites before the children of Israel, and he said in the sight of Israel: 'Sun, stand still over Gibeon; and Moon, in the Valley of Aijalon.' So the sun stood still, and the moon stopped, till the people had revenge upon their enemies. *Is* this not written in the Book of Jasher? So the sun stood still in the midst of heaven, and did not hasten to go *down* for about a whole day. *And there has been no day like that, before it or after it, that the Lord heeded the voice of a man; for the Lord fought for Israel*" (Joshua 10:12-14).

These verses show some examples of men exercising kingdom dominion on the earth and over the kingdoms of men. If the Old Testament saints had such authority, how much more does the church have today?

Chapter 9: The Authority of the Church over the Spiritual and Natural World

Chapter 9: The Authority of the Church over the Spiritual and Natural World

"Behold, I give you the authority to trample on serpents and scorpions, and over all the power of the enemy, and nothing shall by any means hurt you" (Luke 10:19).

I never understood the full implication of this verse until God gave me this chapter. For a long time I had a hard time believing the "nothing shall by any means hurt you" part. I know Jesus does not lie and if He said it, there is a way to live it. But, because of all the horror stories of how Satan tormented or attacked preachers and believers alike from around the world, and how witches and sorcerers attacked Christians and put curses on them, I was not sure if He really meant what He said.

I was a little nervous when I had to deal with the enemy, fearing retaliation. Only after the Holy Spirit showed me the revelation contained in the above verse did I become confident to face the enemy's forces. After you read this chapter you will walk in a new level of authority and nothing shall by any means hurt you again. It does not matter which part of the world you live in. Don't believe the lie of thinking the enemy is stronger in some part of the world than another. He is the same everywhere. Your victory and defeat depend on what you believe.

Our Right as God's Children

Jesus has given the church *authority* over *all* the *power* of the enemy. He has given authority to us to stop any power of the enemy. The difference between power and authority is this: Power is the strength or physical capacity to do something. Authority is the *right* to exercise that power. Sometimes we don't understand the total implications of that verse. If there is any power left in the enemy, Jesus gave us authority to stop him from exercising that power. Each child of God living in any part of the earth has the right to exercise that authority over the power of the enemy at any time.

Whenever the New Testament talks about the enemy it never talks about the authority of the enemy; it only talks about the power of the enemy. Jesus himself acknowledged that Satan has power. When He appeared to Paul and was telling him about his calling, He told him he was to "open their eyes, in order to turn them from darkness to light, and from the *power of Satan* to God, that they may receive forgiveness of sins and an inheritance among those who are sanctified by faith in Me" (Acts 26:18).

> **Each child of God living in any part of the earth has the right to exercise that authority over the power of the enemy at any time.**

Jesus was talking here. He had no problem acknowledging that the enemy has power. He was not in denial like many are today. But He never talked about the enemy having any kind of authority whatsoever. To tell you the truth, the devil has no authority and no right to operate on the earth. He is an illegal entity operating on the earth; and he is doing what he is doing only because people allow him to do it. He is like a squatter on our land.

Even if someone has the power to do something, if he does not have the authority to do so, he has no right to exercise his power. It becomes illegal. For example, I can make a stop sign and stand on a busy street and make the vehicles stop with that sign. When the drivers see someone holding a stop sign, they will stop their vehicles. But I don't have the authority to do that because I am not part of the police force or the department of transportation. If I do that, I am doing something illegal and the authorities can stop me and put me in jail.

Can you imagine how many things we have been letting the enemy do illegally? Because he has no authority to exercise his power, *everything* he does is illegal. Jesus said, "All authority in heaven and on earth has been given unto Me" (Matthew 28:18b NLT). I want you to notice the "all" in that verse. If Jesus received all authority in heaven and on earth, how much is left for the devil? None! Then why does he seem so powerful? Because the church is letting him get away with doing this. Whatever the enemy is doing, he is doing without Jesus' permission.

We should shout and sing about it for all eternity. If you see any works of the enemy anywhere, he has no right to do them. He has been doing them because the *force* God put on this earth to stop him is not doing anything about it because they don't know how. Lord, have mercy!

> **Whatever the enemy is doing, he is doing without Jesus' permission.**

Focused on the Wrong Thing

In some places, Christians are very focused on what the devil is doing. They talk about how powerful he is and how terrible his operation is in their culture. They have bound every demon that exists—and sometimes even those that don't exist—but still have not seen any victory. They don't understand the difference between authority and power and who has received what. They have the authority to stop the enemy, but they are afraid of the power of the enemy. They don't know how to exercise their authority, so they stand back and watch what he does. That's why Jesus directed me write this book, so that His church can begin exercising their right on the earth on His behalf.

When Jesus died and rose again, the Father exalted Him far above all principalities and powers and every name that is named in heaven and on earth and put all things under His feet.

> "Which He worked in Christ when He raised Him from the dead and seated Him at His right hand in the heavenly places, far above all principality and power and might and dominion, and every name that is named, not only in this age but also in that which is to come. And He put all things under His feet, and gave Him to be head over all things to the church which is His body" (Ephesians 1:20-23a).

The Greek word used for *dominion* here and other places in the New Testament is *kuriotes* which also means "government." [13] Isaiah wrote that the government

---

13. Strong, James. *Strong's Exhaustive Concordance*. Peabody, MA: Hendrickson Publishers, 2007. #G2963.

shall be upon Jesus' shoulders (Isaiah 9:6). Today's world governments are nothing but the playground of the kingdom of darkness. How will this change from being the tool of the devil to being instruments and extensions of God's kingdom? This will happen when the church exercises its God-given authority.

Every spiritual force that is part of the kingdom of darkness is now under the feet of Jesus, and He is the Head of the church. If anything is under the feet of Jesus, it is automatically under the feet of the church because we are the body of Christ. In the spirit, everything has been put under the feet of Jesus and we need to live this out practically. That is the purpose of the church. Without doing anything, just by being part of the body of Christ we have inherent authority over every force of darkness. It is a positional right we receive for being the body of Christ.

> If anything is under the feet of Jesus, it is automatically under the feet of the church because we are the body of Christ.

But the evil forces on this earth do not acknowledge that right now. So Jesus put His church on this earth to actualize and bring it to reality. That is our real job as the body of Christ on this earth. When we accomplish that task, I believe Jesus will return.

Born To Take Authority

Before the fall, Adam had power and authority over all satanic forces as a human. You don't need to shout, fast, scream, or do anything extra to have this authority. Each believer inherits this authority; it is their birthright in the kingdom. That is why Jesus gave the authority and power over demons and sickness to His disciples from the very beginning. They did not pray for it or ask for it, nor did they scream or fast for it. He did not require any spiritual discipline from them prior to receiving this power and authority. All they did was come when He called out for them to follow Him. They inherited it from Jesus as a right from the first day of their calling. They didn't even know how to pray yet!

Keep in mind that when Paul talked about the kingdom of darkness, he never mentioned it having any authority, only power.

> "And you are complete in Him, who is the head of all principality and power.... Having disarmed principalities and

176

powers, He made a public spectacle of them, triumphing over them in it" (Colossians 2:10, 15).

The church—by its very existence in any nation—carries the authority over all the principalities and powers that are operating in that nation. But most do not exercise it. We are seated in Christ far above principalities and powers; they are not above us but under us. But the church has to believe this, otherwise, the enemy will continue to take advantage of our ignorant fear, pretend he is powerful, and play games with us.

"But God, who is rich in mercy, because of His great love with which He loved us, even when we were dead in trespasses, made us alive together with Christ (by grace you have been saved), and raised *us* up together, and made *us* sit together in the heavenly *places* in Christ Jesus" (Ephesians 2:4-6).

We have not only received authority but power also. The power that is made available to us has no limit.

"The eyes of your understanding being enlightened; that you may know what is the hope of His calling, what are the riches of the glory of His inheritance in the saints, and what *is the exceeding greatness of His power toward us who believe, according to the working of His mighty power"* (Ephesians 1:18-19).

The power that is available to us is described as the exceeding greatness of His power. One translation says "the immeasurable" power. But most of us do not realize we have *any* power because the eyes of our understanding are not yet opened. The enemy has blinded us from knowing this power because he knows that once the church realizes this truth, his business is finished. It is important to pray the prayer in Ephesians 1. God, who answers prayer, will enlighten our eyes as we seek Him in this as in all things.

> **The enemy has blinded us from knowing this power because he knows that once the church realizes this truth, his business is finished.**

The Name above Every Other Name

"Therefore God also has highly exalted Him and given Him the name which is above every name" (Philippians 2:9).

THE POWER AND AUTHORITY OF THE CHURCH

A name represents the identity and the authority a person carries. Everything in this universe is known by a name. The name of Jesus is above every name: demons, sickness, people, nature, anything that is named: not only in this age but in the age to come. In a kingdom, if something is written in the name of the king and sealed by the signet ring of the king, it is irrevocable.

> "You yourselves write a decree concerning the Jews, as you please, in the king's name, and seal it with the king's signet ring; for whatever is written in the king's name and sealed with the king's signet ring no one can revoke" (Esther 8:8).

Why did the Father give Jesus a name above every other name? In many cultures, if someone writes a law or rule or decree about or against anything, someone else who has more authority than that person can revoke that law, rule, or decree and cancel it. This is especially true when one kingdom overthrows another kingdom. The new kingdom can change or establish new laws in that land. Whatever the previous king had decreed was made void when he was dethroned.

Jesus is King of Kings. There is no king or name above His. Everything has been made subject to Him because He created everything.

> "For by Him all things were created that are in heaven and that are on earth, visible and invisible, whether thrones or dominions or principalities or powers. All things were created through Him and for Him. And He is before all things, and in Him all things consist. And He is the head of the body, the church" (Colossians 1:16-18a).

We are dealing with two different kingdoms, the kingdom of God and the kingdom of darkness. The kingdom of darkness was holding us prisoner under the dominion of sin. When Jesus destroyed and delivered us from the power of darkness, He transferred us to His kingdom. The authority of the kingdom of darkness was shattered right then and there, never to be regained.

> "He has delivered us from the power of darkness and conveyed us into the kingdom of the Son of His love" (Colossians 1:13).

If you were a prisoner of a kingdom, and another king came and subdued that kingdom and rescued you and took you with him into his new kingdom, you would no longer be bound by any laws and accusations the previous king had against you. You could have been the worst criminal ever in the previous kingdom, but once you have been brought into the new kingdom you are now under a new law. You are under a new kingdom with a different government and laws.

Stop acting like a prisoner! That's why we read in the Bible, "Therefore if the Son makes you free, you shall be free indeed" (John 8:36). Though they are brought from the kingdom of darkness to the kingdom of light, many think and behave the same way they used to. So they do not enjoy anything the new kingdom has to offer.

Every law of a nation is signed into action by that nation's head of state. It is by that name, and the authority vested in that name, that a law is put into place. Once it is enacted, that law applies to every citizen of the state.

Jesus is the name above every other name, so whatever the enemy has written or decreed or held against you, you can nullify using the name of Jesus. Once the name of Jesus is used, no one can question its authority because there is no authority above His name. Say hallelujah. Wow! This is powerful.

> **Whatever the enemy has written or decreed or held against you, you can nullify using the name of Jesus.**

That is why Paul says in Romans 8:33-34: "Who shall bring a charge against God's elect? *It is* God who justifies. Who *is* he who condemns? *It is* Christ who died, and furthermore is also risen, who is even at the right hand of God, who also makes intercession for us."

Jesus wiped out the handwriting (the accusations) that were written against us, taking them out of the way, and nailing them to the cross. Colossians 2:14 says: "Having wiped out the handwriting of requirements that was against us, which was contrary to us. And He has taken it out of the way, having nailed it to the cross." No one can rewrite what Jesus wiped out. Your record is clean.

Exercising Our Authority

As a church, we can take authority over all the power of the enemy in whichever city or town we are in and declare it powerless. Take authority over every specific area the enemy is exercising his power over you, and render it powerless. Uproot and tear those areas out and tell them never to operate in that region again.

For example, if substance abuse or alcoholism are major issues in your town, you can take authority over the spirits that are destroying lives through drugs, alcohol, and substance addiction and declare them powerless. Take away their right from operating in that area. This will advance the kingdom of God in your region. If idol worship is a problem, say, "I stop the growth of false religion in _____(name the town). Every principality and power that is operating behind this false religion, I forbid you from operating in Jesus' name." Town by town, city by city, and eventually an entire nation will come under the administration of the kingdom of God through this practice.

What we usually see now is a church fighting with the powers of the enemy for years without realizing the authority God has given them. Specifically identify which power of the kingdom of darkness is operating in your area and do not let them operate there anymore.

You can use this authority for personal evangelism as well. Take authority over the spirit that is ruling in any person that you meet and take the right from that spirit's exercise of power over them. Then you share the gospel and see what happens.

Where Do We Send These Evil Spirits?

You don't send an evil spirit to a dry place, to hell, or to be tormented. There is no biblical evidence to do so. Every time you cast a demon out of a person or dispossess a land or region from the enemy, you always send those spirits under the feet of Jesus because that is where they belong. As the church, we are in the business of bringing His enemies to His footstool. You speak and say, "I surrender them under the feet of Jesus." That's where they belong and they have to obey.

There is one particular Scripture that has been quoted in the New Testament from the Old Testament more than any other. It is the one in which the Father tells the Son to sit at His right hand until He brings all His enemies to be His footstool. It is quoted seven times in the New Testament. I might have quoted it seven times in this book. Please read this verse as it is the key to this whole book.

"But this Man, after He had offered one sacrifice for sins forever, sat down at the right hand of God, from that time waiting till His enemies are made His footstool. For by one offering He has perfected forever those who are being sanctified" (Hebrews 10:12-14).

When the church accomplishes this mission, Jesus will come to rule and reign on the earth. He is coming for a victorious and triumphant church.

Chapter 10: A House of Prayer for All Nations

Chapter 10: A House of Prayer for All Nations

"My house shall be called a house of prayer for all nations" (Mark 11:17b).

God's House

A nation goes where it's church goes. So please stop blaming the politicians and the government about what is happening in your country. The destiny of nations depends on the prayers of the house of God. What is the house of God in the New Testament? There are two applications to the term "house of God." One is political and the other is spiritual. In the political sense every nation has a governing body that is called a "house," for example the "House of Representatives." When Jesus says, "My house," first He is referring to the governing body of His kingdom.

Secondly, Jesus is referring to the place where He dwells. Where does Jesus dwell in the New Testament? He is in heaven, but when a person is born again He comes to dwell inside that person. They become His house. In the New Testament, the house of God is not a building made of hands. Unfortunately, many think the house of God is a building made of mortar and bricks because to many people, church means a building we meet in on Sunday morning. A facility. But Jesus did not come to dwell in a building.

> "Jesus answered and said to him, 'If anyone loves Me, he will keep My word; and My Father will love him, and We will come to him and make Our home with him' " (John 14:23).

> "He who eats My flesh and drinks My blood abides in Me, and I in him" (John 6:56).

"Do you not know that you are the temple of God and *that* the Spirit of God dwells in you?" (1 Corinthians 3:16).

"Or do you not know that your body is the temple of the Holy Spirit *who is* in you, whom you have from God, and you are not your own?" (1 Corinthians 6:19).

Let the Word of God transform your mind. When you think about the church, picture your brethren, not the building you meet in. The church is made of these living stones assembled wherever that may be, and *it could be anywhere.*

"You also, as *living stones,* are being built up a *spiritual house,* a holy priesthood, to offer up spiritual sacrifices acceptable to God through Jesus Christ" (1 Peter 2:5).

"For we are God's fellow workers; you are God's field, *you are* God's *building*" (1 Corinthians 3:9).

"In whom the whole *building,* being fitted together, grows into a holy temple in the Lord" (Ephesians 2:21).

"But if I am delayed, *I write* so that you may know how you ought to conduct yourself in the *house of God,* which is the church of the living God, the pillar and ground of the truth" (1 Timothy 3:15).

It was understood that the church consisted of all the believers. Each individual is a house of God, and Jesus wants to dwell in us as a corporate body and be made manifest to the world through us. When we come together as the church, we make a dwelling place for God—the Bible calls it a spiritual building.

"In whom the *whole building*, being fitted together, grows into a holy temple in the Lord, in whom you also are being built together for a dwelling place of God in the Spirit" (Ephesians 2:21-22).

"But Christ as a Son over His own house, *whose house we are* if we hold fast the confidence and the rejoicing of the hope firm to the end" (Hebrews 3:6).

It is God's eternal plan to dwell in man. When Adam fell into sin, it became impossible for a time. But through Jesus' death and redemption, that plan was reinstated. Once God dwells in us, we become the house of God. The Bible says, "Christ in you, the hope of glory" (Colossians 1:27). Wherever we go, God goes with us. We are His agents that release His purposes on this earth, and cancel the purposes and plans of the enemy.

God is a Spirit, but it was His desire from the beginning to work in partnership with man as a Father with His children. He made mankind for Himself so He would have a family. God can do anything He wants, but He chose to work with us and purposefully stays within His own prearranged laws. If He is to operate on this earth He needs a physical body. God gave us a physical body for Him to dwell in, and work through. Our body is the only temple God has on the earth today. Imagine the things we do with, and to, our bodies? Our bodies are temples created by God in which He is to abide. As it says in Romans 12:1, we are to submit our bodies to Him as a sacrifice and do the things He has for us to do.

> **Our body is the only temple God has on the earth today. Imagine the things we do with, and to, our bodies?**

In the Old Testament, the house of God was first a tent and later a temple, a building made by people's hands. When Jesus was on this earth He talked about the time David ate the bread of the priest, the showbread. Jesus referred to the temple as a house of God. "How he entered the *house of God* and ate the showbread which was not lawful for him to eat, nor for those who were with him, but only for the priests?" (Matthew 12:4). This is mentioned in Matthew, Mark, and Luke's gospels.

A House of Prayer

Why did Jesus say that His house shall be called a house of prayer for all nations? God's desire is to see His will accomplished *on this earth as it is in heaven.* The responsibility of the church is to find out what that will is for its community and nation and pray it through until it manifests on the earth. The destiny of a nation depends on the church. Specifically, the destiny of all nations depends on *the prayers of the church.*

Unfortunately, most churches do not take time to pray. We limit our prayer time to pre-service prayer, men's prayer, and city prayer, but we're supposed to be a local body with a global perspective. One of the main things we should do as a church when we come together is to pray and declare the will of God over our lives, our community, and our nation. Most churches do not even know what God's will is for them or their nation. They have given it to the devil, thinking they can't do anything to bring any change. That is not true.

Many believers complain about what is going on in their nations. *Unless the church prays, nothing is going to change.* People want their government to fix the problems, but God wants to fix those problems through the church. In Matthew 16:19 Jesus gave the keys of the kingdom to Peter (to the church) and told him that whatever he stops on this earth will be stopped by heaven and whatever he allows will be allowed by heaven. The command to bind and loose was given in this context.

> **People want their government to fix the problems, but God wants to fix those problems through the church.**

In the Old Testament, God used individuals to do this, but in the New Testament, He uses the church. Moses was sent to Egypt to deliver God's people. He had the keys to open and close heaven over Egypt. When Moses spoke what God told Him to speak, whatever he spoke happened in Egypt. Pharaoh was the king in the natural, but Moses held the keys of authority in the spirit.

Elijah is another example. He told King Ahab there would be no rain in Israel until he spoke (1 Kings 17:1). What did that mean? The prophet had authority to open and close heavens. The king was just a person riding on the back of a horse, but Elijah made decisions in the spirit. Joseph, Daniel, and Esther are some of the other examples of how God's people were put in high positions to influence governments to accomplish God's purposes. If one person could do that kind of ministry in the Old Testament, what should we be doing as a church, the body of Christ, today?

Praying for Leaders in the New Testament

"Therefore I exhort first of all that *supplications, prayers, intercessions,* and *giving of thanks* be made for all men, for kings and all who are in authority, that we may lead a quiet and peaceable life in all godliness and reverence. For this *is* good and acceptable in the sight of God our Savior, who desires all men to be saved and to come to the knowledge of the truth" (1 Timothy 2:1-4).

These verses are both powerful and interesting at the same time. There are four different words and four different kinds of prayers Paul is asking us to pray. They all are plural words he is using. There must have been a reason for him to use those four specific types of prayers. He could have just used one word and told us to pray for all men and leaders.

The reason we don't have a quiet and peaceable life on this earth today is because the church is not praying these prayers for all men and for people in authority. Instead of peace, we see a war-torn world. Thousands of children are dying daily of starvation and malnutrition. Families lie in ruin more than ever before. Is there an answer for all these problems? Is there a way to change them? There is. The church must start praying and then the Lord will show us the next step.

How do we pray for all men on the earth? When it says men it is not talking about the male species but the human race. The church is supposed to pray for the human race all over the earth. If each of us prayed for all the people living in our immediate communities, towns, or cities, it would make a big difference.

Then, he says we are supposed to pray for kings and all who are in authority. People who are in authority and in government need the prayers of the church. Why do we need to pray for them? We need to pray for their protection from the evil forces, that they will not be used to execute the purpose and will of the kingdom of darkness in our nations. Satan

> Satan and his forces will target the people in authority in order to influence and use them to accomplish his agenda.

and his forces will target the people in authority in order to influence and use them to accomplish his agenda. The church is the only force that can stop this from happening.

There are four different kinds of prayers mentioned here too. First, there are "supplications." These are earnest and humble prayers. It is like going before a king with a petition in hand to address him. We are supposed to ask for the salvation of all men, because it is God's will that none should perish. Instead of praying a general prayer for all men, it is good if we identify and target individuals.

When I see certain people at the store or other places, the Holy Spirit sometimes prompts me to pray for them. I whisper a prayer for that person to God, mainly to bless them and to give them a breakthrough in some area of their life. If I see they are struggling with something, I address that in my prayer too.

The second word Paul uses is simply *prayers*. It means to ask or declare. There are different kinds of prayers. Praying in the Spirit and praying with our understanding are just two of them. There are prayers we pray based on knowledge. We know a person's requests and we pray for those needs. In our nations, we know what needs to be done. We pray and declare that to happen by faith.

The third word Paul uses is *intercessions*. To intercede means to stand for or against someone on behalf of someone else. There are times we need to stand for or against what is going on in our nations. Today, many go out into the street to protest and we don't make any progress. We should be on our knees instead. His house shall be a house of prayer for all nations.

> Today, many go out into the street to protest and we don't make any progress. We should be on our knees instead.

The last thing we are supposed to do is to "give thanks" for the answers to our prayers. Paul directs us to be thankful in all circumstances. Doing this keeps us centered on Christ and His ability in every situation; it also shields us from depression and discouragement.

In the next chapter I deal with how to pray and legislate things in the spirit. Knowing what we know now, we are able to enter into a very important aspect of church life.

Chapter 11: Kingdom Legislation

Chapter 11: Kingdom Legislation

"For the kingdom is the Lord's, and He rules over the nations"
(Psalm 22:28).

Read the introduction of this book again before you read this chapter. One of the reasons the church exists today is to execute the purposes of God on the earth. We read in Ephesians 3:10 that one of the purposes of the church is to make known the wisdom of God to the principalities and powers in the heavenly places. The question is how do we do this through the local church? The incident I shared in the introduction is one of the best examples of how we do this practically. We are going to look in the Bible and see how God used His people to do the same thing.

What do I mean by *legislation*? To legislate means to bring to effect or to cancel a law or enforce the reign and standard of the kingdom of God on the earth. If we don't at least do this in the lives of people who are attending the local church, we are wasting our time and the time of the people.

When we come together as a church and do not legislate anything in the earthly realm (what God wants done in our community, nation, or the earth), then we have not come together properly as the church. When we come together, if we have not addressed the spiritual cause of any issues or problems that our community, city, or nation faces, then we have done nothing to benefit the kingdom of God.

> **When we come together as a church and do not legislate anything in the earthly realm, then we have not come together properly as the church.**

The problem could be anything: politics, war, sickness, drugs, terrorism, abortion, racism, prostitution; the list is endless. Governments are trying to pass new laws against the church and against God's moral standard. The work of the devil is to destroy the foundation of life on the earth. Even though we just had fellowship, sang songs, and drank coffee together, our social time might have benefitted us, but it did not benefit God and His kingdom. If you are not facing any issue at the moment where you are, you should at least enforce the reign and the Lordship of Jesus Christ over your family, community, and nation.

Praying the Heart of God

We need to pray to know what is in the heart of God for our community, nation, and the earth. For us to know that, we need to have an intimate relationship with the Holy Spirit who is now here on earth. The Holy Spirit is the Steward of the kingdom of God sent to help the church. The Holy Spirit knows and communicates what is in the heart and mind of God (1 Corinthians 2:11).

Many nations are going in the direction they are because the church is not exercising its authority over the legal matters of the nations. The kingdom of darkness is prospering its will and executing it through people in government. How much more should the kingdom of God be doing this? Unless the church rises up and stops this in the spirit, nothing will change. There is no point in blaming government or people in power for what is going on. You have to see and detect the *force* behind the legislation and address it in the spirit through prayer.

Why would people in any nation ask their government to legalize abortion? Why would human beings with any kind of common sense legalize public drug use? Most people are not aware that there is a kingdom that is working behind these people and their governments. This kingdom hates human beings and implements its will to steal, kill, and destroy. In the end, this kingdom's desire is the complete destruction of civilization and morality in every nation.

Jesus put His church, the governing body of His kingdom, on the earth to withstand that kingdom and to institute His will on the earth. Instead of allowing Satan to plunder and kill, He wants to see His church exercising the authority He has given us to cancel those plans before they manifest in the natural. But what have the churches been doing? They have been singing people to hell.

You Have Keys!

How do we exercise that legal authority over nations? To help us, Jesus gave us the keys of His kingdom. Imagine a king giving the keys of His entire kingdom to you! You have the right to go into any chamber of his kingdom and open any door, to allow or stop anyone from coming in or going out, and doing whatever they want to do. You can see or use anything the king has in his kingdom. His entire possessions, wealth, authority, and riches are at your disposal, but you use those keys only to bind the thieves that come to steal from the kingdom. You don't use a key to bind the devil, a thief! What stupidity this is! What a loss. Can you see what we have been missing?

Jesus did not give us ropes or the keys to His car! He gave us the keys of the kingdom of heaven. Imagine the wealth, riches, authority, power, wisdom, knowledge, and understanding of His kingdom. It is unlimited. He has given all that for our disposal to use anytime we choose.

The Bible does not say He gave us just one key, or some keys. Jesus has given us a keychain with *all* the keys of His kingdom. He gave us these keys for whatever pertains to overseeing this earthly realm in relation to heaven. Whatever heaven likes to see happening on this earth, He has given all of those keys to exercise His authority on His behalf. Through us He wants to stop the kingdom of darkness from accomplishing any of its plans.

> The Bible does not say He gave us just one key, or some keys. Jesus has given us a keychain with *all* the keys of His kingdom.

Every chamber in a kingdom has a door, and a key to open and close that door. The kingdom of God is not any different from any other kingdom. It has an economic chamber, administrative chamber, educational chamber, transportation, communication, business, etc. What has the church been doing with the keys Jesus gave us? We used them to bind demons and that's about it.

Exercising Our Legal Authority over Nations and Cities

If you know the government is trying to pass any laws against the moral standard of the kingdom of God, the *ekklesia*—the General Assembly—has to gather together and cancel in prayer that law from coming into effect. We must take authority over the spirits that are influencing the government to implement the will of Satan, cancel them and render them powerless because the kingdom of God rules over the kingdoms of men. In some cases, even after the church prayed, nothing seemed to change. We still need to continue to do our part and let God be the Judge.

When a church rises up to exercise its God-given authority, people in governments and other religions will come and fall down at the feet of the apostles as it was in the first century, because they will know who really holds the keys of the kingdom. Today, the devil has already infiltrated the church. He continues to use his divide-and-conquer strategy to render us ineffective. We have no corporate voice as the body of Christ. Here and there, little congregations try to do things but they have not been effective. First of all, we need to pray for the unity of the body of Christ and come against those forces that divide us.

I have been to countries where there are at least a hundred churches in one small town with every name you can imagine, but hell is flourishing in accomplishing its agenda. It grieves God when we will not unite and work together. If only those ministers and believers in that town could get a revelation of how a kingdom operates and about the keys Jesus gave them to bring the change that is necessary. It's time for change.

> It grieves God when we will not unite and work together.

Please read Psalm 149:5-9 and meditate on it:

> Let the saints be joyful in glory;
> Let them sing aloud on their beds.
> *Let* the high praises of God *be* in their mouth,
> And a two-edged sword in their hand,
> To execute vengeance on the nations,
> And punishments on the peoples;
> To bind their kings with chains,
> And their nobles with fetters of iron;
> To execute on them the written judgment—
> This honor have all His saints.
> Praise the Lord!

You may have grown up in a democratic nation and have no idea how a kingdom operates. Why do you think there is so much written about kingdoms and kings in the Bible? It is there for you so you can read, study, and learn how a kingdom operates.

Throughout the Bible, whenever God speaks to our purpose concerning this earth, He always puts His kingdom first and then calls us kings. Because He is King, His children are naturally princes and princesses. When He talks about the church He does the same. What do kings do? They rule. They decree and legislate laws and projects into effect. They serve justice to the needy and poor. Then they destroy or thwart their enemy's plots and uprisings.

Our relationship with God is as children to their Father. Our position on earth as the representatives of God's kingdom is as kings. There are different terms God uses to describe our position as His church. Let's look at a couple of them.

General Assembly

In the book of Hebrews, the Bible calls us the General Assembly of God or His kingdom. The term "general assembly" is a fascinating term; it is actually a political term. In our modern day another place this term is used is in the United Nations. Heads and representatives of different nations come together to address issues the world is facing and then they pass resolutions and legislate policies concerning international relationships and what needs to happen in different countries with regard to the problems they are facing. Whatever they decide is the rule of law for all nations.

> "But you have come to Mount Zion and to the city of the living God, the heavenly Jerusalem, to an innumerable company of angels, *to the general assembly* and church of the firstborn who are registered in heaven, to God the Judge of all, to the spirits of just men made perfect" (Hebrews 12:22-23).

Can we imagine ourselves as the General Assembly of the kingdom of God when we gather as a church? Can you imagine hundreds of the General Assembly of the kingdom of God coming together every Sunday all over the world just to sing some songs and to hear a little sermonette? What good are we doing for ourselves, for our countries, and the kingdom of God by doing this?

Those verses from Hebrews are a perfect example of how the kingdom of God operates. Mount Zion, the city of God and heavenly Jerusalem, is the capital city of the kingdom of God. An innumerable company of angels (those that wait to execute God's will are innumerable) is waiting to execute our orders. There is one General Assembly in heaven and there is one on earth. The one on the earth is the church of the firstborn and the one in heaven are the saints who have gone before us. The Bible calls them the cloud of witnesses (Hebrews 12:1). The names of these firstborn (which is every believer in Christ) are written in heaven. God is the Judge of all.

When we come together on a Sunday morning or anytime, we are a gathering of the General Assembly of the kingdom of heaven on earth. An innumerable company of angels is waiting to execute what we declare over nations. That is why the Bible says, "My house will be called a house of prayer for all nations." It is through

> **An innumerable company of angels is waiting to execute what we declare over nations.**

prayer, or speaking or declaring, that we execute the will of God here on earth. You do not need to close your eyes to pray. You can keep your eyes open. The important thing is to speak what the Spirit of God is saying at that time.

Unfortunately, when the General Assembly comes together these days they don't give any orders. Instead, they do the same old rituals or some kind of humanistic presentation that motivates people, but nothing changes in the spirit. They are worried about who is going to win the game that afternoon or consumed with some need of their flesh. Many of the songs we sing are self-centered and continuously asking God for things we need. Those innumerable angels are waiting to execute our orders, but we aren't giving any orders. We need to address something in the spirit world to shift it from the direction it is going to bring about those changes and manifest them in the natural.

When you come together as the General Assembly of God, address the issues your communities and nation are facing in prayer. In this case prayer means to declare, decree, give orders, command, etc. This is not a *Please Lord, if this is your will, just do it, in spite of us, even-though-we-are-just-worms-and-dust-of-the-earth kind* of prayer. This is you as a child of the Most High, exercising your God-given rights and authority on the earth to bring the will of God to manifestation!

You will also declare a thing, and it will be established for you; so light will shine on your ways" (Job 22:28).

Ambassadors for Christ

"Now then, we are *ambassadors* for Christ, as though God were pleading through us: we implore *you* on Christ's behalf, be reconciled to God" (2 Corinthians 5:20).

The Bible calls us ambassadors for Christ, which is also a political term. It is a person sent to a foreign country to represent their native country and its government. When they speak they do not speak on their own authority, but on behalf of the head of their country. When they speak, it is as if the president or the head of that country spoke.

When you become an ambassador of a country, it is the duty of the government who sent you to provide for every need you have. You don't get a flight and land in the capital city of that country and take a taxi to a hotel. You don't look in the phone book or call a friend to see if you can find a place to rent. No, that's not the way ambassadors operate. Your accommodation, food, transportation, schooling for your children, and everything else you need is prepared for you before you arrive there.

All you have to do is show up. There are a few things to keep in mind. As an ambassador you cannot just speak your mind, because whatever you speak can affect the relationship between the two countries. If someone touches you or does you any harm, it becomes an international issue and war could start between the two countries. They almost respect the ambassador as they respect the country and the leader that country represents. Ambassadors are often used to prevent wars and make treaties.

> **Ambassadors are often used to prevent wars and make treaties.**

"And for me, that utterance may be given to me, that I may open my mouth boldly to make known the mystery of the gospel, for which I am an *ambassador* in chains; that in it I may speak boldly, as I ought to speak" (Ephesians 6:19-20).

From the beginning of time, God always had someone here who administered His kingdom. It didn't matter if it was one man against the most powerful nation or a small number of people against the mightiest armies. His kingdom and His ambassadors always rule over the kingdoms of men. His kingdom always has authority over any king, government, or ruler. Below are some examples.

When you read the Bible you will notice something very important. God's people and the church always had authority over the government or the king of the nations they were living in. For some reason, today's church does not think like that. I don't understand why? I am going to show you from the scriptures a few examples of it so you will know for sure that you and I serve the same God the people in the Bible served.

Abraham Versus the Kingdom of Gerar

From Genesis to Revelation, God Almighty always makes sure His purpose is accomplished. The church is supposed to be the agency today through which God accomplishes His will on the earth.

In Genesis we see that when Abraham went to stay in Gerar, he was afraid and told the people that Sarah, his wife, was his sister. Abimelech, the king took Sarah to be his wife. I am sure Abraham cried out to God that night for his wife. God intervened on behalf of Abraham. "But God came to Abimelech in a dream by night, and said to him, 'Indeed you are a dead man because of the woman whom you have taken, for she is a man's wife' " (Genesis 20:3).

Wow! I like the language God used in the above verse. He told the king in a dream that he was a dead man because he took Sarah. In verse 7 of that passage, God continued to say, "Now therefore, restore the man's wife; for he is a prophet, and he will pray for you and you shall live. But if you do not restore her, know that you shall surely die, you and all who are yours."

God told King Abimelech that if he did not restore Sarah to Abraham, Abimelech and all his people would be dead. That means he and his whole kingdom would be brought to nothing because Abraham was God's prophet. Can you imagine the impact one man can have against a whole nation?

In the New Testament we are called the seed of Abraham. He is the father of our faith. In Psalm 105:15 we are instructed to not touch His anointed and do His prophets no harm.

In fact, Abraham had another similar experience with Pharaoh, the king of Egypt. God plagued the king for his sake and delivered Sarah from the hands of the Egyptians too (Genesis 12:14-20). What a mighty God we serve!

Esther Versus the Kingdom of Persia

Esther was a Jewish girl taken into the palace of King Ahasuerus of Persia to be his wife. At this same time, there was a man named Haman who hated the Jews and wanted to destroy them. He conspired against them and influenced the king to write a decree to destroy the entire Jewish race from the face of the earth. This was not a small kingdom. His kingdom extended from Ethiopia to India.

The decree was written and was sealed with the royal signet ring. This meant it could not be revoked. Esther asked Mordecai her uncle and all the Jews who were in Shushan to fast with her for three days. On the third day Esther went before the king, which was against the law, to request that he and Haman come for a banquet she would prepare.

God gave Esther favor with the king, and the plot Haman was planning against the Jews was revealed to the king. Ironically, Haman was hanged on the same gallows he prepared for Mordecai. God gave them a great victory against their enemies. God can rewrite any decree of any king or government, no matter how great and powerful they are. The kingdom of God rules over the kingdoms of men.

> God can rewrite any decree of any king or government, no matter how great and powerful they are.

What if the church had the same revelation and operated in it today around the world? Do you think any plot the devil conceived could prosper against us? We would have to abort every plan of the enemy against nations and people. I was in Africa when I initially wrote this chapter. God brought me there to minister at a leadership conference. There were pastors and leaders from eight different nations in attendance. In many of the nations in Africa, people have been robbed and stolen from by the enemy. The church has to rise up and enact kingdom legislation in each of these African nations to restore what is rightfully theirs in Jesus' name.

Moses Versus the Kingdom of Egypt

When God sent Moses to Egypt to deliver His people, he went there as the ambassador of God. He was not just an old man walking with a rod in his hand. It might have seemed like that outwardly, but the authority he was representing was the God of heaven's authority.

> "And you shall say to him, 'The *Lord God of the Hebrews has sent me* to you, saying, "Let My people go, that they may serve Me in the wilderness" ' " (Exodus 7:16).

> "So the Lord said to Moses: 'See, I have made you *as God* to Pharaoh, and Aaron your brother shall be your prophet' " (Exodus 7:1).

Wow! Did you understand what you just read? Moses was as God to Pharaoh. That means that whatever Moses spoke over Pharaoh and Egypt could not be nullified, not by any government official or army, or even the demonic forces that ruled Egypt.

When Moses spoke it was as if God Himself was speaking. He was careful to speak only those things he was commanded by God to speak. If Moses had spoken destruction over Egypt, it would have been destroyed. God appointed Aaron his brother as the spokesman, or prophet, for Moses because of his speech impediment.

> **Whatever Moses spoke over Pharaoh and Egypt could not be nullified, not by any government official or army, or even the demonic forces that ruled Egypt.**

Whatever God told Moses to speak he spoke, and it was done as he said, executing God's will over Egypt: one man against the most powerful nation of that time. Do you see the power and the authority God has given to His church?

What Moses and others did in the natural we do in the spirit. We don't go to the presidents' and prime ministers' offices, unless the Lord says to do so. We do this in the spirit through prayer. When the church speaks, it is as if God Himself is speaking because we are His body.

Jeremiah Versus Nations and Kingdoms

How do we legislate kingdom purposes through prayer? If you want to see what the New Testament church is supposed to be doing in the spirit, you need to see what Jeremiah was called to do. He was appointed by God over nations and kingdoms to execute kingdom purposes. If he saw any nation or kingdom rising against the will and purpose of God, God gave him authority to root out, to pull down, to destroy, and to throw down, then to build and to plant.

Many of the Old Testament prophets' ministries were called to the nations. They prophesied the destinies and judgments over nations and things happened just as they prophesied. They spoke the destruction of many nations that no longer exist.

Jeremiah had an exceptional prayer ministry. He was called by God before he was born and was ordained a prophet to the nations. God raised Jeremiah up to determine the fate and destiny of many nations. Again, it was one man against several nations and their kings and armies.

> "Then the Lord put forth His hand and touched my mouth, and the Lord said to me: 'Behold, I have put My words in your mouth. See, I have this day set you over the nations and over the kingdoms, to root out and to pull down, to destroy and to throw down, to build and to plant' " (Jeremiah 1:9-10).

I can only imagine the thoughts going through Jeremiah's head. How on earth am I going to do all this? I feel like a child; how am I going to overthrow nations and kingdoms? I am not a king and I don't have an army. I am not trained to use any weapons. But, in the spirit, he was someone special. When he spoke the Word of the Lord, it was like cruise missiles that went and hit the nations and kingdoms and accomplished exactly what he spoke. Not even one word missed its target. Whatever he declared over a nation happened.

Jeremiah never physically pulled down any king from his throne. He did not wage physical war against any nation to destroy it. He did not root out any country in the physical sense. Jeremiah was engaged in spiritual warfare that dealt with spiritual and cultural influences that were ruling nations at that time.

If one man had such power and authority in the Old Testament over nations and kingdoms, how much more does the firstborn, the General Assembly, *the ekklesia*, have over nations and kingdoms now? God raised up Old Testament prophets to speak to the destinies of nations. May the Lord raise up such prophets now in the nations of the world who are not covetous or lucrative—men and women who will declare and decree His kingdom purposes.

The Bible is full of examples of how God spoke over nations and kingdoms through His people. Most were fulfilled as they had spoken, but there are still some prophecies yet to be fulfilled. God's purpose shall stand. His counsel will endure (Isaiah 46:10).

Jeremiah was a single person. He did not have an army, nor any natural weapons, but God put him over nations and kingdoms to root out, to pull down, to destroy, to throw down, and then to build and plant. There were six things he was supposed to do to nations and kingdoms. Imagine if God put you over the nations and kingdoms of today to do the same. What would you do?

Root Out

The first thing Jeremiah was supposed to do was "to root out." What was he supposed to root out? Everything the heavenly Father did not plant must be rooted out. Church, this is the word of the Lord for you today. Everything your heavenly Father did not plant, you need to root out of your life, community, and nation.

> **Everything your heavenly Father did not plant, you need to root out of your life, community, and nation.**

> "Jesus replied, "Every plant not planted by my heavenly Father will be uprooted" (Matthew 15:13 NLT).

Do you see anything in your life that was not planted by your heavenly Father, but by your culture or your natural parents instead? If it is hindering you from fulfilling your purpose, root it out. Do not even leave a trace of it. Many times we cut off the branches and deal with what we see on the surface, but until we dig it out from the root, it will keep growing back. Dig it all out and throw it into the fire of God. Then it will cease to have power over you and will no longer operate in your life.

As far as I know, we all have things in our lives that were not planted by God. They are the weeds that hinder us from receiving and walking in the fullness God has for us. They must go no matter how *holy* they look. As a church, we need to identify those areas in our community where the kingdom of darkness has set down roots, and root them out through our prayers. Anything in our life or nation that does not line up with the Word of God must be brought into alignment with the Word through prayer.

Pull Down

The second thing Jeremiah was called to do over nations and kingdoms was "to pull down." What do we need to pull down? We need to pull down strongholds that control people and their way of thinking. Do you know why you think and act the way you do? Strongholds are made of thoughts and imaginations and they form our way of thinking. A person in another country does not think and act the way you do. This is because of the strongholds that were formed in your mind by culture, upbringing, knowledge, and experience. Most often these strongholds work in opposition to the knowledge of God. They must be pulled down if we are to renew our mind with the Word of God and activate the mind of Christ.

> "For the weapons of our warfare *are* not carnal but mighty in God for *pulling down strongholds*, casting down arguments and every high thing that exalts itself against the knowledge of God, bringing every thought into captivity to the obedience of Christ" (2 Corinthians 10:4-5).

I believe Paul and his team practiced this before they went into a new territory to do ministry. Before the church can do this in a region, they have to prepare themselves by removing ungodly strongholds from their own minds. Do not go into the camp of the enemy when you have things in your life that belong to him. That wouldn't be a wise thing to do.

> **Do not go into the camp of the enemy when you have things in your life that belong to him.**

The church needs to pull down strongholds that control people's minds. That is one of the reasons it does not matter how much a person hears the Word or teaching. The reason they are not able to change is because of the strongholds *that control* their mind. For some people, it does not matter how many times you tell them something, they will look at you like they have not heard one thing you said. We need to identify those strongholds and pull them down in prayer.

Our prayers are like intercontinental ballistic missiles. Every manmade missile has a range it can reach, but the prayers we pray are not limited to a specific range. They can topple and bring to nothing the counsel of the ungodly on a different continent. All it takes is for you to believe that it will happen when you pray. That's it. If you believe it, then it will happen. If you don't believe it, then it does not matter how long or loud you pray, it will not bring any result.

The most powerful prayers I have ever prayed are those I prayed in a very normal voice or even those I whispered. Some think that unless they pray loudly or scream at the top of their lungs, it will not bring any result. That is not true. To tell you the truth, those prayers we scream may not bring any results at all because it is not our power or energy that brings the results, but the faith that is contained in the words we speak.

> **Prayers we scream may not bring any results at all because it is not our power or energy that brings the results, but the faith that is contained in the words we speak.**

I have found from experience that unless I am relaxed, the power of God cannot flow through me to the person or the situation I am praying for. The more relaxed I am, the more results I see; the more tense I am, the fewer the results. In order to relax I need to have my total trust in God and not in my own spirituality or how I feel at that moment.

There are times we may need to shout and declare if we are addressing something to change in the natural. If your prayer is horizontal then it's okay to shout and scream, but when you are asking God, let your voice be respectful because you are talking to our King. When Jesus came to resurrect Lazarus, we see this principle.

> "Then they took away the stone *from the place* where the dead man was lying. And Jesus lifted up *His* eyes and said, 'Father, I thank You that You have heard Me. And I know that You

always hear Me, but because of the people who are standing by I said *this,* that they may believe that You sent Me.' Now when He had said these things, He cried with a loud voice, 'Lazarus, come forth!' " (John 11:41-43).

When Jesus was talking to the Father, we don't see Him crying out. But when He was talking to dead Lazarus (the situation) we see that He cried out with a loud voice.

Destroy

The third thing Jeremiah was supposed to do was to "destroy." What do we need to destroy? Jesus came to destroy the works of the devil. Jesus has given us authority over serpents and scorpions and over all the power of the enemy (Luke 10:19).

> "He who sins is of the devil, for the devil has sinned from the beginning. For this purpose the Son of God was manifested, that He *might destroy the works of the devil"* (1 John 3:8).

I do not see any difficulty finding any "works of the devil" in our society. The church has authority in the spirit to destroy those works. Church! Wake up! Gird up your loins and take up the sword of the Spirit and fight. This is not the time to keep the sword in its sheath. Do not give any rest to your sword.

We see evil works all around us. If there is sickness in your family, abuse, drug problems in your community or school, or if the government is trying to pass a law that is against the moral standards of the Bible, then the church has the authority to destroy those plans before they come into effect.

Many times the church doesn't do anything about these things. They just talk between people about what is happening and never have a unified prayer to abort those plans of the enemy before they materialize. Oh, how I wish the church would wake up from her sleep and take her place and execute the will of God on this earth. Many lives could have been saved and spared from peril and destruction.

> **Whatever works you see of the enemy in your life, community, or nation, the church has the authority to destroy.**

God has not put any limit on His church. Jesus said whatever we bind on earth will be bound in heaven. That is an all-inclusive phrase. Whatever works you see of the enemy in your life, community, or nation, the church has the authority to destroy.

Throw Down

The fourth thing Jeremiah was called to do over nations and kingdoms was to "throw down." Everything that was not built on the foundation of God must be thrown down.

> "And Jesus said to them, 'Do you not see all these things? Assuredly, I say to you, not *one* stone shall be left here upon another, that shall not *be thrown down*' " (Matthew 24:2).

Jesus was talking about the temple in Jerusalem. To a Jew, the temple was the most spiritual place on earth, where God dwelt and where they came to meet Him. When they swore, they swore by the temple. How come Jesus did not protect the temple from being destroyed? Was not the temple the most holy place where the presence of God dwelt? In Jesus' time the temple became more important than God Himself. It became a center for political and religious corruption and abuse. They began to honor the temple more than the God who helped them build it so He could dwell in it. Jesus said it must be thrown down and not even one stone must remain upon another.

I was surprised by Jesus' statement! The disciples might have been shocked to hear that. That's a horrible thing to tell a Jew. Why did He not protect His own temple? He realized that the temple would become the biggest hindrance to what God was doing on the earth in that day. In Matthew 23 He had a lengthy discourse about the temple.

> "Woe to you, blind guides, who say, 'Whoever swears by the temple, it is nothing; but whoever swears by the gold of the temple, he is obliged *to perform it*.' Fools and blind! For which is greater, the gold or the temple that sanctifies the gold? And, 'Whoever swears by the altar, it is nothing; but whoever swears by the gift that is on it, he is obliged *to perform it*.' Fools and blind! For which is greater, the gift or the altar that sanctifies the gift? Therefore he who swears by the altar, swears

by it and by all things on it. He who swears by the temple, swears by it and by Him who dwells in it. And he who swears by heaven, swears by the throne of God and by Him who sits on it" (Matthew 23:16-22).

Many of us have traditions, rules, and altars we admire and hold more dear than God Himself. They may be religious rules, habits, rituals, or just traditions that were handed down to us by our forefathers, which have no spiritual value and do not have any positive effect on our relationship with God in any way. They must be thrown down. We need to seek Him to find out what He is doing *right now*. Do not worship a place, method, an object, or even a church building. They will all be thrown down. The church needs to throw down those sites and traditions people love more than they love God.

Building and Planting

After a church does the above four things, then they can move to the next stage: building and planting. In many cultures, the church has no effect on people and communities because they try to build without doing the above four steps. Before we build or plant anything, the ground needs to be prepared. Things that need to be rooted out must be rooted out; strongholds that need to be pulled down must be pulled down; evil works that need to be destroyed must be destroyed; and anything that stands in our way must be thrown down.

Then the church needs to partner with God in building up people and nations and plant the right things in the minds of the people.

I have heard many people say that God needs to raise up a Joseph or Daniel for our generation. When I said that to God, He said, "That's why I have the church on the earth today." He is not going to raise up individuals like Joseph or Daniel. The church is supposed to raise up the Josephs and Daniels for today.

Daniel Versus the Kingdoms of Babylon and Persia

Daniel is another example of a person God used to overthrow kingdoms of men and to establish the kingdom of God on the earth through his prayer life.

In the book of Daniel we also see what it means to establish God's kingdom on this earth and how to execute His will.

Many get confused when they hear the word *kingdom*. What comes to their mind is the picture of a natural kingdom with palaces, thrones, and armies of men. That is not what it means today when Jesus talks about His kingdom in the New Testament.

King Nebuchadnezzar had a dream. The dream troubled him so much that he gathered his magicians and demanded they tell him the dream and its interpretation. The magicians and soothsayers could neither bring up the dream nor could they tell its interpretation. The king ordered all the wise men to be killed and Daniel was among them. This dream might be one of the most important dreams mentioned in the Bible that pertains to the future of the world. Can you imagine God speaking to a heathen king about the future of the world through a dream?

Daniel and his friends joined their hearts and prayed, and God revealed the dream and its interpretation to Daniel in a night vision. This incident happened because God wanted to let King Nebuchadnezzar know that there is a God in heaven that reigns over the kingdoms of men and that He is the King of all Kings.

> "But there is a God in heaven who reveals secrets, and He has made known to King Nebuchadnezzar what will be in the latter days. Your dream, and the visions of your head upon your bed, were these" (Daniel 2:28).

The last part of the interpretation of this dream revealed the time we are in now.

> "And in the days of these kings the God of heaven will set up a *kingdom* which shall never be destroyed; and the *kingdom* shall not be left to other people; it shall break in pieces and consume all these *kingdoms*, and it shall stand forever" (Daniel 2:44).

We are living in the time where God's kingdom is already in operation on the earth through the church. We need to break in pieces the tactics of the kingdom of darkness and overthrow its agendas from taking place.

Elijah and Elisha are other examples of people God used to legislate His will over nations and people as they followed His instructions.

The Church

How did the church legislate kingdom authority in the New Testament? The church is the governing body of the kingdom of heaven on the earth. It has authority over every aspect of life in the natural and over the spiritual because Jesus, who is the Head of the church, has received all authority in heaven and on earth. We act on His behalf in whatever level He instructs and guides us to do. We see many examples of this in the New Testament. We see the church exercising its spiritual and legal jurisdiction on a personal level and on a national level.

Personal Level

When Jesus mentioned the church the second time in Matthew, He spoke of it involving the solution of a social problem between two people. He said to bring the matter before the *ekklesia*. Whatever the *ekklesia* decided was the final answer. The church is the highest court of God's kingdom on this earth. Jesus told the disciples that whoever's sins they forgive would be forgiven and whoever's sins they retained would be retained against them (John 20:23).

> **The church is the highest court of God's kingdom on this earth.**

In Acts 5 we read about Ananias and Sapphira who sold their possessions but kept back a portion and brought a certain part of it, and laid it at the apostles' feet, saying it was the whole amount. Peter knew by the Holy Spirit what they had done and revealed the scheme and rebuked Ananias for lying to the Holy Spirit. Immediately, Ananias fell down and died on the spot.

Young men rose and buried Ananias, and his wife did not even know about it. Three hours later when his wife came in, Peter asked her if they had sold the land for such a price. She said yes and he rebuked her for agreeing together to lie to the Holy Spirit. She fell down at the feet of Peter and breathed her last (Acts 5:1-10).

In his first letter to the Corinthian church, Paul instructed them to exercise kingdom legislation on a personal level. There was a believer who was involved in an immoral act and he was not willing to repent. Paul did not say, "Well, the grace of God will cover it, let him continue his lifestyle." No. He said that when they came together as a church, they should commit such a person to Satan for the destruction of his flesh, so that his spirit might be saved in the day of redemption. Wow! If the church commits a person to the hands of Satan, that means the church has spiritual jurisdiction over individuals (1 Corinthians 5:4-5).

In 1 Timothy 1:20, Paul says he delivered two other individuals (Hymenaeus and Alexander) to Satan that they may learn not to blaspheme. Paul had many spiritual encounters with people who were demon-possessed or who were in opposition to his work. One was a man named Bar-Jesus who bewitched people and kept them under the power of sorcery. Paul spoke over him that he would not see the sun for a while and he was immediately struck with blindness (Acts 13:6-11).

> If the church commits a person to the hands of Satan, that means the church has spiritual jurisdiction over individuals.

National Level

"Now about that time Herod the king stretched out *his* hand to harass some from the church. Then he killed James the brother of John with the sword. And because he saw that it pleased the Jews, he proceeded further to seize Peter also. Now it was *during* the Days of Unleavened Bread. So when he had arrested him, he put *him* in prison, and delivered *him* to four squads of soldiers to keep him, intending to bring him before the people after Passover. Peter was therefore kept in prison, but constant prayer was offered to God for him by the church" (Acts 12:1-5).

The above verses say King Herod began to mess with the General Assembly or *ekklesia* of God on this earth. He killed one of the apostles (ambassadors) and arrested Peter and put him in prison, surrounded by soldiers.

Picture this in your mind: Herod, a political king of a natural kingdom, arrested one of God's sons, an apostle, and put him in prison. He was bound with two chains and laying between two soldiers. I believe the ends of those two chains were either fastened to the wall or tied to the two soldiers in case

Peter tried to escape at night. Peter was a high-profile prisoner and the king intended to bring him out to the people after the Passover to execute him.

The Bible says the church offered constant prayer for Peter. In other words, the General Assembly (*ekklesia*) came together and began declaring the will of God for Peter, which was for him to be free from prison. The natural law said he was under arrest and the king had pronounced a death sentence over him. There was no way he was going to come out unless there was someone who had more authority than the king and intervened to overthrow the law of the land.

Naturally, there was no one to speak to the king for Peter, but in the spirit, Peter was an ambassador of the kingdom of God. When you touch an ambassador of a country, it becomes an international incident. The kingdom of God has power and authority over the kingdoms of men to nullify any law or legislate any law it chooses, but God cannot automatically intervene unless someone from the earth intercedes on behalf of that person and cancels the plan of the enemy.

While the *ekklesia* was exercising their God-given authority, Peter was sleeping inside the prison cell. One among the innumerable angels of the Lord was dispatched from heaven in response to the prayers of the church to execute what they declared. The angel came and tapped Peter. Peter himself did not believe what was going on. The chains that bound him fell off of his body. This was a high-level, supernatural prison break. Metals were cut into pieces without any noise and gates opened on their own as the guards slept. Peter was set free and the soldiers, who had been watching Peter, were put to death the next day.

The prayers of the General Assembly not only set Peter free, but something else powerful happened. I believe they prayed against King Herod too, maybe for him to be removed from power. And God was waiting for an opportunity. In the same chapter, we read that when Herod gave a speech the people shouted,

> If the *ekklesia* recognizes its authority and declares the will of God over that nation, it has to change.

saying his voice was the voice of a god and not a man. Immediately, an angel of the Lord struck him because he did not give glory to God. He was eaten by worms and was dead (Acts 12:20-23).

The church in a nation can change any policy or rule of the government or king. It's just a matter of time. If the *ekklesia* recognizes its authority and declares the will of God over that nation, it has to change. There is no question about it.

We know the story of Rome and what happened to it. It was one of the most anti-Christian empires that ever existed on the earth. But in a matter of years that empire was totally turned around by the prayers of the church. Another modern example is what is happening now in communist China. There is nothing impossible with God. He is only waiting for someone on earth to believe and declare His will.

Jesus said that if two of us agree on this earth and ask anything in His name, He will do it (Matthew 18:19). It takes a minimum of two people to sign and execute a deed: The person executing the deed and another as a witness.

We have turned this glorious church into little clubs of social gatherings, which have no spiritual jurisdiction or power of any kind over anything. We have "feel good" meetings where people are entertained to feel better about themselves with a little motivational speech, and then continue to live the same way they were before they came in. Lord, have mercy!

> We have turned this glorious church into little clubs of social gatherings, which have no spiritual jurisdiction or power of any kind over anything.

Paul and Silas Versus the City of Philippi

During one of Paul's missionary journeys he had a vision in the night of a man from Macedonia standing and pleading with him, saying, "Come over to Macedonia and help us" (Acts 16:9). Immediately they went there and reached an influential city called Philippi.

There they met a girl who had the spirit of divination that brought much gain to her masters. Paul cast the demon out of her and the whole city turned against Paul and Silas. They were brought before the magistrates, beaten, and thrown in prison; the jailor was commanded to keep them securely. Having received such a charge, the jailor put them in the inner prison and fastened their feet in the stocks.

KINGDOM LEGISLATION

At midnight, Paul and Silas were praying and praising God. Suddenly, God sent an earthquake that shook the foundation of the prison. All the doors of the prison were opened and everyone's chains were loosed. The jailor was afraid and was about to kill himself, but Paul intervened and stopped him. He and his household were born again and baptized that same night.

In the morning, the magistrates sent word to let them go, but Paul—being a Roman citizen—hesitated and asked the magistrates to come and get them out. They had been beaten openly and put in prison. It was illegal to take these actions against a Roman citizen. When the magistrates realized they were Roman citizens, the magistrates were afraid and came and pleaded with Paul and Silas and released them. Again, the kingdom of God rules over the kingdoms of men.

The Bible is full of examples of how God overthrew kingdoms and changed the laws of the land as a result of the prayers of His people. Whenever you come across an incident or an event where God intervened on behalf of His people, it was His kingdom versus the kingdom of darkness that was ruling the kingdoms of men, and the kingdom of God will always prevail.

Chapter 12: Why Is the Church Unable to Use the Authority God Gave Us? – Part 1

Chapter 12: Why Is the Church Unable to Use the Authority God Gave Us? – Part 1

"And Jesus came and spoke to them, saying, 'All authority has been given to Me in heaven and on earth' " (Matthew 28:18).

Lack of Unity

The main reason there is no real spiritual power manifesting in our midst is because there is no real unity. We are trained and programmed to be individualistic and self-centered, especially in Western cultures where kids are programmed to have everything their own way from the time they are born. They don't have to share much, even with their siblings. And we wonder why they become so selfish when they are grown!

> We are trained and programmed to be individualistic and self-centered, especially in Western cultures where kids are programmed to have everything their own way from the time they are born.

When I was growing up, we had one bicycle for three of us. I shared a room with my brother until I was eighteen years old. I thought it was natural to share until I reached the United States where everything is individualistic. But we see in the Bible that from the birth of the church, its unity was the foremost component behind every spiritual breakthrough. On the day of Pentecost, it says they were all in one place in one accord.

In the early church everything was considered "in common" and everyone shared what they had with others according to their need. Imagine that happening in today's church! If a pastor suggested such a thing, the congregation would view him suspiciously and probably throw him out!

In family life, it's not any different: we have two individuals living together, but not "married" in anything. Everything is separate and individualistic: yours and mine—not ours.

How is God to work through such a situation? Keep in mind it takes a minimum of two people to come into agreement to accomplish something as a church. If there is one thing needed in the church today it is unity. Whenever we need to execute kingdom legislation it takes at least two people to execute it.

> "Again I say to you that if two of you agree on earth concerning anything that they ask, it will be done for them by My Father in heaven. For where two or three are gathered together in My name, I am there in the midst of them" (Matthew 18:19-20).

These are kingdom statements. If two people come into agreement and ask anything in prayer, God will answer that prayer. Paul might have addressed the issue of unity in the church more than any other subject in his epistles.

> "Now I plead with you, brethren, by the name of our Lord Jesus Christ, that you all speak the same thing, and *that* there be no divisions among you, but *that* you be perfectly joined together in the same mind and in the same judgment. For it has been declared to me concerning you, my brethren, by those of Chloe's *household,* that there are contentions among you" (1 Corinthians 1:10-11).

These verses make it very clear how Paul emphasized the issue of unity. Without unity, the prayers we pray will not get answered, whether it is in a church or in a family. But we don't see unity among churches, or even within churches. That is one of the reasons we do not see many of the mighty acts of God in our midst and nations. One local church tries to outsmart the other or asks God to do something special through them so they can feel special. God will not allow that.

> **The devil is well aware that if there is unity in a church or a family, he is powerless against them, so he will do anything he can to cause dissention.**

The devil is well aware that if there is unity in a church or a family, he is powerless against them, so he will do anything he can to cause dissention.

When the Word of God is being preached from the pulpit, the enemy is busy in the congregation throwing contradictory thoughts into people's minds, so that what is being preached won't take root and will have no effect in people's lives. This issue must be addressed in prayer before the Word is preached.

Ignorance of Our Authority and Power

Many believers are ignorant about the authority and power God gave us. Others are walking around as if they do not belong on the earth. They are too spiritual for their own good and miss their purpose altogether. I pray that this book will wake them up from their sleep so they will begin to exercise their God-given rights and use the resources He put on the earth for the good of humanity.

That is why the Bible says, "My people are destroyed for lack of knowledge. Because you have rejected knowledge, I also will reject you from being priest for Me; because you have forgotten the law of your God, I also will forget your children" (Hosea 4:6).

There are many reasons for a nation to remain poor: lack of people with the right vision, lack of understanding about the natural resources God has put in that nation, lack of technology to extract and put those resources to work, and so on.

The Church Is Married to the World

Something has happened to the gospel message in the past fifty years. People began to use it for personal gain. They began to focus on how much wealth and success they could gain using the gospel and the promises of God. Imagine the apostles doing something like that in their day!

Our prosperity theology has created a monster, and now we have no idea what to do with it. Did Peter and Paul offer the people a faster (hybrid) donkey and a bigger fishing boat if only they would believe and put their trust in Jesus or give an offering? Or did Peter and Paul give themselves to Jesus, not even loving their own lives, being willing to die for Him instead? Something has gone drastically wrong in the messages we have been preaching. Our focus has changed from Jesus and His kingdom-centered gospel to the human-centered gospel. Lord, have mercy!

221

Another reason we are not able to exercise the power and authority God has given us is because we (the church) are married to the world. It is a command in the Bible to not love this world or the things in it.

> "Do not love the world or the things in the world. If anyone loves
> the world, the love of the Father is not in him" (1 John 2:15).

Why would God command us not to love this world or the things in it? What is the danger behind this? And how many of us do love the things of this world? We not only love this world and the things in it, but we are married to it and try to use God to get more stuff out of the world. That is the ultimate goal of many Christians today. All their spirituality is geared toward having more of this world. Where does it say that in the Bible?

There is a difference between the earth and the world. The earth is the physical planet and the world is the system by which the earth and everything on it functions. In technical terms, earth is the hardware, and the world is the software by which it operates. The world and the kingdom of God are two different operating systems, and both operate by principles that are opposite to each other. They are like water and oil; no matter how much we try, they will not mix.

Many of us do not understand the different implications of the word *world* in the Bible. It could denote the planet Earth, the human race, the age we are living in, or the age to come. Below are two examples.

> "For *God so loved the world* that He gave His only begotten
> Son, that whoever believes in Him should not perish but have
> everlasting life" (John 3:16).

When it says God so loved the world, it is talking about the human race. In 1 John 2:15 though, He is talking about the world system and the things of this earth through which the kingdom of darkness operates on the earth. How did the world system that we live in today with all its glitter and glamour come into existence and who is its god?

Everyone who is not born again is part of the kingdom of darkness, or the world, and Satan rules over them. The Bible calls him the god of this world.

> "In whom *the god of this world* hath blinded the minds of
> them which believe not, lest the light of the glorious gospel of

Christ, who is the image of God, should shine unto them" (2 Corinthians 4:4 KJV).

"We know that we are children of God and that the world around us is under the control of the evil one" (1 John 5:19 NLT).

"So don't be surprised, dear brothers and sisters, if the world hates you" (1 John 3:13 NLT).

"Of judgment, because *the ruler of this world* is judged" (John 16:11).

He is also known as the prince of the power of the air. We read in Ephesians 2:2, "In which you once walked according to the course of this world, according to the *prince of the power of the air,* the *spirit* who now works in the sons of disobedience."

He is also known as the prince of this world.

"Now is the judgment of this world: now shall the prince of this world be cast out" (John 12:31 KJV).

Jesus called him the prince of this world.

"Hereafter I will not talk much with you: for the prince of this world cometh, and hath nothing in me" (John 14:30 KJV).

"Rulers of the darkness of this *world*" (Ephesians 6:12 KJV).

Through the media we can see what the devil as the god of this world is doing. Unfortunately, even Christians allow this to freely flow into their homes. Through the media they fill themselves with junk and then come to church on Sunday and fall asleep when the Word is being preached. They try to live for God while their minds are filled with the trash of this world. It will never happen.

> A person is only as good as his mind, just like a computer is only as good as its processor and software.

A person is only as good as his mind, just like a computer is only as good as its processor and software. Some Christians know more about what is going on in this world than what is in the Bible. Others know more about their football team and players than the names of the books and characters in the Bible.

The average American watches twenty hours of TV per week. Do you know how much time the average American spends reading the Bible or praying in a week? Fifteen minutes at the most. Do you know how much time a pastor in America spends with the Lord in a week? Twenty-five minutes. Many preach ready-made sermons they buy from other ministries or resources. You try to send these Christians to win the world for Christ and they will get whipped by the enemy and come back home crying like a puppy. God, have mercy on us!

This World Has a Spirit That Is Not of God

> "Now we have received, not the *spirit of the world*, but the Spirit who is from God, that we might know the things that have been freely given to us by God" (1 Corinthians 2:12).

How does the spirit of this world operate? Its purpose is to influence you to love the things of this world more than God and His kingdom. Just evaluate your passions: what does your heart beat for? If you are more passionate for the things of this world than the kingdom of God, then you are ruled by the spirit of this world. If you feel your life is attached to something in this world and you cannot live without that thing, you are under the influence of this spirit, rather than being led of God.

> **If you are more passionate for the things of this world than the kingdom of God, then you are ruled by the spirit of this world.**

The spirit of this world works so subtly that most people are not aware they live for it. Most Christians believe that if they go to church on Sunday morning, they are doing God a favor. They believe they are good Christians and living for God. Many speak in tongues without having any fruit of the Spirit evident in their life.

Many churches have turned into nothing but entertainment centers. People are so used to being entertained in the world and by the world that they expect the church to do the same for them. They do not come to church to worship God or to be trained. They come to show themselves off and watch a production that is put together by the elegant choir and media. Sunday schools are nothing more than playgrounds. Children go there to play video games and run around. They are not trained in the Word or in character.

They have been taught that the one who can jump the highest will get the candy or the one who runs the fastest will win the trophy. Everything is based on talent; almost nothing is based on character. Where did that come from? It came from the entertainment system of the world. That is what they teach in the world. The one who runs the fastest or shoots the ball the best is the greatest. They do not care if he is a homosexual or slept with twenty women, or about any foul in his personal character.

How did the devil become the god of this world? When and how did the current world system that we know begin? How does the devil use the world to blind the minds of men from knowing the only true God? We are going to look into the Bible to see how the devil, with the help of man, created a counterfeit kingdom known as the world system.

It has been God's plan from the beginning that man would dwell in His kingdom on earth. When God created Adam He put him in the garden of Eden, which was a visible form of the kingdom of God operating on this earth. Man had everything he needed in the garden and never lacked anything. He never became sick or poor. It was a place of plenty, peace, and joy.

God's presence was indwelling the garden. He came down to commune with man every evening. We are created to live in communion with God. Only God can fill the void in our soul. Man disobeyed God's command and sinned. As the result of disobedience and sin, man was removed from this kingdom and began to live on his own.

The Counterfeit Kingdom

The enemy used that opportunity, and with man's cooperation he began a counterfeit form of the kingdom of God on earth, which is called the world system or the kingdom of darkness. That is why Satan is known as the god of this world. The Bible uses the word *world* as a synonym for the kingdom of darkness. Know that the enemy always makes a counterfeit of what God has created.

Satan's desire is to be like God; he wants to be worshiped and he wants to be a king like God Almighty. It is unfortunate for him that he cannot create at all. He cannot create anything new. He can only distort and copy what God has already made. He did not want us to live in the garden, enjoying the blessings and the presence of God. He wanted to deceive us into living in a counterfeit kingdom instead.

The initial thing the devil did was to deceive and defeat us, and steal the stewardship of the earth from us. He came to Eve in the form of a serpent and deceived her and influenced her to disobey God. Man fell into the trap and was deprived of everything that God had given him.

> The initial thing the devil did was to deceive and defeat us, and steal the stewardship of the earth from us.

Suddenly man was left alone outside the garden with no food, no shelter, no peace, and no one to fellowship with. Instead of asking God to help him, man continued to walk on his own. The enemy used that as an opportunity to establish a counterfeit kingdom. He offered a pseudo power, wealth, luxury and the glory that man had in the garden. Through man he slowly began to introduce his kingdom on the earth. He learned from God how His kingdom worked and copied it—the only difference was that it was not real; it was only a substitute of what God originally had for man. Many took it as an opportunity and joined the devil in accomplishing his will instead of God's.

The devil and the evil spirits had access to this earth and the animal kingdom before Adam disobeyed, but they had no right to do anything on the earth without man's permission. The devil was waiting for an opportunity to snatch the earth out of the hands of man, because it was to Adam God had given dominion over the earth. Man fell into temptation and the devil received the right to establish his kingdom on the earth. But how did he establish his kingdom?

After Adam and Eve were sent out of the garden (the kingdom of God), they had two sons, Cain and Abel. During the course of time, Cain and Abel brought offerings to God. God was pleased with Abel's offering and rejected Cain's. In anger, Cain killed Abel. Being angry is not sin. It's what you do in your anger that is important to God. Cain was the first murderer and the Bible says he was from the evil one (1 John 3:12). This means the devil took hold of Cain's fallen nature and began to use him to accomplish his purpose on the earth. The Lord cursed Cain and he ran away from the presence of the Lord.

The Bible says in Genesis 4:16, "Then Cain went out from the presence of the Lord and dwelt in the land of Nod on the east of Eden." The devil began to unfold his age-old plan through Cain and his descendants. Please know that Lucifer was in the garden of God in the East before he fell. "You were in Eden, the garden of God" (Ezekiel 28:13).

Cain went to live in a land called Nod after the fall, which is east of Eden. Why did he choose the East and not any other direction? I believe there is a spiritual connection. If you study any heathen worship or even some so-called churches, when they worship they always look toward the east: Hindus, Muslims, and some Eastern churches all look toward the east while they do their rituals. In India, the Hindus worship toward the east. They are worshiping the sun god and facing east because the sun rises in the east.

Cain found a wife (probably one of his sisters) and began to multiply. They began to expand and explore to create a city to live in and leave a mark on history. In Genesis 4 we read the genealogy of Cain and his children and we see how they began to develop different skills and technologies.

> "And Adah bore Jabal. He was the *father* of those who dwell in tents and have livestock. His brother's name was Jubal. He was the *father* of all those who play the harp and flute. And as for Zillah, she also bore Tubal-Cain, an *instructor* of every craftsman in bronze and iron. And the sister of Tubal-Cain was Naamah" (Genesis 4:20-22).

Jabal, Jubal and Tubal-Cain were descendants of Cain. They began to excel in technology, arts, agriculture, and music. That was the first known *world* or the *kingdom of darkness*. Meanwhile, the children of God were waiting for the seed of the woman to be born to rescue them from the clutches of sin and the enemy. This is true even today. While the people of this world excel in their work, believers have been waiting for the rapture or revival for more than two thousand years.

> While the people of this world excel in their work, believers have been waiting for the rapture or revival for more than two thousand years.

This is where it all began. The devil took the opportunity and went with it while Seth and his descendants waited around for God to show up. Music and technology do not come from the devil. God created music, but the devil—who likes to be worshiped as god—stole what God created. As the church, we need to take back what was stolen from us, heal that which was made crooked, and build back that which was demolished.

In Genesis 5, we read the genealogy of Adam and Seth, but we do not read about anyone doing anything innovative. They ate and slept and gave birth to children. They were only fruitful in their body. That is all that is mentioned there. For hundreds and hundreds of years that is what they did. Does that sound familiar to you? They were waiting and hoping for the Lord to do something for them. There is nothing wrong with waiting and hoping for the Lord to do something. There is a time to do that. Remember, God created man to work and to have dominion.

The Church Has Always Been Depending On the World

Seth and his children began to depend on Cain and his children for agriculture, shelter, music, and technology. That means that if they wanted any food, tents, entertainment, or tools they had to go to the *world* to get it. It is the same today; believers wait around for God to do things and watch their favorite TV program or run to a ball game after church. They are going to see the children of the devil (most of them) making millions of dollars; they clap, jump, and shout for them. They sit in their easy chairs and sip drinks while the children of the devil excel in their works. They remain poor, broke, or barely surviving. When they come to church, they have no voice to praise their God. This needs to change.

Men began to multiply on earth and their wickedness increased. God found only one man righteous out of all the people who were alive. The devil and his kingdom were flourishing. They built cities and towns and named them after themselves and their children. It grieved God and He decided to destroy the world and its inhabitants with a flood. The flood came and only Noah and his family were rescued. The Bible says that only Noah found grace in the sight of the Lord, not his whole family or three sons. The flood destroyed the people and living creatures, but as you and I know, a flood cannot kill demonic forces.

The demonic forces did not give up. They were just waiting for an opportunity to repeat what they had previously done, to rebuild their kingdom. Right after the flood, Noah planted a vineyard and drank of the wine and was drunk. He lost his senses and became uncovered in his tent. The devil influenced Noah's son, Ham, and he went in and saw the nakedness of his father and told his brothers outside (Genesis 9:20-23).

When Noah woke up from his drunkenness and realized what Ham had done to him, he cursed him. Cain was cursed and it gave the devil an open door to work through him and his descendants. After the flood, the first person who was cursed was Ham and the devil began to work through him to create a world system without God. The kingdom of darkness again began to operate on this earth.

> After the flood, the first person who was cursed was Ham and the devil began to work through him to create a world system without God.

Again, we see the same pattern we saw before the flood. The sons of Ham began to multiply and expand on this earth in technology and in other areas. The Bible says in Genesis 10:6-12,

> "The sons of Ham were Cush, Mizraim, Put, and Canaan. The sons of Cush were Seba, Havilah, Sabtah, Raamah, and Sabtechah; and the sons of Raamah were Sheba and Dedan. Cush begot Nimrod; he began to be a mighty one on the earth. *He was a mighty hunter before the Lord; therefore it is said, 'Like Nimrod the mighty hunter before the Lord.' And the beginning of his kingdom was Babel,* Erech, Accad, and Calneh, in the land of Shinar. From that land he went to Assyria and built Nineveh, Rehoboth Ir, Calah, and Resen between Nineveh and Calah (that is the principal city)."

The False Church

One of Ham's grandsons was called Nimrod and he built Babel or Babylon, the first kingdom. Babylon is a counterfeit kingdom or system that has been operating here ever since. Just like God has His church, His governing body on earth, the devil has his false church, called Babylon. The church is described as a bride and Babylon is described as a prostitute, also a woman.

We read in the book of Revelation about Mystery Babylon, the great mother of harlots and abomination of the earth. God will judge the Babylonian system of this world and will destroy it (Revelation 17-18) because the devil has been deceiving people using its wealth and glamor for a long time.

All the Gentile nations and kingdoms came out of Ham and Japheth. Where did they come from? They came from the *east*. Do you see the same pattern here? God came down and confused the people and their language and dispersed them throughout the earth. What we see again in the history of the world is the repetition of what happened before the flood.

We do not see Shem's descendants doing much on this earth except eating and begetting children. They did not obey the command of the Lord to be fruitful, multiply, subdue the earth, and take dominion. They only obeyed the first part of the command (Genesis 11:10-32).

Similarly, the church today depends on the world for technology, methods, expertise, and almost everything else. That is not what God intended. He wants His children in leadership positions. We borrow from the world; we use their technologies, methods, money, and tactics and bring them to a church to apply them and help the church "grow." There are church growth experts available. If you hire them, they will come and train the pastor and leaders. They say that if you follow their techniques for a certain length of time, they can guarantee a certain increase in numbers in the church. Would you call that a New Testament church or a man-run business?

> Man is mesmerized by this world and what it has to offer and has misunderstood it as the kingdom of God for too long.

That is the origin of the world system on this earth. Unfortunately, man is mesmerized by this world and what it has to offer and has misunderstood it as the kingdom of God for too long.

The current world system is made up of seven ingredients. They are the seven gates of hades that Jesus referred to in Matthew 16, through which the kingdom of darkness has been operating on the earth until today. They are: 1) Culture 2) Religion 3) Government 4) Economy, 5) Education System 6) Media & Entertainment 7) Science & Technology.

Culture

Social and Moral Values
Race
Manners
Customs

Traditions
Language
Superstitions

Most people take pride in their culture, language, or race and think it is better than any other. Instead of realizing our true identity, value, and worth as a child of God, the devil—through various cultures—offers false identity, fear, and pride, causing people to fight against each other. When you receive Jesus you become part of His kingdom, which has its own culture. Unfortunately, many do not *crucify* their culture when they come into God's kingdom and remain in the old. Racism and the caste system are alive and well today. The kingdom culture is to love one another, and to be a blessing to each other.

The devil brought customs and manners to keep people divided and under the bondage of false identity and superstitions. Every culture is supposed to be a support system in fulfilling our God-given purpose. But now most cultures work against anything that is of God. As His children we need to reestablish kingdom culture and values into our society.

Religion

Origin of the World and Purpose of Creation
Faith in God(s)
Rituals (What to Do to Keep That God Happy)
Types of Worship
Conduct toward Fellow Humans and Nature
Life after Death
Beliefs about the Spirit World

Instead of having a relationship with God, Satan introduced religion and substituted it in place of God. Instead of worshiping the true God, he introduced false gods and goddesses. Religious people seldom seek for a relationship with God; they adhere more to rituals than relationship. Do not be satisfied with rituals and mantras when so much more is available. Every religion has a trace of truth in it, but not the whole truth. The Bible calls religious people the seed of the serpent (Genesis 3:15, Matthew 3:7; 23:33;

> **Every religion has a trace of truth in it, but not the whole truth.**

John 8:44). There are more people killed on this earth today because of religion than any other cause.

Government

> State and Federal
> International Political Organizations
> Kings, Presidents, Prime Ministers
> Legislative and Judiciary
> Military

Instead of being ruled by God as our king in a theocracy, the devil brought about systems of various types of governments and political systems. They are called the rulers of darkness (Ephesians 6:12). It was God's desire to be our king and be the king of the earth. Throughout the history of the world there have been many tyrants and kings who oppressed their people and killed millions of them for power. The devil uses governments more than anything else to execute his will on earth over people. That is why when the Israelites asked for a king like other heathen nations, it displeased the Lord. He knew what the fruit would be. As the governing body of God's kingdom, we need to have influence on the governments of this earth. More on this later.

> **The devil uses governments more than anything else to execute his will on earth over people.**

Economy

> Money
> Business
> Banks
> Precious Stones and Metals
> Real Estate
> Agriculture

Instead of living in His kingdom and enjoying God's blessings, the enemy came up with a system called money. Today, everything is based on how much money a person has. People are divided on the basis of how much money they make. They will kill and steal or do anything to have more money. The devil uses money to control people more than any other thing. Money has a vice

232

grip on our lives and how we live. Jesus said there are only two masters on this earth: money and God. That is why He said we cannot serve both God and mammon (Luke 16:13). We will serve one and hate the other. Remember the story of the rich young ruler. Most people's motive is to make more money. Because of this, they serve money as their master. Either you will master money or money will be your master. Once you seek and discover the kingdom, your provision is attached to your purpose.

> **Either you will master money or money will be your master.**

Education System

> Schools
> Colleges of Different Kinds
> Universities

Instead of learning about God, His character, His kingdom, and each one's purpose, the devil introduced an education system which does not honor God. God originally intended the education system to train people to live in His kingdom and to learn His ways and their individual purpose. Man was created to operate in revelation knowledge, and you can live in the kingdom of God only by revelation knowledge, not by intellectual knowledge. The knowledge of good and evil came because of sin.

The education system we have today has nothing to do with God or leaning on His ways, but mostly glorifies Satan and the ways of man. Once you are born again you can begin to receive revelation knowledge. All the treasures of wisdom and knowledge are hid in Christ (Colossians 2:3). The church needs to redeem the education system from the hands of the enemy and establish excellent schools and universities that teach the ways of God and train men and women to discover their God-given purpose.

Media & Entertainment

Media	**Entertainment**
TV/Internet	Movies
Telephone	Music
Print	Arts and Sports

THE POWER AND AUTHORITY OF THE CHURCH

We have lost the joy of the Lord and the joy of our salvation, and the devil has used this as an opportunity to introduce things from his kingdom as substitutes to make and keep people happy. Instead of enjoying God, His love, joy, and fellowship, the devil introduced entertainment to bring false joy and happiness to people. The movies and sports we enjoy today are all part of it. In truth, there is nothing better than being with God and enjoying His presence and fellowship. There is unspeakable joy in His presence. Today, we lack true joy so we try to substitute it with fleshly entertainment. The most familiar word of our culture is *fun*. If something is not fun, then people don't want to do it. Because we lost that joy-filled fellowship with God, we need something of this world to fill that place.

> **Instead of enjoying God, His love, joy, and fellowship, the devil introduced entertainment to bring false joy and happiness to people.**

God came down to the garden every evening to fellowship with man. They walked and talked and enjoyed each other. Adam did not need any other form of entertainment to keep him happy. Today, people come home each evening and go straight to their entertainment centers or other devices. They watch TV and see what the devil is doing.

Everything the devil made has to do with meeting the carnal needs of our flesh. The fall flipped the order of our nature that God created. To God we are first a spirit being; then He gave us a soul and body to operate on the earth. Most humans now operate the other way around, which is body first, then soul, and very few even recognize that they have a spirit. The devil devised a system to satisfy our body first; everything in this world is focused on making our body happy or making us feel better. But the flesh is never satisfied.

The pleasures this world has to offer will never meet the real need for joy and peace that only come from knowing God. That is why some of the most successful entertainers are some of the most miserable people on earth. Many are on drugs or addicted to sex or alcohol, and some even commit suicide at an early age. The more successful they get, the further removed they become from real life. Do not follow the lifestyle of those who are entertaining you. They are entertaining your senses at the expense of their own lives.

The Bible says the joy of the Lord is our strength. We need to regain our true joy that comes from our relationship with God. There is fullness of joy in His presence and pleasures forevermore (Psalm 16:11). When you discover God's kingdom you will discover righteousness, peace, and joy in the Holy Spirit. When our mind is corrupted or if our will is taken captive by the devil through the things of this world, we will not be able to receive anything from God. We can call ourselves Christians but there will be nothing to prove it other than the *Christianese* we speak. A little leaven leavens the whole lump (Galatians 5:9).

Science & Technology

> Natural Science
> Applied Science

To blind people about the existence of God and a Creator, the devil introduced a system called science. You will never hear science or scientists try to prove that there was no Krishna, Buddha, or Mohammed. They only try to disprove God and anything that Jesus did or said as the Creator of the universe. The devil is using that as his tool. Evolution is a good example.

You may ask, "Is there any truth in science?" Of course, there is. There is some trace of truth in every religion on earth too. There is always a bit, but it is not the whole truth. Most religions teach about helping the poor. That does not mean they are doing it based on God's love.

What is destroying the current generation is media, entertainment, and technology. The time they are supposed to be spending developing their talents and abilities is spent in front of a screen playing games or chatting with their friends. Unless we make a deliberate choice and change the way we raise children I don't see the current generation making any difference for God in the future.

These are seven arteries through which the devil operates his kingdom and deceives the whole world. Some call it the world system. The book of Revelation calls it the seven mountains on which the "mystery, Babylon the great, the mother of all harlots and the abominations of the earth" sits (Revelation 17:5).

> "So the great dragon was cast out, that serpent of old, called
> the devil and Satan, who deceives the whole world; he was

235

cast to the earth, and his angels were cast out with him"
(Revelation 12:9).

Believe it or not, the whole world is deceived by the devil. There is a strong possibility every believer is deceived in at least one area of their life. The problem with deception is that when we are deceived we won't know we are deceived. Satan is a liar and the father of all lies. He influences the people of this world through one of those seven segments to believe in his lies. Most do not recognize the power that operates behind the lies or their source because he disguises himself. He appears to be harmless and hides from the light so that no one notices him other than those who are living in the light and revelation of God. As someone said, when the devil comes to us, he comes with everything we ever wished, not with horns and hooves.

Chapter 13: Why Is the Church Unable to Use the Authority God Gave Us? – Part 2

Chapter 13: Why Is the Church Unable to Use the Authority God Gave Us? – Part 2

"Wisdom is better than weapons of war" (Ecclesiastes 9:18a).

Blinded and Deceived

We need to discern what is of God and what is of the devil. As the old saying goes, "All that glitters is not gold." It is very easy to fall prey to the temptations of the enemy.

If you take any unbeliever from anywhere in the world today, you can be sure that the god of this world is using one of the seven components by which this world is made to blind his or her mind from believing the glorious gospel of Christ. He uses either culture, religion, government, money, education, entertainment, or science to blind people's minds. There are also spirits that are specifically assigned to control each of those components or gates.

Similarly, if you take nations and even continents, you will find the devil uses one of those world systems to blind the people in that country or region. For example, in the East, he uses religion as the predominant means to blind the people so they will not believe in Jesus. In the West, he uses money and entertainment. The same devil works over both hemispheres, but he uses different tactics or packages based on the culture and region and the mindsets that have been formed.

Then he deceives people to believe that what one has is better than the other. For example, people in the West look at the religions in the East and can't imagine how they worship those idols. In the same way, people in the East look at the West and can't imagine how they spend so much money on junk and having fun. The same enemy works behind both but through different deliberate means. Please read the following verse carefully.

"In whom the *god of this world* hath blinded the minds of them which believe not, lest the light of the glorious gospel of Christ, who is the image of God, should shine unto them" (2 Corinthians 4:4 KJV).

Sadly, many in the church have also been deceived by the spirit of this world. They think they love Jesus, but they have little in their lives to reflect that. If they do a real evaluation they will find that they have been serving this spirit and not Jesus, and that they have been living for themselves all along. They are worshiping themselves as gods. They will follow God as long as it makes them happy, but the minute their flesh gets uncomfortable they will abandon their faith.

> They will follow God as long as it makes them happy, but the minute their flesh gets uncomfortable they will abandon their faith.

Paul said, "But I fear, lest somehow, as the serpent deceived Eve by his craftiness, so your minds may be corrupted from the simplicity that is in Christ. For if he who comes preaches another Jesus whom we have not preached, or if you receive a different spirit which you have not received, or a different gospel which you have not accepted—you may well put up with it!" (2 Corinthians 11: 3-4).

Wow! That means there are different types of Jesus being preached today; there are other spirits than the Holy Spirit and there are other gospels than the gospel of the kingdom. The Jesus that is being preached today is Jesus, the sugar daddy. He doesn't require anything and doesn't require us to change. He just gives out blessings all day long. The gospel most people preach these days is the gospel of self-gratification. We need to renounce it. People follow Jesus to the extent their flesh is happy. The moment their flesh is not happy, they will draw back from their commitments and covenants because of selfishness and pride.

We need to *renounce* the spirit and the god of this world from being our lord before we can *reach* the world with the real gospel of the kingdom. Many believers are deceived by the spirit of this world, thinking it is the Holy Spirit. What is the difference? The spirit of this world will influence you to love the things of this world and live for them. The Holy Spirit will influence you to love God and other people more than anything else.

God chooses people from the world, brings them into His kingdom, and trains them to go back into the world to influence it. You cannot be in the mud and help someone get out of the pit.

> "If you were of the world, the world would love its own. Yet because you are not of the world, but I chose you out of the world, therefore the world hates you" (John 15:19).

> "As You sent Me into the world, I also have sent them into the world" (John 17:18).

Now you know what this world is all about and how it was made and who is behind everything that happens. Knowing this, how can the church reach the world? You cannot remain married to the world and change it at the same time. I do not believe the church needs to act and look like the world to reach the world. All it takes for the church to win the world is for the church to act like the *church*. This present world system has been operating on earth since Adam. The first century Christians did not win the world by acting and looking like the world. They turned the world upside down!

So how do we live on the earth without being a part of the world system? There is an answer for that in the Bible too. As long as we live here we need to use the world, but we must make sure our trust and dependency is not in the world and its system, but in God alone.

> **As long as we live here we need to use the world, but we must make sure our trust and dependency is not in the world and its system, but in God alone.**

> "And those who use this world as not misusing *it*. For the form of this world is passing away" (1 Corinthians 7:31).

The best example is the fish that lives in the ocean. A fish may live in the ocean for years and use its salt water for its survival, but the water's saltiness will not get inside the fish. When you cook a fish from the ocean, you still need to add salt. Though we live in this world and use the things of this world for our survival, we should not live for the things of this world and become contaminated by them. Our motivation and goal for living should not be to have more of this world.

All That Is in This World Is Not of God

> "For *all that is in the world*—the lust of the flesh, the lust of the eyes, and the pride of life—is not of the Father but is of the world" (1 John 2:16).

Everything in this world caters to satisfying those three things: the lust of the flesh, the lust of the eyes, and the pride of life. Just like the flesh is an enemy of the spirit, the world is an enemy of the church because the world is the kingdom of darkness. Those who want to be a friend of the world become an enemy of God.

> "Adulterers and adulteresses! Do you not know that *friendship with the world* is enmity with God? Whoever therefore wants to be *a friend* of the world makes himself an enemy of God" (James 4:4).

We do not hear very many messages on these verses today because if they are preached, people will get offended and not come back the next Sunday. This is because they are living for the things of this world and are more passionate about them than they are for Jesus. If you do not believe me, call for prayer and fasting in your church and see how many show up. We are married to this world. As long as we are married to this world we cannot change or influence it. We can only flow along with it and watch what they do.

The church has adopted the same lifestyle, music, entertainment, and other worldly ways of doing things and lost its own peculiar essence. In many places there is no difference between people who go to church and unbelievers. Both groups have the same problems, struggle with the same issues, use the same language, and have the same or a higher rate of divorce. What are we trying to do as the church? Anytime you water down the message of the gospel or the songs we sing for worship to please the crowd, you miss God entirely.

They brought the music of the world into the church to attract the world to the church. What happened? We almost lost all worship or praise songs. Most of the songs we sing do not mention Jesus or God. Most of them sound like Indian Bollywood romantic songs. "I want to be with you and I want to be where you are, I long for you…" They use pronouns like "I" or "you" to please the public instead of using Jesus or God. When you dilute the gospel to please the people, you lose the very essence and power of it. As a result, we have become a powerless church.

When the rich young ruler came to Jesus and said he wanted to follow Him, Jesus told him to go and sell everything he had and then come and follow Him. The young man walked away because he had many possessions and was not willing to give them up. Jesus did not run after him to change His requirement. He did not say, "Just sell half and then come and follow Me." He did not lower His standard. In Christendom today we have lowered our standard to fit everyone and make everyone happy. What is the result? We lost our significance.

What can be done to win the people of this world? We need to train believers in *character* and *skill* and send them into the world to *preach* the gospel of the kingdom. When I say "preach," I mean to demonstrate the gospel of the kingdom in the area in which you are called. If a believer is trained in the area of economy, he or she may work for a bank or for a financial firm, or own one and run it according to kingdom principles.

> **When I say "preach," I mean to demonstrate the gospel of the kingdom in the area in which you are called.**

One of the reasons the people of the world lead in most arenas of life is because whatever they do, they do it with excellence. The church became lazy and does not do things with excellence, which is why we are not attractive to the world. Instead, the reverse is true: The church is attracted to the world because they do jobs with excellence.

Jesus very specifically said, though we are in this world, we are not *of* this world. But we are not taught clearly what that means. If you want to know the difference between the world and the kingdom of God, please read the prayer of Jesus in John 17. He separated the two and prayed only for those who believe in Him, not for the whole world. The gospel of John mentions the word *world* more than any other book in the Bible; it is used sixty-two times in the NKJV.

Satan uses the world system to rule over nations, regions, and people. We (the church) are God's army and He sends us into the world to overcome it, preach the gospel of the kingdom, and establish God's kingdom. It is the same as a nation sending its army to invade and conquer another nation. We are in a battle—a spiritual battle. The good news is our enemy is already defeated. We fight a defeated foe.

> "For we are not fighting against flesh-and-blood enemies, but against evil rulers and authorities of the unseen world, against mighty powers in this dark world, and against evil spirits in the heavenly places" (Ephesians 6:12, NLT).

The enemy will use the world and its system to fight back using the unbelievers. That is why Jesus said, "I will build my church and the gates of hell shall not prevail against it."

The same way we try to evangelize the world, the demonic powers are using the world system and are operating behind it to *evangelize us* with their agenda. What is behind all the propaganda about same-sex marriage and their fight to get accepted in society? They are trying to evangelize and win supporters for their cause. What is the reason behind all the propaganda and the media war about evolution or abortion? They are trying to *evangelize you* to believe their message.

> "We know that we are of God, and the whole *world* lies *under the sway of* the wicked one" (1 John 5:19).

Because we are born again, we are not supposed to function by the *operating system* of this world, but by the operating system of the kingdom of God. That is why it is so difficult for us to receive the benefits of the kingdom of God. We have been programmed from our childhood with the world and its system and it is difficult to reprogram our mind according to the kingdom principles. Actually, that process is called repentance.

What We Should Do to the World

The world (the kingdom of darkness) has an agenda, and that is to allure and deceive the church and invade it with its principles, methods, and culture, thereby disarming the church of any power. As long as the church looks like the world, it is not a threat to the kingdom of darkness in any area. Many are living as slaves to this world and its system.

We need to overcome this world system if we are going to enjoy the benefits of God's kingdom. Do not fall prey to it. It will try to lure you into it by offering its various products. Remember when the devil came to tempt Jesus, he offered Him all the kingdoms of the world and their glory if He would fall down and worship him (Matthew 4:8-9).

Wow! Imagine the devil asking Jesus to worship him. If he is so bold to do that to Jesus, how much more will he try to tempt the frail men and women of this earth? Because most are waiting to have some wealth and a little bit of glory, they will do anything to gain it. Jesus overcame the devil by overcoming this world and what it has to offer.

> "These things I have spoken to you, that in Me you may have peace. In the world you will have tribulation; but be of good cheer, I have overcome the world" (John 16:33).

> "For whatever is born of God overcomes the *world*. And this is the victory that has overcome the world—our faith" (1 John 5:4).

We need to be crucified to this world and all its passions. Many today don't understand or cannot differentiate what is of the world and what is of God because we have been so programmed by it from birth. From the moment we are born again, it is our responsibility to renew our mind from the way it was programmed. For that to happen, we need to seek His kingdom first. The more we discover how His kingdom works and operates, the more our way of thinking changes. We need to be crucified to this world, which means we should not be seduced by anything the world has to offer.

> "But God forbid that I should boast except in the cross of our Lord Jesus Christ, by whom the world has been *crucified* to me, and I to the world" (Galatians 6:14).

Paul wrote that he had betrothed us as a virgin to Christ:

> "For I am jealous for you with godly jealousy. For I have betrothed you to one husband, that I may present you as a chaste virgin to Christ. But I fear, lest somehow, as the serpent deceived Eve by his craftiness, so your minds may be corrupted from the simplicity that is in Christ" (2 Corinthians 11:2-3).

The Church Should Look Different

Our anticipation, lifestyle, and relationship with Christ should be clearly reflected in the way we live. We should be like a virgin waiting to see her bridegroom on her wedding day. When a virgin is engaged to marry, her whole lifestyle is different than a normal person's. She won't get entangled in any other relationship. Everything she does will be to prepare to meet and please her love. Her foremost love will be toward her bridegroom, and everything else in life will be secondary to her. Her utmost devotion and commitment will be toward her soon-coming bridegroom, to please him at any cost. She will not be swayed by any other guy who may try to lure her away and break her commitment to her fiancé.

If you look at the church today, does she resemble this woman? If you were the bridegroom, would you marry such a bride? If I were the bridegroom, I wouldn't marry a bride like the church because the only intention the majority of the church has is to use me to get things that benefit them. They are not interested in what is important to me, nor am I their first love. They love a lot of things of this world and treat me like a side-business. Who wants to marry a bride like that? What would make anyone think Jesus would come back to marry a bride like that?

There is not much difference today between those who call themselves Christians and the people in the world. That was not the way it was in the Old Testament between the people of Israel and the people of other nations, or with the early church. Their differences were not just the temple in Jerusalem.

Everything about them was different: Their culture, their ways of doing things, the way they dressed, everything was different from the people in the world. They never borrowed, but lent to other nations. There was no sick among them. There was no one who had a need that was not met. Other nations were jealous of Israel and their blessings. They were hated because of their favor and lifestyle, not because of their hate speech against the social ills of their day!

It was the same in the early church. The people of the world looked at the church and were jealous and afraid (Acts 2:43; 5:5). They wanted to have what the church had. Now, no one wants what the church has. In fact, the church has almost become a nuisance in most societies. They do not add much value to their communities and their nations.

This has to change. We need to divorce this world and return to the Lord Jesus Christ as our first love. We don't hear any more teachings about holiness, sanctification, or separation from the world. We hear more about personal success, money, prosperity, and grace. Preachers don't preach from the epistles to the churches much either. Many just share a story from the Old Testament or a parable from the Gospels and give a pep talk on Sunday morning.

Very few fully understand the basic doctrines of the church or the New Testament. They preach that there is no more judgment for a believer. Nor do believers need to repent of their sins. I don't think they ever read the messages to the seven churches in the book of Revelation. Additionally, there is not a single epistle that Paul wrote to the churches or leaders that does not contain some kind of warning to believers to live soberly in this evil and wicked generation—or face judgment from God.

Do yourself a favor. Read Paul's letters and all the letters to the churches and mark the verses in which they warn of judgment for believers who are not living a holy life. Epistles were written to and for believers, not unbelievers. You will be very surprised how many times they warn believers. What I hear from today's preachers is not to worry about your sins and mistakes because the grace of God will cover everything. That is true, but it is not the whole truth. Don't be deceived.

> To call sin a weakness and say there is no judgment for a believer in Christ is a lie from the pit of hell. There is no such teaching in the Bible.

To call sin a weakness and say there is no judgment for a believer in Christ is a lie from the pit of hell. There is no such teaching in the Bible. There is no judgment for the Adamic sin we inherited by birth, for which Jesus died on the cross, for us, and all of humanity. But for everything else we do while we are in this body, we will need to give an answer to the Lord on the day of reckoning and will receive a reward according to our works.

Read the messages to the seven churches in the book of Revelation and you will see how severely Jesus deals with them. He never said to any of the churches, "Just live the way you are living and don't worry about the sin. My grace will cover it all." No, He never said that. When He told Paul His grace was sufficient, He was not talking about sin.

Because we know who we are and what the church is supposed to be doing, the question is where do we begin? How do we reach this world? I am happy to share the answers to those questions.

Reaching the World

Before we go out to reach the world, we need to understand it better. I explained that previously in this chapter. How did people in the Bible reach their world? What kind of methods did they use? If we look at the world from the east to the west, you will see a pattern in the diagram below.

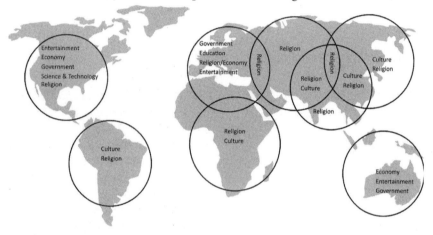

This map shows how the kingdom of darkness operates in different continents. How the devil operates in India is different from how he operates in the United States. We have to know what "device" he uses to blind the people in each continent and deal with it accordingly.

In Asia and the Middle East, the predominant force the devil uses to blind people is religion. In the United States, it is primarily economy and entertainment that he uses to blind people from receiving the gospel. As I mentioned before, he uses one of those seven segments of which the world is made to blind each individual who has not yet received Jesus. It is the responsibility of the church to expose these demonic devices and train people to go out into the world to win souls for the kingdom.

There was a time when I thought that when Jesus said to go into all the world and preach the gospel, He was talking about going into different countries.

I began to travel to other countries, and the results I saw were minimal. I became very disappointed in my endeavor. I also went to some countries where they claimed the majority of the population was already Christian, but the situation there was even worse. Hell had more influence than the whole church combined. That was discouraging too.

I went to God in desperation and asked Him why this was. I asked Him, "If You are the most powerful God and the church is the body of Christ, then why does Your kingdom seem so weak and ineffective? The church has been trying to evangelize countries for many centuries, but has not been very successful."

That's when God began to speak to me about how He reaches the world. He began to show me His way of doing things. He said, "It does not take a majority to change a nation, but a minority and most of the time just one person." He began to tell me about people like Joseph, Daniel, Esther and others He used to reach nations.

> **It does not take a majority to change a nation, but a minority and most of the time just one person.**

In order to evangelize the nations, we need to evangelize the world system. When you evangelize the world system, the nations get evangelized automatically. For example, there are many ministries and outreaches that try to reach children. There is an easy way to reach the children in a community. Start a Christian school. You don't need to go running after the children; the children will come to you. And not only the children, but the parents will come to you too! Depending on the quality of the school, you will attract a similar quality of children and families. The best example is someone chasing flies to catch them. It will be very difficult to catch a fly by chasing it, but there is an easy way to catch a fly, put something sweet outside and all the flies you want will come to you.

In most countries, I believe big companies have more influence than the church. In each country there are companies that are highly influential. Even the government depends on these companies for its income and acts as their puppet. What if a Christian owned a company like that in a country? Do you think it would grant the church more influence? Or do you think standing on the street corner and shouting, "You are going to hell if you don't believe in

Jesus!" would be a better plan? Which one of those methods will give a better witness for Jesus, our Lord and King? You make the choice.

Kingdom Strategies

In the first century the apostles evangelized the world system and they reached almost all known countries with the gospel in their lifetime. The reason we are taking centuries to reach countries is because we do not understand what the world is made of and how a kingdom operates. Once we understand the world system and train the believers and our children to reach it, we will be much more effective and strategic and we will see great results in less time.

Paul did not conduct any crusades, as we know them today. At least we do not read about it in the books he wrote. He was not running around conducting revival meetings either. He was very strategic in his approach because he knew that for a nation to come to Christ, he needed to reach the system by which that nation operated. As I said earlier, crusades will save souls but they will not save a nation. I am all about nations because God is all about nations.

> "In the middle of its street and on either side of the river was the tree of life which bore twelve fruits, each tree yielding its fruit every month. The leaves of the tree were for the *healing of the nations*" (Revelation 22:2).

If you look at the churches and the cities Paul selected to establish a new work, those also were very strategic. Corinth was an important city in ancient Greece. Ancient Ephesus was a port city and a hub. If Paul started a church there, it would spill into cultures all over Asia Minor, and that is exactly what happened. He did not just choose any place to preach the gospel. He chose the most prominent and influential cities because he knew that in order to reach any nation you need to go to the top first and not the bottom. He operated with a kingdom mindset.

> **If you look at the churches and the cities Paul selected to establish a new work, those also were very strategic.**

We are very good at showing Jesus as the healer, prophet, and preacher. But not everyone is physically sick, especially most wealthy people. Not everyone will have a chance to be prophesied over, but everyone needs products to survive here on earth. Almost everyone needs a school, college, or university to study at or a place to send their children. We lack witnesses in those key positions and that is why it is taking so long to reach the nations.

Kingdom Methods

Those people who are supposed to be witnessing in these areas are sitting in the pews depressed and feeling useless because they don't have a healing or prophetic gift. They are asking Jesus to get them out of here as soon as possible. Now is the time for you to shake off the dust and stand up for Jesus in whatever capacity He has called you. Everyone is created to be a witness for Jesus, but not everyone is called to use the same method.

Everyone is gifted with at least one natural gift and one spiritual gift. Remember the parable of the talents. You might not have developed those gifts. Unless you start using them, they will not become strong in your life. God put those gifts in us in seed form. We need to nurture and grow them by using and learning more. The more you use any gift, the better you become at it, and the more you learn about it, the better you can teach others about it.

> The more you use any gift, the better you become at it, and the more you learn about it, the better you can teach others about it.

Jesus said to go into all the world and make disciples of all the nations, teaching them to observe all things that He commanded. The church has been good at preaching and making converts. When new converts come to church, they should be trained to become disciples. They should be taught to seek His kingdom *first*. We have to train believers to live in the kingdom and then how to go into the world.

There are many colleges and seminaries that train people to preach the gospel, but they have totally left out training people how to go into the world. The main reason is they do not know what the word "world" means. I am referring to its seven components: 1) Culture 2) Religion 3) Government 4) Economy 5) Educational system 6) Media and Entertainment 7) Science and Technology. Each believer is anointed or gifted to influence one of those spheres at some level.

The following diagram will show us how the church is supposed to function in relation to the kingdom of God and how it is supposed to reach the world with the gospel of the kingdom. The church is the only visible form of the invisible kingdom of God. We need to train our people to discover their natural and spiritual gifts and send them out into the world to influence it.

Go into All the World and Preach the Gospel Mark 16:15

The chart below shows how the church should reach the world, which results in transformation of individuals and nations by administering the kingdom of God.

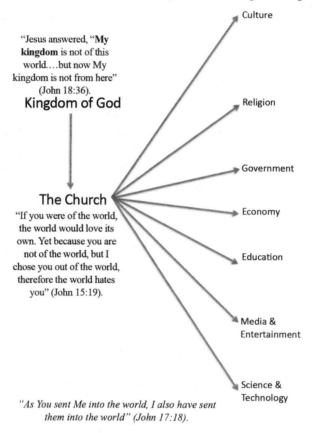

"Jesus answered, "**My kingdom** is not of this world....but now My kingdom is not from here" (John 18:36).
Kingdom of God

The Church
"If you were of the world, the world would love its own. Yet because you are not of the world, but I chose you out of the world, therefore the world hates you" (John 15:19).

Culture

Religion

Government

Economy

Education

Media & Entertainment

Science & Technology

"As You sent Me into the world, I also have sent them into the world" (John 17:18).

Jesus said to go into the world. That means we are in the kingdom of God, trained and equipped to go out to war, to fight and invade the world and its systems. When I say war and army, please don't picture thousands of people marching in unison with weapons in their hands. That is the picture of the armies of this world. Jesus' kingdom is not of this world and that is not the way His army operates. Our mission is more of a covert operation than open confrontation. We infiltrate the systems of this world with a kingdom mindset and influence it for God.

If the world is made up of the seven different spheres that I mentioned above, how do we preach the gospel to these areas? If one of today's preachers goes to preach using conventional methods to reach the people, they will not receive it. For example, what is the best way to *preach* the gospel to the top universities and colleges in this country? Do they invite any of our pastors to preach in one

> **Our mission is more of a covert operation than open confrontation. We infiltrate the systems of this world with a kingdom mindset and influence it for God.**

of their chapel services or speak at a commencement and try to convince them of the gospel? Maybe a very few, but most do not have a chapel service because they are not run by Christians. Do we start a top university or college and train young people in the ways of the Lord? Or do we go in there as professors as witnesses of Jesus to the next generation? Which are the most effective ways? What will have the greatest impact?

Years ago, I heard that one famous evangelist spent more than four million dollars to conduct one crusade in India. There were huge gatherings of people for three days. Many might have become converts but when he left, India remained the same. I wrote a letter to him, asking him to consider spending money like that to establish a Christian college or university instead. Generations might be impacted.

When I say, "go into all the world" I am not talking about cars and airplanes or other modes of transportation that people use when they *go* to preach the gospel. I am talking about the method or package that is used in which the message of the gospel is carried to the people without using words. Francis of Asissi once said, *"Preach the gospel at all times and when necessary, use words."*

Going into the world means to find a way to influence the system by which the world functions, to take it back from the enemy, and establish the will of God in that particular area, to fulfill God's desire to see His will done on earth as it is in heaven. God has a plan for the education system, economy, entertainment, and politics of every country.

The education system, medical field, government, entertainment, and other worldly systems are great vehicles for preaching (demonstrating) the gospel. The enemy is using these fields to propagate his lies and advance his kingdom to keep people in bondage. The church needs to take back these areas for God and use them for His glory. The enemy has blinded believers and kept them away from these influential fields. He has made us believe we are not supposed to be involved in these areas because they belong to the devil and his kingdom instead. That is a deception and built on lies. The Bible does not tell us that.

Every single person God used in the Bible was used to influence one or more of the components this world is made of. This chart shows the person God used and which components they influenced with the kingdom mindset. He took them out of the world and trained them and sent them back to influence or bring change to their world. If we are going to reach this world for Jesus and for His kingdom, I believe that this is the only way we are going to accomplish what God has intended for centuries. Let the real church arise!

> **Every single person God used in the Bible was used to influence one or more of the components this world is made of.**

Examples of People God Used in the Bible to Reach Their World

	Culture	Religion	Government	Economy	Education	Media & Entertainment	Science & Technology
Noah	✓	✓	✓	✓	✓	✓	✓
Abraham	✓	✓	✓	✓			
Joseph			✓	✓			
Moses		✓	✓				
Elijah		✓	✓				
Elisha		✓	✓				
David			✓	✓		✓	
Abigail				✓			
Ruth	✓	✓		✓			
Bezalel							✓

	Culture	Religion	Government	Economy	Education	Media & Entertainment	Science & Technology
Esther	✓		✓				
Daniel		✓	✓				✓
Paul	✓	✓	✓				
Peter		✓	✓				
Jesus	✓	✓	✓	✓	✓	✓	✓
Jonah	✓	✓	✓				
Solomon			✓	✓	✓	✓	✓

One of the reasons the church and the world are in the shape they are in right now is because we do not know how to witness for Jesus effectively. We have been following what we know of tradition but that is not the whole truth. When we understand who Jesus is and learn how to witness for Him, we will see the change we are looking for. In order to do that He has endowed us with the power of the Holy Spirit, but we have not been using His power properly. The next chapter covers that.

How did God use His people to influence the world system? There are six methods or ways by which God reaches the world. As a church we need to train our people in those methods. We have to be very deliberate and intentional in our training. Everything we do as a church has to be geared toward developing people and our future generations to use those methods to reach the world.

The below chart will show you the methods God uses to reach the world.

The Six Methods by Which God Reaches the World

	Power	Prayer	Business/Product/ Service	Wisdom/Skill	Government	Love
Moses	✓	✓	✓	✓	✓	
Elijah	✓	✓				
David			✓	✓	✓	
Samuel		✓	✓		✓	
Solomon			✓	✓	✓	
Elisha	✓	✓				

THE POWER AND AUTHORITY OF THE CHURCH

	Power	Prayer	Business/Product/ Service	Wisdom/Skill	Government	Love
Bezalel			✓	✓		
Esther		✓			✓	
Mordecai					✓	
Nehemiah					✓	
Daniel		✓		✓	✓	
Joshua				✓		
Jeremiah		✓			✓	
Abraham		✓	✓		✓	
Jonah					✓	✓
Stephen	✓			✓		
Jesus	✓	✓	✓	✓	✓	✓
John						✓
Paul	✓	✓	✓	✓	✓	✓
Joseph of Arimathea			✓		✓	
Job			✓	✓		
Tabitha			✓			
Mother Theresa						✓
Ethiopian Eunuch					✓	
Lydia			✓			

In the following chapter I am going to share the plan God has given the church in the twenty-first century to reach the world before Jesus' return. It will also show you one of the main reasons we have not been able to reach the world, even though God gave us all the power and anointing we ever needed. Please open up your spirit to receive what the Holy Spirit is saying to the church.

Chapter 14: Kingdom Evangelism

Chapter 14: Kingdom Evangelism

"But you shall receive power when the Holy Spirit has come upon you; and you shall be witnesses to Me in Jerusalem, and in all Judea, and Samaria, and to the end of the earth" (Acts 1:8).

12 People Reached the Entire World

Have you ever wondered how twelve apostles reached almost all the countries of the known world with the gospel in their lifetime? We have been trying to evangelize the world for centuries but have not been very effective. More than half of the planet remains unreached, but we have more Christians, miracle workers, technology, and resources today than at any other time before. Is there a solution? I believe there is. The solution is administering the kingdom of God. The question is how do we do that?

There are over seven billion people on earth today and only two billion are thought to be Christians. That means more than five billion people are yet to be reached. If we use the methods we currently use, based on the results we are seeing, it may take another two thousand years to reach another billion souls. Within that time period, close to a hundred generations will live and die without ever knowing Jesus Christ. Is there a better and speedier way to reach more people? I strongly believe there is, and I am excited to share that with you. That is what I wish to explore in the next two chapters.

We Can Reach Our World

This is not something new I invented. It's been in the Bible all along from the very beginning. It is God's way of reaching the world. It is called "kingdom evangelism." The apostles used the same method and before they died, the majority of the world was Christian. There is only one agency God put on this earth to evangelize the world and that is the church. But the church, as a whole, has lost its mission and is running parallel to the world system.

Why kingdom evangelism? The early church and the apostles lived and ministered in a very hostile society. People like Moses, Joseph, Nehemiah, Daniel, and Esther were all living in environments that were hostile to their faith too. And today we find ourselves in a similar situation: living in a world in which it seems people are becoming more anti-Christian and anti-gospel. But those who lived before all reached their world for God. The question is how did they do it? They did it through kingdom evangelism.

We need to address evangelism with a kingdom mindset, a mindset of one who is part of a kingdom that is trying to take over another kingdom. What approach would they take? Did they go to the enemy's kingdom and sing songs? Or did they reach the poor and preach on their streets? I believe the answer is no. We must make a plan to *influence* each of the components that the kingdom is made of, or the people who are in authority, those governing the kingdom. In this case, the kingdom of God is taking over the kingdom of darkness.

You may have heard of *power evangelism* or *marketplace* or *prayer evangelism*. Personally, I like them all. But if we add kingdom evangelism to them, we will have the missing ingredient and we will see the result we have been looking for, which is to win the nations for Christ. Power and prayer evangelism needs to come under the umbrella of kingdom evangelism, without which we will never see

> The plan God gave me will enable the church to reach any country on this earth within ten to fifteen years, without a single crusade or healing rally!

nations coming to Christ. The plan God gave me will enable the church to reach any country on this earth within ten to fifteen years, without a single crusade or healing rally! But it will take some serious praying, strategizing, planning, and training to accomplish that goal. The good news is you can see your nation come to Christ in your lifetime. That is exciting. I know that's the dream and prayer of every true believer of Jesus Christ. You may ask why ten to fifteen years? It will take that many years to train a generation to influence a culture.

If you look at the world today, the majority does not make the decisions for the general public. It's not the majority that influence and shape a culture, but the few people or that one person at the top that makes decisions for everybody. So if you want to reach a nation, you try to reach those people or train Christians to be in those positions. That is how kingdom evangelism works.

In any arena: business, politics, or entertainment, it's the top three percent of the population that make decisions for the rest of us. They shape the culture of every nation. The rest just follow their lead. Unless we have influence with that three percent, we are not going to see any change for the better in our nations in the near future. You can scream and shout all you want inside the four walls of a building or even on the street, but nothing is going to change unless we learn to think and act like our God. That is what we are supposed to be doing anyway. We are His children after all.

> In any arena: business, politics, or entertainment, it's the top three percent of the population that make decisions for the rest of us.

I am not saying we should have Christian presidents legislate the law for everyone to go to church. No. What I am saying is that if we have a Christian president or have a judiciary that believes the Bible, at least they will not legalize same-sex marriage or abortion. We can decide what our children are being taught in our schools and we can regulate what can be put on public television.

The Early Church

After the church was born, it reached people in every level of society. People from all walks of life were members of the church: the priests, rulers, government officials, widows, business people, and so on.

When the church was birthed on Pentecost, there were leaders and business people from every nation under heaven present in Jerusalem. "And there were dwelling in Jerusalem Jews, devout men, *from every nation under heaven*" (Acts

2:5). The gospel was preached to every nation as a witness. There were devout and prominent men there from every nation.

When we think about Pentecost, we often limit it to an emotional experience. What was God thinking when He sent the Holy Spirit on that day? He had a kingdom mindset. He was thinking about how to influence key people from every nation in one setting. Bang! Mission accomplished. I call that a maximum impact!

Of course it was an emotional experience. When the Holy Spirit came, people thought the disciples were drunk. But what was the objective God was trying to accomplish through all this? Some people like to get emotional, crawl on the floor, and be called Holy Rollers, but that experience does not reach people of influence for the kingdom. We have been trying to duplicate the upper room experience but are not producing the same results they had. It is time for a change. God may have an entirely different strategy to reach the people of our time.

Do you remember the story of Philip the evangelist? An angel of the Lord told him to go by the road from Jerusalem to Gaza. He wanted Philip to meet a very influential man from the government of Ethiopia.

> "Now an angel of the Lord spoke to Philip, saying, 'Arise and go toward the south along the road which goes down from Jerusalem to Gaza.' This is desert. So he arose and went. And behold, a man of Ethiopia, a eunuch of great authority under Candace the queen of the Ethiopians, who had charge of all her treasury, and had come to Jerusalem to worship" (Acts 8:26-27).

This chief financial officer for the queen of Ethiopia is one example of the type of person who used to come to Jerusalem to worship. These are the kinds of people who were present at Pentecost. God took maximum advantage of this opportunity.

When the Gentiles were first reached with the gospel, God sent Peter to a particular man named Cornelius and his family. Cornelius was a centurion of the Roman army, a key person to reaching the Gentiles. A centurion is a commander over groups of a hundred soldiers, a man of influence among all the Jews and Gentiles (Acts 10:22). Why did God send Peter to Cornelius? Why not just ask him to start an outreach to orphans? No, God is a king and whatever He does has a kingdom flavor. I am not saying we should not take care of orphans and widows; we should, but to reach a nation or community we need to start from the top. Another example is the conversation Jesus had with Nicodemus. Nicodemus was a ruler of the Jews (John 3:1).

The Greatest Impact

Jesus was sent at the perfect time to have the greatest effect. The Bible says, "When the fullness of the time had come, God sent forth His Son" (Galatians 4:4). What does it mean by the fullness of the time? Why did it take more than four thousand years for God to send His Son? God waited for the geopolitical setup of the world to be just right to reach more people with the good news of the gospel.

When Jesus was born, the Romans were in charge. The Romans were tolerant of some things and not at all of others. They took over territory and demanded tribute, allowing people to continue as they did before, as long as they did not threaten Roman authority or superiority. They ruled through an army that acted with order and precision, and they built good roads, which made traveling much easier than it had ever been before. They spoke one language, so that anyone who spoke Greek could easily share their message all over the vast Roman Empire.

> God waited for the geopolitical setup of the world to be just right to reach more people with the good news of the gospel.

Their empire was similar to America today. Everyone wanted what the Romans had: language, culture, food, lifestyle, citizenship, everything. If one could have influence in Rome, he had influence everywhere. All over the world today people look to America and want what we have. If you want to reach the world, reach the most influential country, and all other countries will be reached automatically. That is what God meant when He said He sent Jesus at the fullness of the time, or the right time. He is so smart.

If we study the ministry of Paul and the churches he established, we will see that he was operating with a kingdom mindset. He did not go to a city to set up an orphanage or feeding program. God led him to people of influence. In Philippi, Paul and his team met a businesswoman named Lydia. The Lord opened her heart to hear the things spoken by Paul (Acts 16:14). The next convert was the jailor and his family because Paul and Silas were imprisoned as the result of casting a demon out of a girl, and God delivered them from the prison by sending an earthquake (Acts 16:16-33). Later in Thessalonica many prominent men and women believed the gospel and joined Paul and Silas and a new church was established.

> "And some of them were persuaded; and a great multitude of the devout Greeks, and not a few of the leading women, joined Paul and Silas" (Acts 17:4).

> "Therefore many of them believed, and also not a few of the Greeks, prominent women as well as men" (Acts 17:12).

In Corinth we see the same pattern. The first converts in Corinth were a ruler of the synagogue named Crispus and his household (Acts 18:8).

When you reach people of influence, a domino effect takes place. In the eastern world, community is vibrant and plays an important role in a person's life. They don't think individualistically as in the western world. They adhere to the moral and social beliefs of their community leaders. They are watching and thinking about what other people are doing and are influenced by it.

> **When you reach people of influence, a domino effect takes place.**

The church reaches for the poor first because we have lost the kingdom mindset and no longer have a full revelation of who Jesus is. Because of this, we fail to witness effectively. Though many claim to have been preaching the full gospel, the truth is they have been preaching a partial gospel.

You Shall Receive Power

How do we practically implement kingdom evangelism into our daily lives? I have been in ministry a long time and have preached from Acts 1:8 many times; I thought I knew what it meant until the Holy Spirit began to show me a revelation contained in it that I never saw before. We have been limiting the Holy Spirit and His power to only use His gifts. Jesus did not say, "You shall receive gifts when the Holy Spirit comes upon you." If the power is only meant for gifts then Jesus would have said so. I was asking God why the church seemed so powerless in many cultures, even though the Christians were in the majority and they had received the power of the Holy Spirit.

The Holy Spirit began to open up the eyes of my understanding. Every believer who received the Holy Spirit has the power of God residing in him or her. But we have been using that power only for casting out demons, healing the sick, and prophesying over people.

> There is a misconception in the church that if someone does not cast out demons, prophesy, or heal the sick, they are not operating in the power of God.

There is a misconception in the church that if someone does not cast out demons, prophesy, or heal the sick, they are not operating in the power of God. That is absolutely wrong. We cannot limit the power of the Holy Spirit. Those are just some gifts of the Holy Spirit. The Holy Spirit is much bigger than those gifts. He is the Architect of the entire universe.

The power of the Holy Spirit does not manifest the same way through every individual. He differs from person to person. We all use electricity; in the West we call electricity power. We use electricity for various purposes. We have scores of appliances and equipment in our homes that work with electricity. A refrigerator keeps things cold and a heater keeps us warm. A television allows us to see what's going on around the world. A computer helps to do various tasks. But the power that works behind all of these is electricity. It is the same power but with different manifestations.

Same Power—Different Manifestation

The same Holy Spirit that worked through Paul to cast out demons helped Joseph to administer a nation. The same Holy Spirit that helped Joseph to administer a nation helped David kill a giant. It was the same Power but different manifestations. Each believer in a church is like a different piece of equipment, or the Bible calls us vessels. We are unique and different and we each have a different function. So the power of God manifests through us differently. What if everyone was a healer? Then who would teach the adult classes and who would minister to the children? It's time to remove the limits we have put on the Holy Spirit.

"There are diversities of gifts, but the same Spirit. There are differences of ministries, but the same Lord. And there are diversities of activities, but it is the same God who works all in all" (1 Corinthians 12:4-6).

"If the whole body *were* an eye, where *would be* the hearing? If the whole *were* hearing, where *would be* the smelling? But now God has set the members, each one of them, in the body just as He pleased" (1 Corinthians 12:17-18).

In Deuteronomy 8 we read that it is God who gives us power to make wealth. Some people are anointed to create wealth. Some people are anointed to serve. Some people are anointed to minister to children. Some are anointed to be in politics. Again, it is the same power but different manifestations. There are some basic gifts that any believer can exercise: praying for the sick, giving a word to someone who is discouraged, taking authority over demons. But don't get stuck there or try to become a specialist. You might be called to do much more and possibly something different.

> If a believer is a CEO of a national corporation, his position and work ethic are a witness of the gospel to everyone around him, without doing any *preaching*.

That means that if you have a product or mastered an ability, skill, or service, it is a witness of the gospel to unbelievers. If a believer is a CEO of a national or multinational corporation, his position and work ethic are a witness of the gospel to everyone around him, without doing any *preaching*. This is kingdom evangelism.

This revelation answered my long-unanswered question about why the church has been unable to reach the majority of the population of the earth. We have been trying to fly with one wing. In many parts of the world, especially in the West, I believe we have already reached the maximum people we can with the methods that we traditionally know and practice: crusades, revivals, healing rallies, gospel tracts, etc. If the rest of the world is to be reached, the church needs to take hold of this revelation and apply it.

New Age: New Methods

The leaders that God used in the last century for crusades, healings, and tent meetings are ready to pass their baton to the next generation. Some already have. But in every generation, God does something new. If we try to copy our previous generations we will totally miss what God has for us now. There is a new generation that God is raising up. They are not sure of their identity yet because they lack direction and training. Right now they are trying to copy what they have seen from their leaders, but that will not work for them.

> **If you have a product or mastered an ability, skill, or service, it is a witness of the gospel to unbelievers.**

Just look at the churches: most are no longer effective in what they are doing. They are in survival mode and ready to crumble. They are carrying out their traditions and doing fun things to keep people interested. Many know something different has to happen but they lack direction so they try to repeat something that happened in the 60s or 80s.

Let me ask you a question. Would you go back to use anything that you used in the 60s and 80s right now? Your style of clothing, the cars you drove, the electronics and technology you used, or the food you ate? Do you think our children want to do that? No, they wouldn't. Then why do you think the *spiritual* things that worked then would work now? They will not. What God did then was for that generation.

Now is the time for kingdom evangelism. It is evangelism that occurs as a by-product or as a result of the body of Christ worldwide administering the kingdom of God in their communities and nations. This is not a new kind of evangelism. It's a restoration of the true method mentioned all throughout the Bible, a method the church is neglecting because of ignorance and deception.

People like Abraham, Joseph, Daniel, Esther, Nehemiah, and many others never preached a sermon or healed the sick, but they lived their life with a kingdom mindset and executed God's purposes through their lives in nations and over kingdoms. As a result of this process, *kingdom evangelism* took place, meaning nations and kings came to know that there is a God in heaven that ruled over them.

The people who are not yet reached may not come to a crusade or healing rally. We need to employ a different method. "Behold, I will do a new thing, now it shall spring forth; shall you not know it?" (Isaiah 43:19). As you receive this revelation and move according to it, you will be that person God is waiting to use to change the world with the kingdom of God.

Reaching the World

God gave each of us the power of the Holy Spirit to become a witness for Jesus. He said to me, "Before you go out and witness for Jesus, you need to know who Jesus is." I thought I knew who Jesus was because of my background. I had been brought up in a Christian home and had been in church all my life. But when the Holy Spirit began to reveal to me who Jesus is, I understood why the church is not effective in many cultures. It is because we have not only limited the Holy Spirit but also limited Jesus in what we know of Him and how we have been witnessing Him to the world. We have reached the world we could with the knowledge we have of who Jesus is. If the rest of the world is going to be reached, we need to know what we do not know of Jesus and witness for Him accordingly. Then the rest will be history. So lets find out who Jesus really is and learn how to witness for Him.

1) Creator

First, the Holy Spirit said Jesus is the Creator of the universe. Everything you see, and even what you cannot see with your eyes, was created by Jesus. How do we witness Jesus as the Creator?

> "*All things were made through Him,* and without Him nothing was made that was made" (John 1:3).

> "*For by Him all things were created* that are in heaven and that are on earth, visible and invisible" (Colossians 1:16).

> "And to make all see what is the fellowship of the mystery, which from the beginning of the ages has been hidden in God who created all things through Jesus Christ" (Ephesians 3:9).

People with products have influence. Governments of this world for the most part are influenced or controlled by people in business. How do we witness that Jesus is the Creator? The church needs to come up with products that are useful for the people in the world. The majority of our money is spent on products and services. Every day everyone uses products. Every product we use comes out of the earth.

God did not create airplanes, but He created the raw materials necessary to make them and hid them in the earth. God did not create furniture, but He created trees and gave us a brain to imagine and create what we needed from them. God did not create automobiles, but He created everything we needed to make one. Now it's up to us to use our imagination to make what we need. God gave us the earth, but we have not used it the best we can. Unfortunately, we have been waiting to get out of our planet. What a sad dilemma!

> **Governments of this world for the most part are influenced or controlled by people in business.**

In most countries, key companies have more influence than the worldwide church combined. What if some of those companies were run by believers? It is time for the church to reclaim lost territories and to emerge as innovators like our Lord Jesus Christ. The Holy Spirit is the Architect of the Universe in which we exist, and the earth is just one tiny planet in that universe. I once read that the Sun can contain one million earth-sized planets. It is time to take the Holy Spirit out of the box we put Him in. We thought He came just to heal the sick, help us speak in tongues, and give us emotional experiences.

Many people turn their brain off when they are born again. We need to use our brains to come up with products and services that are helpful to humanity and become valuable to our society—not a nuisance! We need to open our minds and become productive and creative.

All the treasures of wisdom and knowledge are hid in Christ (Colossians 2:3). We need to tap into them and solve the problems our communities are facing. Believers need to identify with Jesus as the Creator by designing new software or coming up with a way to heal cancer. There are a great many challenges in today's world. The church must rise to the occasion and come up with the answers. Let us tap into some of that wisdom and knowledge that are hid in Christ our Lord to find the solutions.

2) King

Our God is a King.

> "The Lord *is King* forever and ever" (Psalm 10:16a).

> "For the *king*dom *is* the Lord's, and He rules over the nations" (Psalm 22:28).

He is also called the King of glory (Psalm 24:8).

> "Where is He who has been born King of the Jews? For we have seen His star in the East and have come to worship Him" (Matthew 2:2).

> "Now to the King eternal, immortal, invisible, to God who alone is wise, *be* honor and glory forever and ever. Amen" (1 Timothy 1:17).

There were many in the Old Testament who witnessed God as King on the earth. Why don't we see this in our day? Did God cease from being a king? Let us find that out.

> "For unto us a Child is born, unto us a Son is given; and the government will be upon His shoulder. And His name will be called Wonderful, Counselor, Mighty God, Everlasting Father, Prince of Peace. Of the increase of *His* government and peace *there will be* no end, upon the throne of David and over His kingdom, to order it and establish it with judgment and justice from that time forward, even forever. The zeal of the Lord of hosts will perform this" (Isaiah 9:6-7).

The above verses are prophetic declarations about our Lord Jesus Christ. The first thing it says about Him is that the government will be upon His shoulder. How does government rest upon His shoulders? He is the Head of the church and we are His body on this earth. The shoulder is part of the body, which means the government of this earth is supposed to be on the shoulders of the church. For some reason we made this verse part of our eschatology, meaning something that is going to take place somewhere out there in the future. This is not true according to the verse. That is what religion does. It steals from us what we should have now and gives us a false hope that someday things are going to be better. But faith says, "now."

From the phrase "from that time forward, even forever" we understand that the fulfillment of the prophetic timing began from the time a Son was given. It says that of the increase of His government and peace, there will be no end. That means it is eternal. We all know the Son spoken of here is Jesus. He came two thousand years ago to order His government with judgment and justice from that time forward, even forever. Literally, it began two thousand years ago, but we have not grasped what it really meant.

When the wise men from the East came to see Jesus they came looking for the King who was born in Bethlehem. How did they receive the revelation that Jesus was a king? Because of His star they saw in the East (Matthew 2:2). When He died, He died as a king too. The inscription on the cross was "King of the Jews." When the governor asked Jesus if He was the King of the Jews, He did not deny it. He said, "It is as you say" (Matthew 27:11).

How do we witness to others of Jesus as a king? Believers need to be involved in the political arena of their nations. We have been avoiding politics for too long. Because of that, the unrighteous have taken over governments all over the world. There is no righteous justice system in the world anymore. People with money make their own rules. Any wicked person with money can do almost anything anywhere in the world.

> We have been avoiding politics for too long. Because of that, the unrighteous have taken over governments all over the world.

Isaiah said the government shall be upon the shoulders of Jesus (Isaiah 9:6), not on the shoulders of the devil. Church leaders should encourage believers to get involved in politics, both locally and in the central government of their nations. Otherwise, how do we witness to others that Jesus is King?

One of the main reasons this world is in this chaos is because there are not very many people witnessing Jesus as a king. "When *the righteous are in authority, the people rejoice: but when the wicked beareth rule, the people mourn*" (Proverbs 29:2 KJV).

Anytime I meet someone from any country, they are always complaining about how bad the government in their nation is, and they talk against the leaders of their nations. Just talking negative about your government is not going to change anything for the better. The only way to change anything is if we have witnesses for Jesus in those governments. We need believers in positions of influence for the kingdom causes we are striving for. We must find out why we do not have any influence in government and come up with a solution.

One of the popular messages of the last few years was telling Americans to go back to her roots; that message is dying out as I write this book. America cannot go back to her roots. We need a new strategy.

There were fifty-six men who signed the Declaration of Independence. Out of the fifty-six, fifty-four of them were known to be Christians and attended some form of church. That meant their moral and ethical value system was based on Judeo-Christian ethics. That is why this country was established the way it was. How many people do we have in our government now that are a witness for Jesus? If we are going to take this country back to its roots, we need believers in positions of government—at both the state and national levels—who will witness Jesus as a king.

Again, we are not here to take over governments, but like Joseph and Daniel did, we need to have people witnessing in high places. Everyone God used in the Old Testament is a type of Christ: Moses, Joseph, David, Daniel, and Esther. Every single person God used manifested Christ through their life and His mission on earth. We have received the real deal, and today there are fewer witnesses for Jesus than ever in world governments.

God has anointed many people with His power to be a witness in government, but they have avoided it, thinking it is not God's will for them. The enemy has deceived us to keep us out of this most important aspect of a nation so that he can have free reign without any hindrance. Every government on earth belongs to Jesus, because there is no authority,

> **Why should we give the authority God gave us to the devil and then complain about what he is doing with it?**

natural or spiritual, except from Him. Why should we give the authority God gave us to the devil and then complain about what he is doing with it? Paul calls people in governmental authority "ministers." Did you know that? In Romans 13 he mentioned it two times. I was really surprised when I read this.

"For he is the minister of God to thee for good" (Romans 13:4a KJV).

"For this cause pay ye tribute also: for they are God's ministers, attending continually upon this very thing" (Romans 13:6 KJV).

I am a minister of the gospel. I preach the gospel to groups of people. You can be in charge of finance in the government of your nation and you are also a minister of God. You preach the gospel through your influence, your input, and your decisions. The same Holy Spirit is working through us, but in different manifestations.

There is a wrong teaching in the body of Christ that kings are those people who do business. That is not entirely true. Kings might do business, but their primary role is to be in government.

Each believer is anointed to manifest at least one aspect of Jesus. When we all come together as a body, we have the fullness of God (Ephesians 4:13). Church, this has to happen. It must happen if Jesus is going to return to the earth. He is not coming for a church crying like a baby to get her out of the earth. He is coming for a victorious church.

Every person God used in the Old Testament was a type or shadow of Christ, so that means they were representing or foreshadowing Christ who was to come. Abraham was a prophet, Joseph was a prime minister, and David was a king. Esther was a queen, Moses was a deliverer, and the list goes on. They were all witnesses of the Messiah. Jesus is all of them and more. Jesus said every Scripture testifies of Him.

"You search the Scriptures, for in them you think you have eternal life; and these are they which *testify* of Me" (John 5:39).

3) Judge

"The Lord executes righteousness and justice *for all* who are oppressed" (Psalm 103:6).

"And He commanded us to preach to the people, and to testify that it is He who was ordained by God *to be* **Judge** of the living and the dead" (Acts 10:42).

If the Lord executes righteousness and justice for *all* who are oppressed, how does He accomplish it and why do we not see that happening in our world today? Does our God lie? There are millions of people who are oppressed and in need of justice. The only way God can do it is through His people, the *ekklesia*.

If there was ever a time we needed to witness Jesus as the righteous Judge, it is now. The justice systems of the world are corrupt and have no moral foundation. We need judges that represent the kingdom in every level of our judicial system. Money manipulates almost every part of the justice system in the world today. The person with money can get around any crime.

> **We need judges that represent the kingdom in every level of our judicial system.**

When Jesus shared a parable about persistent prayer He mentioned an unrighteous judge and a widow, and how this widow kept imploring him. He finally gave in and avenged her.

> "Then the Lord said, 'Hear what the unjust judge said. And shall God not avenge His own elect who cry out day and night to Him, though He bears long with them? I tell you that He will avenge them speedily. Nevertheless, when the Son of Man comes, will He really find faith on the earth?' " (Luke 18:6-8).

God is a judge and judges among the mighty.

> "God stands in the congregation of the mighty; He judges among the gods. How long will you judge unjustly, and show partiality to the wicked? *Selah*. Defend the poor and fatherless; do justice to the afflicted and needy. Deliver the poor and needy; free *them* from the hand of the wicked" (Psalm 82:1-4).

Who are those called mighty here? The Hebrew word used for mighty is *El*, the same word used for God in many places in the Bible. God calls us gods with a small "g."

The Supreme Court justices in the United States ruled to amend the definition of marriage. Christians across the country made an uproar in their churches and on social media but that did not change anything. If we need to change the rule, then we need Christians in the positions of lawmakers and judges. We need witnesses for Jesus as judges.

4) Prophet/Shepherd/Healer

The reason I put these three titles together is because we are very familiar with those ministry gifts. We have many prophets, pastors, and evangelists today that witness Jesus very effectively, so I am not going to spend much time on these areas. We are already familiar with Jesus as Prophet, and those who witness for Jesus that way we call prophets. Jesus is also Healer and those who witness for Him in this way we call healing evangelists.

5) Teacher

One of the names people called Jesus while He was on this earth was Teacher. How do we witness Jesus as the teacher? I believe the best schools and universities in any city or country should be under the leadership of Christians. That's the way we should witness Jesus as the teacher. Part of the Great Commission Jesus gave was: "Teaching them to observe all things that I have commanded you" (Matthew 28:20). Catholics have done a tremendous job in this area. In almost any country or city you visit, you will find a Catholic school with excellent standards. Even in Muslim countries, there are schools run by Catholics. Most of the leaders in their countries received their education in those schools. Why do the evangelicals not do such things? We need to sing and preach less and do more with our hands and brain and show the world that our God reigns. I believe God intended all forms of education to be done through the church.

> We need to sing and preach less and do more with our hands and brain and show the world that our God reigns.

6) Father

God called Abraham to be a father of many nations. Why a father? Why not an owner or a king? Nations need fathers. Fatherlessness is a key problem in our society today. Most people grow up without a good father and most do not receive the blessing of a good father. The second most important relationship we have is our relationship with our father. If our relationship with our father is not right, then nothing else will go right.

I cannot emphasize the importance of the blessing of a father. A person who is blessed by his or her father is an unstoppable force on this earth. Even the kingdom of darkness cannot do anything against that person because the blessing that was spoken will work as shield against all opposition. It is the same with cursing. A person who is cursed by his father has little hope. Serious repentance and healing must take place to break that curse. Otherwise, that curse will work like a 'lid" over his or her head; he or she will not go much higher in life.

> A person who is blessed by his or her father is an unstoppable force on this earth.

I have noticed in many cultures that people die at an early age, especially men. When I visited some of these cultures I discovered that none of those people were ever blessed by their parents. The first commandment with a promise is to honor your father and mother so that it may go well with you and you will live long on the face of the earth. Your life span is directly connected to your relationship with your parents. How deep is that?

We need to witness Jesus as Father to the fatherless on this earth. It is not an easy task. I raised orphan children for fourteen years in our ministry and I know the challenges that are involved with it. In the place you were not blessed by your natural parents, God will connect you with a person who will be your spiritual father.

We must make sure we do not abuse or take advantage of those who are entrusted to us. We must not take spiritual fathering to an extreme either. We must make sure everything is balanced with the Word. God is a father to the fatherless (Psalm 68:5).

7) Redeemer

Jesus paid the price and redeemed our lives from death and destruction. There are many ways we can be a witness for Jesus as the Redeemer, but it might take a lot of sacrifice to witness to someone as their redeemer. One of the reasons for the many suicides, child labor, and prostitution in Third World countries is financial debt. People borrow money and are unable to pay it back or pay the interest, so they decide to end their life. Or, they are forced to send their children to work in factories or prostitution.

Most of the time it is not even very much money, less than a thousand dollars, but in many parts of the world that's a lot of money. I have had a few experiences where God helped me to witness as a redeemer in such cases. You won't believe the relief and freedom people feel and the joy you can see in their faces when their burden is lifted. Debt, in any sense, is a burden and a curse.

Slavery is still a problem today. Men, women, and children are sold as slaves in some parts of the world. We can witness Jesus as Redeemer if we pay their ransom and redeem them from slavery. I watched online how Christian women and children are being auctioned off in a Middle Eastern country. Because of persecution, many Christians from Pakistan fled to Thailand to seek asylum. When they arrived they were put in prison by the government for not paying the penalty. There are plenty of opportunities in the world to witness for Jesus as a redeemer.

8) Servant

Jesus said the Son of Man came to serve and give His life as a ransom for many (Matthew 20:28). When we serve we need to serve with a spirit of excellence. Whether you are working in a company or a hotel, in any capacity you serve other people, you serve as a witness for Jesus. You should not preach about Jesus; that's not what I mean by witnessing for Jesus. But by seeing the excellent work you do, people should ask you the reason behind your performance. Then you should say you are a witness of Jesus who also came to this earth to serve others.

> By seeing the excellent work you do, people should ask you the reason behind your performance.

Companies and institutions should stand in line to hire a Christian as their employee. They should be aware of the rare privilege it is to have a believer in Christ working for them. They should know about the increased level of excellence and quality we demonstrate in our work ethic. Church, what would happen in this world if the believers demonstrated the character and quality of Jesus in the workplace?

9) Giver/Rich

Jesus gave His life as a ransom for many (Mark 10:45). We know the famous verse, "God so loved the world He gave His only begotten Son." When you truly love someone you give everything. You give the most precious thing you have.

> "For you know the grace of our Lord Jesus Christ, that though He was rich, yet for your sakes He became poor, that you through His poverty might become rich" (2 Corinthians 8:9).

There is no reason for anyone to be poor on the earth, just as there is no reason for anyone to live in sin. Jesus became poor and paid for the poverty of the entire world. If anyone is living in sin or poverty, it is because of choice or ignorance. Most people are poor because of their ignorance. As kingdom citizens, we need to learn the laws that govern wealth and money and teach others how to create wealth. That's part of our mandate.

People have taken this truth to an extreme and developed a gospel called the prosperity gospel. There is no such gospel in the Bible. The gospel does bring blessings; there is no doubt about it, but we need to keep our focus on Jesus, not on our wealth or creating wealth.

Most of the prosperity preachers we have today do not preach or equip the believers to create wealth. They steal from the sheep and become rich. A true minister of the gospel is always looking for the betterment of the people he is teaching.

> **Most of the prosperity preachers we have today do not preach or equip the believers to create wealth. They steal from the sheep and become rich.**

When I first came to the Unites States, a friend of mine took me to meet a group of businessmen. I was blessed to meet them because their business existed for one sole purpose, to generate income to support ministries. They donated their profit to support missions around the world. I pray that God will raise up more businesses like that.

We need to witness Jesus as the richest person in the universe. God said, "And you shall remember the Lord your God, for *it is* He who gives you *power to get wealth*, that He may establish His covenant which He swore to your fathers, as *it is* this day" (Deuteronomy 8:18).

The church needs to train believers to tap into that power of God to create wealth to establish God's covenant. God knows it takes serious wealth to establish His covenant, so He gave His power to His children to create it. But most of us are still asking God for free money. Do not ask God for free money; ask Him for the power to create wealth. God never gave free money to anyone in the Bible. He always gave an idea or instruction and showed people how to apply an idea or obey instructions. This process generated money that met their need.

> **God never gave free money to anyone in the Bible. He always gave an idea or instruction and showed people how to apply an idea or obey instructions.**

One of the spiritual gifts Paul mentioned in Romans 12 is giving. How can we give if we do not have anything? In order to give, we need to have a way to generate money. This not only speaks about giving money, but about giving our time, love, kindness, forgiveness, and much more.

Don't try to copy someone else. Instead, find out how the power of the Holy Spirit wants to manifest through you to witness for Jesus. There are millions of ways to witness for Jesus. You can be a chef and witness for Jesus through the creativity of cooking. We are uniquely created with particular gifts and talents. Do not limit God and try to put Him in a box. Do not use the Holy Spirit only to prophesy, heal, and speak in tongues. They are a few of His gifts, but that's not the Person of the Holy Spirit. If I give you a car as a gift, that car is not me, the person; that is just one of my gifts. I have given many things as gifts to various people, especially my books, but none of those gifts represent my total being. It is very sad today that many know the Holy Spirit only for His gifts.

Ask the Holy Spirit to help you know Him and to discover your uniqueness; break off the mold that religion and culture have put upon you. *Be the only you who ever lived on the face of the earth.* There is only one David, Moses, and Esther in the Bible. The world has yet to see everything God intended for His church and through His church. Where do we go from here? How do we initiate the change? The next chapter will give you the answer.

Chapter 15: The Game Plan

Chapter 15: The Game Plan

"The kingdoms of this world have become the kingdoms of our
Lord and of His Christ, and He shall reign forever and ever!"
(Revelation 11:15).

If Jesus tarries, by the year 2050 world population is projected to be 9.6 billion people. That is only thirty-four years from now. That means many of you who are reading this book will be alive to see it. The children and youth that are part of our church today are those who are supposed to reach these 9.6 billion people with the gospel. Do you think they are being prepared for such an enormous task? I don't think they are. For many, their passion is for anything else but Jesus Christ. Who is to blame for this? The current church system we have today.

The research proves it. Josh McDowell, author and representative of Campus Crusade for Christ says in his book, *The Last Christian Generation*[14] that various denominational leaders have confessed to him that between sixty-nine and ninety-four percent of their young people are leaving traditional church after high school—and very few return.

> **Between sixty-nine and ninety-four percent of their young people are leaving traditional church after high school—and very few return.**

The reason they leave is not because they do not love God, but because they know they are created to do something greater or different than what the church offers them. They did not receive what they needed when they came to church and have very little to show for it. They see

---

14. McDowell, Josh, and David H. Bellis. *The Last Christian Generation*. Holiday, FL: Green Key, 2006. Print.

unbelievers in the world changing things left and right with new products and innovations while the church sits quietly on the sidelines. The youth today think differently than previous generations.

In the Western world, the majority of current church members are above fifty years old. Just look around when you go to church next and you will see what I am talking about. That means the majority of the Christian population that is alive today may die out by 2050 unless we are willing to take some drastic steps. Let me warn you by the Spirit of God, the things

> **The Christian population that is alive today may die out by 2050 unless we are willing to take some drastic steps.**

that will unfold will not be good for the church and our future generations. What happened to the first century churches and in Europe can happen to the churches that you and I are part of too. That is not God's will.

Right now the church does not have any influence over anything that is going on in our nation, though we say we are the majority. If it continues like this, do you think Christianity as we know it today will have any impact in the Western world thirty-four years from now? Not much. God gave me a plan to take any nation for God within ten to fifteen years without conducting a single crusade, healing rally, street witnessing plan, or any other traditional method in use today. It will be accomplished through administering the kingdom of God. That means if we are diligent and apply the principles written in this book, we will see nations coming to the Lord. That has been the Lord's desire from the very beginning. It does not have to be a far-fetched dream somewhere out there; this is something you can see with your own eyes in your lifetime.

If God promoted His people to positions of authority today, I don't know how many would have any idea what to do. If a churchgoer became the prime minister of a nation, would they really know how to govern that nation? Do we train our children with that kind of a mindset? Do we know the laws that govern the economy of a nation? I recently heard that the Harvard Schools of business and politics are filled with Mormons. Do you know why? They own some of the largest global corporations and businesses.

The Bible is a book of principles, patterns, and types. That means what is mentioned in the Bible is for our example and we have to apply that to our lives. People like Joseph and Daniel were promoted to top levels of leadership in their nations. Unfortunately, the church did not grab that revelation and run with it. We have been waiting for God to raise up Josephs and Daniels. But He is not going to do that.

The reason God raised up Joseph and Daniel in the Old Testament was because there was no other opportunity for them to go and learn what they needed to learn. There were no Christian or Judaic universities or law schools where they could enroll and learn principles of governing nations.

Today, that is not the case. We have hundreds of universities and opportunities where we can send our children to learn those things, but we are not doing it. That's one of the reasons the righteous are not in power. It is our responsibility to apply those principles, learn from those examples, and follow the faith and good deeds of those who went before us. God wants the righteous in authority, but we were deceived and secluded ourselves when the "rapture syndrome" began to infiltrate the church worldwide. We began to be more concerned about what was going to happen after we die than living our life now. Most of the latter part of the twentieth century Christian teachings focused on two things: the end times and the rapture. That is the reason we lost our nations right out from under our nose.

Whenever people ask me about end times and what is going to happen after we die, I tell them I am still trying to figure things out about this life. I know people who left their church because they did not hear much about the end times and the second coming from the pulpit.

So where do we start if we want to reach a nation in ten to fifteen years? First, as parents and leaders, we need to receive the kingdom mindset and train our children with that mindset, a mindset to reign and take dominion. We should not teach them to dominate others, but to exercise God-given dominion over at least one area of life. It is accomplished through mastering at least one subject or talent, ability, or skill.

> We should not teach our children to dominate others, but to exercise God-given dominion over at least one area of life.

We need to teach our children the purpose God had for creating man and how to have dominion. We need to prepare curricula with the intention of teaching people to discover their purpose and reign in one area of life. We need to prepare Sunday school and youth curricula particularly focused on the kingdom of God and its principles and how to administer it in the community and nation we are living in.

To prepare you for this, I strongly recommend you get a copy of my book, *The Three Most Important Decisions of Your Life*. Read it and let your children read it. It's a manual for life on earth. Every teenager and parent on this earth should read that book. Life is only long enough to make three major decisions; once you make them, the rest of your time is spent living out the consequences of those decisions. That book can save them from a lot of unnecessary pain, and most importantly it will help them discover their purpose.

When I see what they do in youth and children's ministry these days, it grieves my spirit. Most of them are just an extension or copy of what is happening in the entertainment world: movies, games, and sugar! I walked into a youth ministry facility in a church and what I saw grieved my spirit. There were five entertainment centers with big screens where kids were gathered around playing video games. Are we preparing the leaders of tomorrow? We have to start training our children when they are little in the ways of God, not in the ways of the world. Most Christian parents' dream is to visit a famous amusement park with their children. What a sad thing. Why don't you visit the Holy Land with your children and walk them through the footsteps of Jesus? Imagine the spiritual impact it would have on their lives and future.

"Train up a child in the way he should go and when he is old, he will not depart from it" (Proverbs 22:6). It does not say to train a child in the way he is going, or the way he would like to go, but the way *he should go*. The first five years are the most important time in a child's life for training. Whatever they see and learn in those five years molds their mindset and will stay with them for the rest of their life. That is why training is needed. If we just

> While our kids are having fun in our churches, other religious groups are training their children to be business owners and community leaders.

have fun all the time, then we won't be able to train them to do anything. While our kids are having fun in our churches, other religious groups are training their children to be business owners and community leaders.

We need to protect our children from the things of this world until they have a kingdom mindset. Once they have the kingdom mindset, they will be able to navigate the world system without being contaminated or influenced by it. It's okay if they watch a movie once in a while, but make sure their little minds are not programmed that way. Once their minds are contaminated with the system and the things of the world, the kingdom of God will not have much impact on their life. The world and the kingdom are like water and oil; they can never be mixed together. They are two different kingdoms. We need to closely watch and separate what is of the kingdom of God and what is of darkness. It is no longer easy to differentiate between the church and the world. The god of this world has infiltrated his agenda into almost everything. We need to use the discerning of spirits before we let anything flow into our homes.

Following are the steps we need to take right now if we are serious about God and His kingdom. If your passion is which sports team is going to win the game next week, forget about this and doing anything for His kingdom.

Global Prayer Network

If we start with anything, we should start with prayer. When God gave me this book to write I did not understand the whole counsel of God about it until the end. In the midst of writing it, I went through some serious battles that the enemy brought against my life. There were times I felt I was going to lose my mind as the devil attacked me. If this book reaches the hands of God's people, it is going to cause some serious damage to his kingdom. One day the devil even came and told me, "If you don't preach this message, I will not attack you."

We know that God is always victorious and makes us triumph in our battles. This book will do you no good if you just read it and say, "Wow, this was a great book!" or "I didn't really like this one." You must take action. One day God dropped the idea in my heart to design a website that will connect people from all over the world and launch a Global Prayer Network to connect believers from all over the world and mobilize them to pray. We are the house of God and we are supposed to be a house of prayer for all nations. The website is not ready yet, but I have started a Global Prayer Network Facebook page. Please visit it and 'like' it and you can post your prayer requests and comments about this book on it.

The mandate is to start prayer cells or micro-churches that meet in homes or residential places in every city and town, large and small. These will pray to destroy the plans of the enemy and execute the will of God for that city and region. What these prayer cells will be doing is coming together once a week or

> **We are the house of God and we are supposed to be a house of prayer for all nations.**

when something is about to happen in your community or nation that is not of God. Then, come together to pray and execute, or legislate, God's will through prayer.

Don't worry about how big or small the problem or the issue looks because whenever two or three are gathered in His name, Jesus promised to be in the midst of them. And if two of us agree and touch anything on earth and ask in prayer believing that God will do it, He promised to do it.

It works like this. If you are a believer in Christ, you are a child of God and an ambassador of His kingdom. You are a "special agent" sent by God to the earth to destroy the works of the enemy. Your responsibility is to be on the lookout to find what is happening around you and in your city and nation. You need to be aware of what is going on in the world.

When an ambassador hears by natural means or receives from the Spirit about what the enemy kingdom is planning to execute, he or she calls another ambassador to inform them about it so they can come together in agreement to thwart that plan before it materializes. That is kingdom legislation. Or they can post that information as a prayer request on the GPN website for the global body of Christ to pray about. We need to stay one step ahead of the enemy at all times. It will happen only through Spirit-led intercession.

This prayer network is not only to pray for communities and nations but also to pray for our personal needs. People from all over the world will be able to post prayer requests for themselves, their communities, and their nations. And people from anywhere in the world will be able to pray for those requests. We will create a prayer chain that is going on 24/7, nonstop, because when it is night in one side of the earth, it is day on the other side.

As you are reading this, we have already started our first GPN prayer cell in India. My goal is to start prayer cells like this in every city of every nation. If you would like to start a prayer cell in your city or town please let us know. I will give a copy of this book to everyone in the group. One of the requirements to be part of this prayer network is to read this book. We invite any prayer cells already established who would like to join us in praying effectively with a kingdom mentality.

Would you like to be a part of such a powerful Global Prayer Network, where believers from all around the world connect in unity for one purpose: to see the kingdom of God established in their lives, communities, and nations? I believe this is an answer to many of our prayers and this will be an answer to many of the problems we face in our lives and nations. If you would like to start a Prayer Cell in your home or area, please contact us.

> **When you pray for the needs of someone else as you pray for your own, God will answer your prayers.**

If you want to share a personal prayer request, you can send it as a private message, but when you see a prayer request on the GPN page please pray for it even if you do not know that person. They are our brothers and sisters in Christ. When you pray for the needs of someone else as you pray for your own, God will answer your prayers.

From time to time I will be giving training about how to pray. Some of this training will be done online. As the Lord leads I will come to any nation to train and launch a prayer cell. What I have seen is that most believers do not know how to pray effectively. Most of our prayer time is spent asking God for material things or blessings that He has already given to us. It will take another book to explain the things God already gave to us.

Please make sure you sign up on the Global Prayer Network page on Facebook and send me a friend request. If you are not on Facebook, you can call us on the number that is mentioned at the end of this chapter. Share our page with your friends and have them join the prayer network as well. There is no charge or monthly fee for joining. You receive all of this free of cost.

Kingdom Ambassadors

We have been called the ambassadors of Christ and His kingdom. God wants to send His ambassadors on diplomatic and special assignments and missions to execute His purposes in the nations of the world. If you would like to be one of those kingdom ambassadors, please let us know. We have further training for you.

As a result of this prayer movement, we will be sending strategic mission teams to different parts of the world to execute the purposes of God. Those who are called to do this and have the means to go, we will train and send you out to the nations to execute kingdom purposes. Based on the events taking place in different nations, kingdom ambassadors will be sent there to address those issues in the spirit through prayer. These will be totally covert spiritual operations. These groups will turn the tide of the events in nations; kings, presidents, and business owners will tremble as a result of what will happen. These teams will receive training before they go out to deal with the rulers of darkness over nations.

When they are on their journey, there will be prayer groups that pray and cover them for their protection and discernment. We need to have a Command Center to manage this kind of operation efficiently. May the Lord provide everything we need for His kingdom purpose.

Kingdom Awareness Conferences

In order to train this generation with a kingdom mindset and to take back what the enemy has stolen from us, God has been instructing me to host Kingdom Awareness Conferences. I have been holding back from it, but with the release of this book I feel it is time to step out and begin the new season God has for us. We intend to do these nationally and internationally.

We are more than willing to come and host a Kingdom Awareness Conference in your area. Whether it is in your house, church, or any other venue, big or small, we will come and train the people and impart the anointing and the grace God has put on me. The number of people attending is not a concern, as long as God is in it and provides for it. If it fits into my schedule, I am open to organizing it anywhere at any time, so please pray about it and let us know. There is no financial prerequisite for any preaching engagements.

Here is a synopsis of some of the ground we will be covering in these conferences. We will elaborate on what is taught in this book. We will cover how to practically train the next generation to take back our nations for God, how to change our democratic mindset to a kingdom mindset, how the kingdom economy works, prayer and intercession, and much more.

Kingdom Training Center

After reading this book, you might wonder, "Wow! Where do we begin? How do we initiate the change?" God wants each of His children to be part of what He is doing on the earth today. Would you like to be part of this movement? Everyone can do something.

There is another thing the Holy Spirit asked me to do. That is to start training centers on every continent and eventually one in every nation to train believers for kingdom evangelism. Some of these will be part of the local churches. Through these Kingdom Training Centers, we will train believers in almost everything a kingdom or nation is made of in order to influence culture, religion, government, education, economy, media and entertainment, science and technology.

> The Holy Spirit asked me to start training centers on every continent and eventually one in every nation to train believers for kingdom evangelism.

There are people in the body of Christ who feel called to particular nations. Everyone's call is unique and different because each individual is gifted to manifest Christ and His kingdom in a unique way. For example, recently I was in Tibet doing prayer walking in the city of Lhasa. It is not permitted to preach the gospel openly in Tibet. If someone is called to reach Tibet with the gospel of the kingdom, they cannot go there and hold open-air crusades because it is prohibited. But a person or group can learn the culture, arts, or music of Tibet and organize events for the general public.

The presentation has to be excellent and professional in quality and people should be attracted to it. The gospel message would have to be very subtly integrated in the presentation. Through this, a group could establish relationships with the local people. Slowly and surely, they would initiate a cultural transformation in Tibet and some people would eventually come to know Jesus as their Lord. As soon as they are born again, we need to teach them to seek the kingdom first. We may have to encounter some persecution, but as we know: The kingdom of God thrives in the midst of any persecution. This is only one example. We could go there with a product to help the people. There are hundreds of ways to penetrate hardcore enemy lines with the wisdom of God, even those that have been closed to the gospel for hundreds of years.

There have to be training programs for arts, media, government, education, technology, and everything must be based on the kingdom perspective with a kingdom mindset. We will eventually have branches of training centers in every nation on this earth. Local churches need to adopt this method and start training programs for their children and youth ministries. The earlier we start training someone to have a kingdom mindset, the better and more powerful it will be when they are grown up. It is obvious that someone or something is shaping the mindset of our children, so why not use the kingdom of God to do the same? Why should we sit and watch while the kingdom of darkness is shaping our culture and the mindset of our generation?

As I said, many Christians have no idea how to administer a kingdom. In order to achieve this, we need extensive training programs and curricula prepared to train believers in Christ to become kingdom-minded ambassadors of Christ. These training centers will address both the natural and spiritual aspects of the kingdom. I am calling anyone whose heart is stirred to be part of this to use their gifts for the kingdom. We need help from believers from all walks of life to develop this program.

> We need extensive training programs and curricula prepared to train believers in Christ to become kingdom-minded ambassadors of Christ.

There will be long- and short-term courses available to train people in politics, economy, entrepreneurship, etc. and at the same time praying for the sick and how to prophesy to individuals and nations. I recently learned that a ministry like ours can be registered with the United Nations as an NGO (non-government organization). Then we will have permission to attend the General Assembly meetings. How many Christian ministries take advantage of that opportunity? I don't think there are very many who do that. There are so many opportunities and methods the church can employ to make a difference in our nations, so let's not waste any more time singing inside the four walls of our churches waiting for the rapture. As the Bible says, "My people are destroyed for lack of knowledge" (Hosea 4:6). It also says, "Where there is no vision, the people perish" (Proverbs 29:18 KJV). It's time for a change.

If God moves on your heart to be part of this ministry and this movement, I request that you take a step of faith and contact us at the number, e-mail, or the address at the end of the book. After reading this book, you know more about the church than ever before. I can't do this alone. I don't want to do it alone! Let's do this together for the kingdom and for our next generation. I am looking for 12 men or women in every city in every nation who are willing to be the ambassadors of the Kingdom of God. They will be spearheading the vision and plan for that city and nation.

Accomplishing this task will require teachers, volunteers, business people, politicians, educators, planners, researchers, intercessors, farmers, administrators, helpers, and anyone in whose heart the Lord moves to join us to bring the kingdom of God to the earth. We are part of the same body, but different members with different functions. I strongly believe this is the "new thing" God wants to do on the earth. Please do not waste your precious time and life looking for something else or waiting for God to do something, when He is knocking at your door. Will you answer the call?

We need prayer and financial partners. Things are going to change and many ministries that God used in the last generation will no longer be in the forefront. Their time is up. The church as we know it today will change dramatically and many are going to fall away from their faith, but God is beginning something new. Please pray about what you read in this book and contact us as soon as you can.

Kingdom-Minded Churches

In addition to the Global Prayer Network, God put the vision in my heart to establish kingdom-minded churches (ekklesia) in all major cities of the world. These churches will administer His kingdom. This will be a new breed of believers who will be moving with kingdom authority to administer His kingdom here on earth. The current church that you and I are a part of is not equipped to administer His kingdom. They are waiting to fly away. God is looking for a new generation who is willing to give it all up for His kingdom, to gain something we cannot lose.

> **God is looking for a new generation who is willing to give it all up for His kingdom, to gain something we cannot lose.**

These churches may not be mega churches; some of them will be house churches or micro churches. If you feel in your spirit that you are supposed to be part of this end-time army of God who wants to take back everything the enemy has stolen from us, we want to hear from you. I call men and women in the name of Jesus Christ from all walks of life from the four corners of the earth whose hearts the Lord has stirred to answer the call, who are willing to do anything and everything to see His kingdom established on the earth.

> "Then everyone came whose heart was stirred, and everyone whose spirit was willing" (Exodus 35:21a).

> "They came, both men and women, as many as had a willing heart" (Exodus 35:22a).

To understand more about how a kingdom-minded church operates, God has given me a book called The Book of Acts in a Kingdom Perspective: *How the early church administered God's Kingdom.* After finishing reading this book I strongly recommend you get that and read and study it. We will announce when this is available. Please don't consider you received everything by just reading this book once. Do a study group with other believers that you know.

The prayer and concern I have is that you will read this book and say it's a powerful book and not do anything differently than you are doing now. That is a scary thought. Or, that something else will grab your attention and you will forget what you read. Please do something with what you learned. If you do not know what to do, please contact me. I will further help you to find your place in the body of Christ. In any case, we would like to hear from you. Don't hold back. Below is our contact information. God bless you.

Prayer of Dedication

Heavenly Father, thank you so much for what You have done for me through Your Son, Jesus Christ. Please forgive me for being selfish and prideful. I want to be part of what You are doing on this earth right now. I live to honor You and Your Son. I give my spirit, soul, and body to be a vessel for Your Holy Spirit. I belong to You. Show me what is my part in bringing Your kingdom to this earth. In Jesus' name I pray. Amen.

Maximum Impact Ministries

P.O Box 631460
Littleton, CO 80163-1460
Phone: (720) 420 9873
Email: mim@maximpact.org
www.powerandauthorityofthechurch.com

Let the *Reformation* Begin!

More Books by Abraham John

Kingdom Mandate: A Wake-Up Call for the Church

The Three Most Important Decisions of Your Life: Kingdom Secrets to Discover and Fulfill Your Destiny

Keys to Passing Your Spiritual Tests: Unlocking the Secrets to Your Spiritual Promotion

Recognizing God's Timing for Your Life: Discerning God's Timing and Purpose Through Your Daily Circumstances

Overcoming the Spirit of Poverty: How to Know and Fulfill Your Purpose

Seven Kinds of Believers: Why All God's Children are not Blessed Equally

Also from Maximum Impact Ministries:

Study Guides

7 Dimensions of God's Glory: Learning to Manifest God's Glory (Free)

7 Dimensions of God's Grace: Learning How to Meet All Your Needs (Free)

7 Kinds of Faith: Learning to Live by Faith (Free)

To place an order:

Maximum Impact Ministries,
P.O. Box 631460
Littleton, CO 80163-1460

Phone: (720) 420 9873
Email: mim@maximpact.org
www.maximpact.org